AF598642

THE BOOK OF EZEKIEL

THE IGNATIUS CATHOLIC STUDY BIBLE

REVISED STANDARD VERSION
SECOND CATHOLIC EDITION

THE BOOK OF EZEKIEL

With Introduction, Commentary, and Notes

by

John Bergsma

with

Scott Hahn and Curtis Mitch

and

with Study Questions by

Dennis Walters

IGNATIUS PRESS SAN FRANCISCO

Original Revised Standard Version, Catholic Edition
Nihil Obstat: Thomas Hanlon, S.T.L., L.S.S., Ph.L.
Imprimatur: + Peter W. Bartholome, D.D.
Bishop of St. Cloud, Minnesota
May 11, 1966

Introduction, commentaries, and notes:
Nihil Obstat: Ruth Ohm Sutherland, Ph.D., Censor Deputatus
Imprimatur: + The Most Reverend Salvatore Cordileone
Archbishop of San Francisco
April 19, 2023

Second Catholic Edition approved by the
National Council of the Churches of Christ in the USA

Cover art: Water from the Temple
(Ezekiel 47) Wood engraving
Published in 1886
iStockphoto.com

Cover design by Riz Boncan Marsella

Published by Ignatius Press in 2023

ISBN 978-1-62164-109-4 (PB)
ISBN 978-1-64229-302-9 (eBook)
Printed in the United States of America ♾

CONTENTS

INTRODUCTION TO
THE IGNATIUS STUDY BIBLE

by Scott Hahn, Ph.D.

You are approaching the "word of God". This is the title Christians most commonly give to the Bible, and the expression is rich in meaning. It is also the title given to the Second Person of the Blessed Trinity, God the Son. For Jesus Christ became flesh for our salvation, and "the name by which he is called is The Word of God" (Rev 19:13; cf. Jn 1:14).

The word of God is Scripture. The Word of God is Jesus. This close association between God's *written* word and his *eternal* Word is intentional and has been the custom of the Church since the first generation. "All Sacred Scripture is but one book, and this one book is Christ, 'because all divine Scripture speaks of Christ, and all divine Scripture is fulfilled in Christ'"[1] (CCC 134). This does not mean that the Scriptures are divine in the same way that Jesus is divine. They are, rather, divinely inspired and, as such, are unique in world literature, just as the Incarnation of the eternal Word is unique in human history.

Yet we can say that the inspired word resembles the incarnate Word in several important ways. Jesus Christ is the Word of God incarnate. In his humanity, he is like us in all things, except for sin. As a work of man, the Bible is like any other book, except without error. Both Christ and Scripture, says the Second Vatican Council, are given "for the sake of our salvation" (*Dei Verbum* 11), and both give us God's definitive revelation of himself. We cannot, therefore, conceive of one without the other: the Bible without Jesus, or Jesus without the Bible. Each is the interpretive key to the other. And because Christ is the subject of all the Scriptures, St. Jerome insists, "Ignorance of the Scriptures is ignorance of Christ"[2] (CCC 133).

When we approach the Bible, then, we approach Jesus, the Word of God; and in order to encounter Jesus, we must approach him in a prayerful study of the inspired word of God, the Sacred Scriptures.

Inspiration and Inerrancy The Catholic Church makes mighty claims for the Bible, and our acceptance of those claims is essential if we are to read the Scriptures and apply them to our lives as the Church intends. So it is not enough merely to nod at words like "inspired", "unique", or "inerrant". We have to understand what the Church means by these terms, and we have to make that understanding our own. After all, what we believe about the Bible will inevitably influence the way we read the Bible. The way we read the Bible, in turn, will determine what we "get out" of its sacred pages.

These principles hold true no matter what we read: a news report, a search warrant, an advertisement, a paycheck, a doctor's prescription, an eviction notice. How (or whether) we read these things depends largely upon our preconceived notions about the reliability and authority of their sources—and the potential they have for affecting our lives. In some cases, to misunderstand a document's authority can lead to dire consequences. In others, it can keep us from enjoying rewards that are rightfully ours. In the case of the Bible, both the rewards and the consequences involved take on an ultimate value.

What does the Church mean, then, when she affirms the words of St. Paul: "All Scripture is inspired by God" (2 Tim 3:16)? Since the term "inspired" in this passage could be translated "God-breathed", it follows that God breathed forth his word in the Scriptures as you and I breathe forth air when we speak. This means that God is the primary author of the Bible. He certainly employed human authors in this task as well, but he did not merely assist them while they wrote or subsequently approve what they had written. God the Holy Spirit is the *principal* author of Scripture, while the human writers are *instrumental* authors. These human authors freely wrote everything, and only those things, that God wanted: the word of God in the very words of God. This miracle of dual authorship extends to the whole of Scripture, and to every one of its parts, so that whatever the human authors affirm, God likewise affirms through their words.

The principle of biblical inerrancy follows logically from this principle of divine authorship. After all, God cannot lie, and he cannot make mistakes. Since the Bible is divinely inspired, it must be without error in everything that its divine and human authors affirm to be true. This means that biblical inerrancy is a mystery even broader in scope than infallibility, which guarantees for us that the Church will always teach the truth concerning faith and morals. Of course the mantle of inerrancy likewise covers faith and morals, but it extends even

[1] Hugh of St. Victor, *De arca Noe* 2, 8: PL 176, 642: cf. ibid. 2, 9: PL 176, 642–43.

[2] *DV* 25; cf. Phil 3:8 and St. Jerome, *Commentariorum in Isaiam libri xviii*, prol.: PL 24, 17b.

farther to ensure that all the facts and events of salvation history are accurately presented for us in the Scriptures. Inerrancy is our guarantee that the words and deeds of God found in the Bible are unified and true, declaring with one voice the wonders of his saving love.

The guarantee of inerrancy does not mean, however, that the Bible is an all-purpose encyclopedia of information covering every field of study. The Bible is not, for example, a textbook in the empirical sciences, and it should not be treated as one. When biblical authors relate facts of the natural order, we can be sure they are speaking in a purely descriptive and "phenomenological" way, according to the way things appeared to their senses.

Biblical Authority Implicit in these doctrines is God's desire to make himself known to the world and to enter a loving relationship with every man, woman, and child he has created. God gave us the Scriptures not just to inform or motivate us; more than anything he wants to save us. This higher purpose underlies every page of the Bible, indeed every word of it.

In order to reveal himself, God used what theologians call "accommodation". Sometimes the Lord stoops down to communicate by "condescension"—that is, he speaks as humans speak, as if he had the same passions and weakness that we do (for example, God says he was "sorry" that he made man in Genesis 6:6). Other times he communicates by "elevation"—that is, by endowing human words with divine power (for example, through the Prophets). The numerous examples of divine accommodation in the Bible are an expression of God's wise and fatherly ways. For a sensitive father can speak with his children either by condescension, as in baby talk, or by elevation, by bringing a child's understanding up to a more mature level.

God's word is thus saving, fatherly, and personal. Because it speaks directly to us, we must never be indifferent to its content; after all, the word of God is at once the object, cause, and support of our faith. It is, in fact, a test of our faith, since we see in the Scriptures only what faith disposes us to see. If we believe what the Church believes, we will see in Scripture the saving, inerrant, and divinely authored revelation of the Father. If we believe otherwise, we see another book altogether.

This test applies not only to rank-and-file believers but also to the Church's theologians and hierarchy, and even the Magisterium. Vatican II has stressed in recent times that Scripture must be "the very soul of sacred theology" (*Dei Verbum* 24). As Joseph Cardinal Ratzinger, Pope Benedict XVI echoed this powerful teaching with his own, insisting that "the *normative theologians* are the authors of Holy Scripture" (emphasis added). He reminded us that Scripture and the Church's dogmatic teaching are tied tightly together, to the point of being inseparable: "Dogma is by definition nothing other than an interpretation of Scripture." The defined dogmas of our faith, then, encapsulate the Church's infallible interpretation of Scripture, and theology is a further reflection upon that work.

The Senses of Scripture Because the Bible has both divine and human authors, we are required to master a different sort of reading than we are used to. First, we must read Scripture according to its *literal* sense, as we read any other human literature. At this initial stage, we strive to discover the meaning of the words and expressions used by the biblical writers as they were understood in their original setting and by their original recipients. This means, among other things, that we do not interpret everything we read "literalistically", as though Scripture never speaks in a figurative or symbolic way (it often does!). Rather, we read it according to the rules that govern its different literary forms of writing, depending on whether we are reading a narrative, a poem, a letter, a parable, or an apocalyptic vision. The Church calls us to read the divine books in this way to ensure that we understand what the human authors were laboring to explain to God's people.

The literal sense, however, is not the only sense of Scripture, since we interpret its sacred pages according to the *spiritual* senses as well. In this way, we search out what the Holy Spirit is trying to tell us, beyond even what the human authors have consciously asserted. Whereas the literal sense of Scripture describes a historical reality—a fact, precept, or event—the spiritual senses disclose deeper mysteries revealed through the historical realities. What the soul is to the body, the spiritual senses are to the literal. You can distinguish them; but if you try to separate them, death immediately follows. St. Paul was the first to insist upon this and warn of its consequences: "God ... has qualified us to be ministers of a new covenant, not in a written code but in the Spirit; for the written code kills, but the Spirit gives life" (2 Cor 3:5–6).

Catholic tradition recognizes three spiritual senses that stand upon the foundation of the literal sense of Scripture (see CCC 115). **(1)** The first is the *allegorical* sense, which unveils the spiritual and prophetic meaning of biblical history. Allegorical interpretations thus reveal how persons, events, and institutions of Scripture can point beyond themselves toward greater mysteries yet to come (OT) or display the fruits of mysteries already revealed (NT). Christians have often read the Old Testament in this way to discover how the mystery of Christ in the New Covenant was once hidden in the Old and how the full significance of the Old Covenant was finally made manifest in the New. Allegorical significance is likewise latent in the New Testament, especially in the life and deeds of Jesus recorded in the Gospels. Because Christ is the Head of the Church and the source of her spiritual life, what was accomplished in Christ the Head during his earthly life prefigures what he continually produces in his members through grace. The allegorical sense builds up the virtue of faith. **(2)** The second is the *tropological* or *moral* sense, which reveals how the actions of God's people in the Old Testament and the life of Jesus in the New Testament prompt us to form virtuous habits in our own lives. It therefore draws from Scripture warnings against sin and vice as well as inspirations to pursue holiness and purity. The moral sense is intended to build up the virtue of charity. **(3)** The third is the *anagogical* sense, which points upward to heavenly glory. It shows us how countless events in the Bible prefigure our final union with God in eternity and how things that are "seen" on earth are figures of things "unseen" in heaven. Because the anagogical sense leads us to contemplate our destiny, it is meant to build up the virtue of hope. Together with the literal sense, then, these spiritual senses draw out the fullness of what God wants to give us through his Word and as such comprise what ancient tradition has called the "full sense" of Sacred Scripture.

All of this means that the deeds and events of the Bible are charged with meaning beyond what is immediately apparent to the reader. In essence, that meaning is Jesus Christ and the salvation he died to give us. This is especially true of the books of the New Testament, which proclaim Jesus explicitly; but it is also true of the Old Testament, which speaks of Jesus in more hidden and symbolic ways. The human authors of the Old Testament told us as much as they were able, but they could not clearly discern the shape of all future events standing at such a distance. It is the Bible's divine Author, the Holy Spirit, who could and did foretell the saving work of Christ, from the first page of the Book of Genesis onward.

The New Testament did not, therefore, abolish the Old. Rather, the New fulfilled the Old, and in doing so, it lifted the veil that kept hidden the face of the Lord's bride. Once the veil is removed, we suddenly see the world of the Old Covenant charged with grandeur. Water, fire, clouds, gardens, trees, hills, doves, lambs—all of these things are memorable details in the history and poetry of Israel. But now, seen in the light of Jesus Christ, they are much more. For the Christian with eyes to see, water symbolizes the saving power of Baptism; fire, the Holy Spirit; the spotless lamb, Christ crucified; Jerusalem, the city of heavenly glory.

The spiritual reading of Scripture is nothing new. Indeed, the very first Christians read the Bible this way. St. Paul describes Adam as a "type" that prefigured Jesus Christ (Rom 5:14). A "type" is a real person, place, thing, or event in the Old Testament that foreshadows something greater in the New. From this term we get the word "typology", referring to the study of how the Old Testament prefigures Christ (CCC 128–30). Elsewhere St. Paul draws deeper meanings out of the story of Abraham's sons, declaring, "This is an allegory" (Gal 4:24). He is not suggesting that these events of the distant past never really happened; he is saying that the events both happened *and* signified something more glorious yet to come.

The New Testament later describes the Tabernacle of ancient Israel as "a copy and shadow of the heavenly sanctuary" (Heb 8:5) and the Mosaic Law as a "shadow of the good things to come" (Heb 10:1). St. Peter, in turn, notes that Noah and his family were "saved through water" in a way that "corresponds" to sacramental Baptism, which "now saves you" (1 Pet 3:20–21). It is interesting to note that the expression translated as "corresponds" in this verse is a Greek term that denotes the fulfillment or counterpart of an ancient "type".

We need not look to the apostles, however, to justify a spiritual reading of the Bible. After all, Jesus himself read the Old Testament this way. He referred to Jonah (Mt 12:39), Solomon (Mt 12:42), the Temple (Jn 2:19), and the brazen serpent (Jn 3:14) as "signs" that pointed forward to him. We see in Luke's Gospel, as Christ comforted the disciples on the road to Emmaus, that "beginning with Moses and all the prophets, he interpreted to them in all the Scriptures the things concerning himself" (Lk 24:27). It was precisely this extensive spiritual interpretation of the Old Testament that made such an impact on these once-discouraged travelers, causing their hearts to "burn" within them (Lk 24:32).

Criteria for Biblical Interpretation We, too, must learn to discern the "full sense" of Scripture as it includes both the literal and spiritual senses together. Still, this does not mean we should "read into" the Bible meanings that are not really there. Spiritual exegesis is not an unrestrained flight of the imagination. Rather, it is a sacred science that proceeds according to certain principles and stands accountable to sacred tradition, the Magisterium, and the wider community of biblical interpreters (both living and deceased).

In searching out the full sense of a text, we should always avoid the extreme tendency to "overspiritualize" in a way that minimizes or denies the Bible's literal truth. St. Thomas Aquinas was well aware of this danger and asserted that "all other senses of Sacred Scripture are based on the literal" (*STh* I, 1, 10, *ad* 1, quoted in CCC 116). On the other hand, we should never confine the meaning of a text to the literal, intended sense of its human author, as if the divine Author did not intend the passage to be read in the light of Christ's coming.

Fortunately the Church has given us guidelines in our study of Scripture. The unique character and divine authorship of the Bible call us to read it "in the Spirit" (*Dei Verbum* 12). Vatican II outlines this teaching in a practical way by directing us to read the Scriptures according to three specific criteria:

1. We must "[b]e especially attentive 'to the content and unity of the whole Scripture'" (CCC 112).

2. We must "[r]ead the Scripture within 'the living Tradition of the whole Church'" (CCC 113).

3. We must "[b]e attentive to the analogy of faith" (CCC 114; cf. Rom 12:6).

These criteria protect us from many of the dangers that ensnare readers of the Bible, from the newest inquirer to the most prestigious scholar. Reading Scripture out of context is one such pitfall, and probably the one most difficult to avoid. A memorable cartoon from the 1950s shows a young man poring over the pages of the Bible. He says to his sister: "Don't bother me now; I'm trying to find a Scripture verse to back up one of my preconceived notions." No doubt a biblical text pried from its context can be twisted to say something very different from what its author actually intended.

The Church's criteria guide us here by defining what constitutes the authentic "context" of a given biblical passage. The first criterion directs us to the literary context of every verse, including not only the words and paragraphs that surround it, but also the entire corpus of the biblical author's writings and, indeed, the span of the entire Bible. The *complete* literary context of any Scripture verse includes every text from Genesis to Revelation—because the Bible is a unified book, not just a library of different books. When the Church canonized the Book of Revelation, for example, she recognized it to be incomprehensible apart from the wider context of the entire Bible.

The second criterion places the Bible firmly within the context of a community that treasures a "living tradition". That community is the People of God down through the ages. Christians lived out their faith for well over a millennium before the printing press was invented. For centuries, few believers owned copies of the Gospels, and few people could read anyway. Yet they absorbed the gospel—through the sermons of their bishops and clergy, through prayer and meditation, through Christian art, through liturgical celebrations, and through oral tradition. These were expressions of the one "living tradition", a culture of living faith that stretches from ancient Israel to the contemporary Church. For the early Christians, the gospel could not be understood apart from that tradition. So it is with us. Reverence for the Church's tradition is what protects us from any sort of chronological or cultural provincialism, such as scholarly fads that arise and carry away a generation of interpreters before being dismissed by the next generation.

The third criterion places scriptural texts within the framework of faith. If we believe that the Scriptures are divinely inspired, we must also believe them to be internally coherent and consistent with all the doctrines that Christians believe. Remember, the Church's dogmas (such as the Real Presence, the papacy, the Immaculate Conception) are not something *added* to Scripture; rather, they are the Church's infallible interpretation *of* Scripture.

Using This Study Guide This volume is designed to lead the reader through Scripture according to the Church's guidelines—faithful to the canon, to the tradition, and to the creeds. The Church's interpretive principles have thus shaped the component parts of this book, and they are designed to make the reader's study as effective and rewarding as possible.

Introductions: We have introduced the biblical book with an essay covering issues such as authorship, date of composition, purpose, and leading themes. This background information will assist readers to approach and understand the text on its own terms.

Annotations: The basic notes at the bottom of every page help the user to read the Scriptures with understanding. They by no means exhaust the meaning of the sacred text but provide background material to help the reader make sense of what he reads. Often these notes make explicit what the sacred writers assumed or held to be implicit. They also provide a great deal of historical, cultural, geographical, and theological information pertinent to the inspired narratives—information that can help the reader bridge the distance between the biblical world and his own.

Cross-References: Between the biblical text at the top of each page and the annotations at the bottom, numerous references are listed to point readers to other scriptural passages related to the one being studied. This follow-up is an essential part of any serious study. It is also an excellent way to discover how the content of Scripture "hangs together" in a providential unity. Along with biblical cross-references, the annotations refer to select paragraphs from the *Catechism of the Catholic Church*. These are not doctrinal "proof texts" but are designed to help the reader interpret the Bible in accordance with the mind of the Church. The *Catechism* references listed either handle the biblical text directly or treat a broader doctrinal theme that sheds significant light on that text.

Topical Essays, Word Studies, Charts: These features bring readers to a deeper understanding of select details. The *topical essays* take up major themes and explain them more thoroughly and theologically than the annotations, often relating them to the doctrines of the Church. Occasionally the annotations are supplemented by *word studies* that put readers in touch with the ancient languages of Scripture. These should help readers to understand better and appreciate the inspired terminology that runs throughout the sacred books. Also included are various *charts* that summarize biblical information "at a glance".

Icon Annotations: Three distinctive icons are interspersed throughout the annotations, each one corresponding to one of the Church's three criteria for biblical interpretation. Bullets indicate the passage or passages to which these icons apply.

Notes marked by the book icon relate to the "content and unity" of Scripture, showing how particular passages of the Old Testament illuminate the mysteries of the New. Much of the information in these notes explains the original context of the citations and indicates how and why this has a direct bearing on Christ or the Church. Through these notes, the reader can develop a sensitivity to the beauty and unity of God's saving plan as it stretches across both Testaments.

Notes marked by the dove icon examine particular passages in light of the Church's "living tradition". Because the Holy Spirit both guides the Magisterium and inspires the spiritual senses of Scripture, these annotations supply information along both of these lines. On the one hand, they refer to the Church's doctrinal teaching as presented by various popes, creeds, and ecumenical councils; on the other, they draw from (and paraphrase) the spiritual interpretations of various Fathers, Doctors, and saints.

Notes marked by the keys icon pertain to the "analogy of faith". Here we spell out how the mysteries of our faith "unlock" and explain one another. This type of comparison between Christian beliefs displays the coherence and unity of defined dogmas, which are the Church's infallible interpretations of Scripture.

Putting It All in Perspective Perhaps the most important context of all we have saved for last: the interior life of the individual reader. What we get out of the Bible will largely depend on how we approach the Bible. Unless we are living a sustained and disciplined life of prayer, we will never have the reverence, the profound humility, or the grace we need to see the Scriptures for what they really are.

You are approaching the "word of God". But for thousands of years, since before he knit you in your mother's womb, the Word of God has been approaching you.

One Final Note. The volume you hold in your hands is only a small part of a much larger work still in production. Study helps similar to those printed in this booklet are being prepared for *all* the books of the Bible and will appear gradually as they are finished. Our ultimate goal is to publish a single, one-volume Study Bible that will include the entire text of Scripture, along with all the annotations, charts, cross-references, maps, and other features found in the following pages. Individual booklets will be published in the meantime, with the hope that God's people can begin to benefit from this labor before its full completion.

We have included a long list of Study Questions in the back to make this format as useful as possible, not only for individual study, but for group settings and discussions as well. The questions are designed to help readers both "understand" the Bible and "apply" it to their lives. We pray that God will make use of our efforts and yours to help renew the face of the earth!

INTRODUCTION TO EZEKIEL

Author Jewish and Christian tradition has always received the Book of Ezekiel as the work of the Judean prophet Ezekiel, who is identified as the "son of Buzi" and one of the priests taken into exile to Babylon along with King Jehoiachin in 597 B.C. If the "thirtieth year" mentioned in Ezekiel 1:1 is the prophet's age when he began writing, then he was born about 622 B.C. The last dated oracle in the book comes from around 571 B.C., so we may guess that he died shortly thereafter, perhaps in 570 B.C.

Many modern scholars regard Ezekiel as the author of the book on the basis of the following evidence: **(1)** the Hebrew of the book seems to reflect the transition from preexilic Standard Biblical Hebrew to postexilic Late Biblical Hebrew that took place during the sixth-century Babylonian Exile; **(2)** the unique, even idiosyncratic literary and theological style of the book remains constant throughout the work, suggesting a single author; **(3)** the literary characteristics of the book (careful record-keeping, attention to dating, overriding concern with the Temple and liturgy, extensive reuse of priestly and legal terminology from the Mosaic Law) suggest the author was a priest; **(4)** the dates and historical references in the book always fit with our knowledge of the ancient Near East in Ezekiel's lifetime; **(5)** there is no awareness in the book of any of the events of the postexilic time period and the return of the exiles to Judah and Jerusalem; **(6)** the vision of the restoration of Israel in chapters 40–48 is actually at significant odds with how events transpired historically, making it hard to imagine as the work of a later author.

It is true that in European, especially German, scholarship, there continues to be a tradition of attempting to identify many different layers of editing in the Book of Ezekiel, extending long after the life of the prophet. There is no direct evidence to support these theories: they usually rest on certain long-held assumptions in continental scholarship, for example, that the priestly material of the Pentateuch (much of Exodus–Numbers) is postexilic (fifth century B.C.) in origin. Since the Book of Ezekiel uses this material extensively, so the argument goes, the book must be even later. However, the tradition of the postexilic origin of the priestly materials of the Pentateuch rests on no direct evidence and is increasingly being called into question on linguistic, historical, and other grounds. Many scholars feel the proper way to argue would be, since Ezekiel uses the priestly materials of the Pentateuch, and his book fits securely into all that is known of the culture, language, and history of the early sixth century (ca. 592–572) B.C., therefore the priestly materials of the Pentateuch must be older than Ezekiel.

Date The Book of Ezekiel is one of the most clearly organized of all the prophetic books. The prophet follows a strict chronological order in recording his oracles and reflects his priestly training in the care he takes to mark down exact dates on which revelations have come to him. With few exceptions, Ezekiel dates his prophecies from the beginning of the exile of King Jehoiachin (ca. 597 B.C.). Some scholars reconstruct the dates of his revelations roughly as follows:

Ezek 1:1	593 B.C
Ezek 8:1	592 B.C.
Ezek 20:1	591 B.C.
Ezek 24:1	588 B.C.
Ezek 26:1	587–586 B.C.
Ezek 29:1	587 B.C.
Ezek 29:17	571 B.C.
Ezek 30:20	587 B.C.
Ezek 31:1	587 B.C.
Ezek 32:1	585 B.C.
Ezek 32:17	585 B.C.
Ezek 33:21	585 B.C.
Ezek 40:1	573 B.C.

Thus, with small variations, there is a chronological flow from earlier to later prophecies, the only exception being Ezek 29:17–21. The references to external historical events found in Ezekiel's oracles make a good match with our reconstruction of the history of this time period from extrabiblical sources. Since such accuracy would be very difficult for a later writer or editor to re-create, there is justification in taking the book as it presents itself: a roughly chronological account of the experiences and activities of the prophet within a twenty-two-year period between 593 and 571 B.C.

Title The book takes its name from the prophet whose life and work it claims to record, Ezekiel, son of Buzi. Ezekiel is an English rendering of the Hebrew *Yeḥezqē'l,* meaning "God strengthens." Indeed, the strength of God—manifested in either the power to destroy or the power to restore—is a common motif throughout the book. The statement in 3:14 that "the hand of the LORD [was] strong [Heb. *ḥazaqah*] upon me" may be taken as emblematic of Ezekiel's entire life and ministry. In the Greek Septuagint, the book became *Iezekiēl,* and in the Latin Vulgate, *Liber Hiezechielis Prophetae,* "The Book of Ezekiel the Prophet".

Place in the Canon It is clear that ancient Judaism held Ezekiel to be an authoritative book: in Sirach, the prophet is listed among the heroes of Israel's history (Sir 49:8–9); many of the Dead Sea Scrolls (notably the Damascus Document and the Temple Scroll) show the significant influence of Ezekiel's thought and language; and the book was translated into Greek for the edification of Hellenistic Jews in the Diaspora outside the land of Israel. Nonetheless, there was strong resistance to receiving Ezekiel into the canon of rabbinic (postbiblical) Judaism because of three issues: most importantly, because of the differences between Ezekiel's laws and rituals in Ezek 40–48 and those of Moses in the Pentateuch; secondly, because the surreal visions of the divine chariot (Heb., *merkavah*, chaps. 1–3, 10) were considered dangerous for the spiritually immature to read; and thirdly, because of the scandalous description of Jerusalem as a prostitute in Ezek 16 and 23. The rabbis debated Ezekiel's canonicity into the fifth century A.D., but at some point in the early medieval period a consensus was reached in favor of the book's inspiration, although restrictions were placed on how and by whom the book could be read.

The Church never disputed Ezekiel's canonicity. In the early canonical lists, it typically followed Isaiah and Jeremiah as a major prophet. It has become apparent that, like Jeremiah, Ezekiel circulated in Hebrew in at least two distinct editions, a shorter and a longer. The Septuagint translation reflects the shorter edition, whereas the traditional Jewish Hebrew text (proto-Masoretic) on which St. Jerome based the Vulgate is 4 to 5 percent longer. As is the case with Jeremiah, the additional material consists largely of amplifications and clarifications that make the book easier to understand for later generations of readers. While the shorter edition looks original, the longer edition is also quite ancient.

Structure Ezekiel was a high-ranking priest serving in the Jerusalem Temple and would have received the best literary education available in the kingdom of Judah. This is reflected in the composition of his book, which is more clearly organized and structured than almost any other prophetic text. Record-keeping was essential to the priestly ministry, and Ezekiel carefully records the day, month, and year when he received divine revelations. These date notations provide a thread of continuity throughout the book (1:1; 8:1; 20:1; 24:1; 26:1; 29:1, 17; 30:20; 31:1; 32:1, 17; 33:21; 40:1). The dates follow chronological order—with only a few exceptions—so that the reader moves in order from the earliest to the latest oracles.

The book may be divided into four unequal parts: **(1)** Chapters 1–24 recount the ministry and messages of Ezekiel prior to the destruction of Jerusalem; **(2)** chapters 25–32 contain oracles of judgment against Gentile nations; **(3)** chapters 33–39 convey oracles of postexilic restoration for the people of Israel and the city of Jerusalem; and **(4)** chapters 40–48 are a tightly integrated vision of a new Temple and liturgy, situated in a land of Israel that has been resettled, redistributed, and restored to peace and prosperity.

Thus, like the other major prophets, Ezekiel consists of a section devoted to the lifetime and ministry of the prophet himself (chaps. 1–24; cf. Is 1–12, or Jer 1–25); a section of "oracles against the nations" (chaps. 25–32; cf. Jer 46–51, Is 13–30); and a section comprising oracles of restoration for the age to come (chaps. 33–48; cf. Is 40–66; Jer 30–33).

The Prophet and His Times Very little is known about the life of Ezekiel other than what he tells us in his book. In fact, his name is mentioned only three times in the entire Bible (Ezek 1:3; 24:24; Sir 49:8). If the "thirtieth year" mentioned in 1:1 is the thirtieth year of the prophet's lifetime, then he was born ca. 622 B.C. and presumably grew up in a priestly family that resided in or near Jerusalem. About 597 B.C., Nebuchadnezzar, king of Babylon, captured Jerusalem and exiled the Judean king (Jehoiachin) and all the middle and upper classes of Judean society to various locations in Babylon (2 Kings 24:10–17). Ezekiel was among these and was deported to a place "by the river Chebar" (1:3). He was married, but his wife passed away (24:15–18), and he did not remarry, nor is mention made of any children. He enjoyed some respect and esteem among his fellow exiles in Babylon (e.g., 20:1), even if the substance of his prophecy often went unheeded (e.g., 3:7; 33:32). His visions and behavior were sometimes shocking and provocative (e.g., chaps. 4–5, 12, 16, 23), and his language can be very graphic and blunt (e.g., 23:19–20), leading some modern scholars to question his mental health. Yet no insane person could produce a literary masterpiece like this book, and to attribute his style or oracles to mental illness is to fail to appreciate the seriousness of his efforts to shock his contemporaries out of their moral and spiritual complacency. Furthermore, Ezekiel is not all darkness and judgment. Although most of his oracles were condemnations of Israel, Judah, and the nations, his last major vision (chaps. 40–48), presumably recorded near the end of his life, is a profoundly hopeful revelation of a purified and restored Israel, focused around a perfect Temple.

The period of Ezekiel's ministry was one of the most tumultuous in Israel's history. The Northern Kingdom of Israel had long been destroyed (ca. 722 B.C.) by the Assyrians, but the Southern Kingdom of Judah, under the Davidic kings, held out against the Assyrians and, after 612 B.C., the new threat of Babylon. The Babylonian king Nebuchadnezzar reduced Judah to a vassal state in 605 B.C., taking hostage members of the royal court (including Daniel and his companions). In 597 B.C., Nebuchadnezzar put down a Judean rebellion by capturing Jerusalem and exiling most of the populace, leaving behind only the lower classes who worked the land and a small royal court in Jerusalem. In this exile, King Jehoiachin—the last ruling descendant of David in direct succession—and Ezekiel were taken to Babylon. In 587 B.C., Jehoiachin's uncle and successor, Zedekiah, revolted unsuccessfully, and Nebuchadnezzar had Jerusalem and its Temple destroyed, exiling most of the rest of the city's populace in 586 B.C.

The exile of 597 B.C. was much larger and more significant in Judah's history, because it was largely the descendants of this exile who preserved Judah's sacred books and returned to rebuild Jerusalem and Judean culture after the fall of Babylon in 539 B.C. But the exile of 586 B.C. is better remembered because of the trauma of the Temple's destruction and the end of the Davidic monarchy. The Book of Ezekiel begins between these two exiles, with the prophet already exercising his ministry in Babylon in 593 B.C. Most of the book (chaps. 1–33) is taken up with Ezekiel's prophecies against Judah and other nations during the crisis years leading up to the revolt and destruction of Jerusalem in 586 B.C. (see 33:21). The oracles of chapters 34–39 seem to be set in the immediate aftermath of the destruction of Jerusalem. The long concluding oracle (chaps. 40–48) comes about fourteen years after the fall of the city and a long period during which the prophet recorded no revelations. It seems to be his valedictory vision concerning Israel's future.

The Message of the Prophet Although not a "weeping prophet" like Jeremiah, Ezekiel maintains perhaps the most rigorously pessimistic view of the spiritual condition of Israel of any of the prophets. In his oracles against Israel and Judah in the first half of the book (chaps. 1–24), he describes the people as obsessed with idolatry, a kind of spiritual adultery that he notoriously likens to an unfaithful wife with a voracious appetite for other lovers (chaps. 16, 23). Ezekiel does not even see the people as capable of repentance of themselves. Nonetheless, there is hope with God. God's presence moves from Jerusalem out to Babylon, to accompany the exiles (chaps. 8–11), because it is with the exiles that the future of the nation rests (11:14–25). Yet this is not because of the righteousness of the exiles! They, too, are unrepentant, and ultimately their salvation will require a divine act, a kind of spiritual surgery in which, at some future date, God will remove their "heart of stone" and give them a "new heart" and a "new spirit" (36:26) that will be "my (God's) spirit" (36:27).

A large part of the book, however, is taken up delivering oracles of judgment on the nations surrounding Israel (chaps. 25–32, 38–39). From these, we recognize that the Lord is not the God of Israel alone, but the Creator and master of the whole earth, who calls all nations to account for their actions and judges world rulers for their arrogance and their crimes.

In Ezekiel's final vision (chaps. 40–48), Israel's infatuation with idolatry is finally annihilated, and God regathers the nation as a perfect twelve-tribe unity around a centrally located, massive, symmetrical, and perfect Temple, where a righteous Son of David humbly monitors and participates in the national worship, setting an example for all his people. Faithful celebration of the liturgy has been a dominating concern for Ezekiel from the beginning of the book and throughout; thus, it is fitting that his vision of eschatological peace and salvation for Israel focuses on the purified liturgical life of the people as their source of life, peace, and joy.

Christian Perspective. Ezekiel is very different from Isaiah or Jeremiah, but he shares with them the same overarching "bad news, good news" message: the bad news is that Israel is under God's judgment for violation of the Mosaic covenant; the good news is that a new covenant is coming, which Ezekiel calls a "covenant of peace" (34:25) or "everlasting covenant" (37:26). In particular, Ezekiel explicitly recognizes the limitations of the old Mosaic covenant (20:25) as "ordinances by which they could not have life", thus anticipating the treatment of the Mosaic Law in the Gospels and Paul. Jesus recognizes that "not good" laws were given to Israel because of sin, the "hardness of heart" (Mt 19:8; Mk 10:5). Likewise, Paul speaks of the law being "added because of transgressions" (Gal 3:19). The belief that there were limitations and accommodations in the old or Mosaic covenant is not a Christian innovation, but an insight of the Israelite prophets themselves.

Of all the New Testament, it is the Johannine literature that is most heavily influenced by Ezekiel. The Shepherd discourse of Ezek 34 is an important background text for understanding the Feeding of the five thousand (Jn 6:1–15, but also Mk 6:34–44) as the act of the Christ, the Good Shepherd, both God and Son of David, who feeds the tribes of Israel (twelve baskets) on the mountain heights where there is good pasture (cf. Mk 6:39; Jn 6:10). The same chapter of Ezekiel is the inspiration for the Good Shepherd discourse (Jn 10:1–18). The Lazarus narrative (Jn 11) assumes the background of the Vision of Dry Bones (37:1–14), especially 37:13: "And you shall know that I am the LORD, when I open your graves, and raise you from your graves, O my people." Against the background of this verse, it is clear that John regards the resurrection of Lazarus as proof of the divinity of Jesus Christ. Ezekiel 47, the vision of the River of Life from the Temple, lies behind Jn 7:37–39, which alternatively translated reads: "Jesus stood up and proclaimed, 'If any one thirst, let him come to me; and let him drink who believes in me. As the Scripture has said, "Out of his heart shall flow rivers of living water."' Now this he said about the Spirit...." John's quote, "Out of his heart shall flow rivers of living water", is a paraphrase of 47:1–12, which shows a River of Life flowing out from the heart of the Temple. Jesus identifies himself as Ezekiel's New Temple (cf. Jn 2:21) from which flows the River of the Spirit, a sign of which is the flow of blood and water from the side of Christ in Jn 19:34. This imagery occurs again in Rev 22:1–5. The entire Book of Revelation is filled from beginning to end with allusions to Ezekiel (e.g., compare Rev 18 with Ezek 27), notably the end (Rev 21–22), where John the seer recapitulates the prophet's journey to see and measure the new Temple City of God (Rev 21:10, 15, etc.).

The early Church saw Christ's fulfillment of Ezekiel's vision of the eschaton perpetuated in the ministry of the Sacraments, in which Christ continues to be present to his people. Ezekiel's predicted sprinkling with "clean water" (36:25) finds its realization in Baptism, which is also the River of Life (47:1–12), the River of the Spirit that brings life to the nations, bestowing the "new heart" and "new spirit" (36:26) necessary to be a partaker of the "everlasting covenant" of peace (37:26). In the Eucharist, Christ the divine Shepherd (34:15) continues to feed his sheep with "fat pasture" (34:14) in the "heavenly Jerusalem" (Heb 12:22), the true "mountain heights of Israel" (34:14) so that they may eat and be satisfied (Mk 6:42). Because of the concentration of baptismal typology in 36:16–28, the passage was used for mystagogical preaching by the Church Fathers and is the seventh and final Old Testament Reading for the Easter Vigil liturgy.

OUTLINE OF EZEKIEL

1. Ezekiel's Ministry before the Fall of Jerusalem (chaps. 1–24)

A. The Fifth Year of the Exile (1:1—7:27)
B. The Sixth Year of the Exile (8:1—19:14)
C. The Seventh Year of the Exile (20:1—23:49)
D. The Ninth Year of the Exile (24:1–27)

2. Ezekiel's Oracles against the Nations (chaps. 25–32)

A. Judgment on Ammon, Moab, Edom, Philistia (25:1–17)
B. Judgment on Tyre and Sidon (26:1—28:26)
C. Judgment on Egypt and Pharaoh (29:1—32:32)

3. Ezekiel's Ministry after the Fall of Jerusalem (chaps. 33–39)

A. Ezekiel the Watchman (33:1–20)
B. Judgment on the Survivors in Judah (33:21–33)
C. The Book of Comfort (34:1—37:28)
D. Prophecy against Gog (38:1—39:20)
E. The Restoration of Israel (39:21–29)

4. Ezekiel's Vision of the Temple (chaps. 40–48)

A. Dimensions of the New Temple (40:1—42:20)
B. The Glory of the Lord Fills the New Temple (43:1–27)
C. The Liturgies of the New Temple (44:1—46:24)
D. The Water Flowing from the New Temple (47:1–23)
E. The Tribal Territories in the Promised Land (48:1–35)

THE BOOK OF

EZEKIEL

The Vision of the Four Living Creatures

1 In the thirtieth year, in the fourth month, on the
fifth day of the month, as I was among the exiles
by the river Che'bar, the heavens were opened, and
I saw visions of God. [2]On the fifth day of the month
(it was the fifth year of the exile of King Jehoi'achin),
[3]the word of the LORD came to Ezek'iel the priest,
the son of Buzi, in the land of the Chalde'ans by the
river Che'bar; and the hand of the LORD was upon
him there.
4 As I looked, behold, a stormy wind came out of
the north, and a great cloud, with brightness round
about it, and fire flashing forth continually, and in the
midst of the fire, as it were gleaming bronze. [5]And
from the midst of it came the likeness of four living
creatures.* And this was their appearance: they had
the form of men, [6]but each had four faces, and each
of them had four wings. [7]Their legs were straight,
and the soles of their feet were like the sole of a calf's
foot; and they sparkled like burnished bronze. [8]Under
their wings on their four sides they had human
hands. And the four had their faces and their wings
thus: [9]their wings touched one another; they went
every one straight forward, without turning as they

1:1: Rev 19:11. **1:5, 18:** Rev 4:6.

1:1–3 These verses function to introduce the prophet and his book. They identify the prophet's age (30 years), specify the year, month, and day the prophet received his first vision (July 31, 593 B.C.), his location (by the Chebar canal near Nippur in Babylon), his profession (priest), and his father (Buzi).

1:1 the thirtieth year ... fourth month ... fifth day of the month: The prophet does not specify the date from which he counts but the best explanation is from his birth. If so, the prophet was born about 622 B.C. Thirty years old was the typical age for priests to begin their ministry (Num 4:3, 23, 30). **the river Chebar:** The Chebar canal, known from a few ancient texts to have been near Nippur, an ancient and culturally important city in southeast Mesopotamia, about 70 miles southwest of Babylon, near the town of Afak in modern Iraq.

1:2 fifth year: 593 B.C. **King Jehoiachin:** Exiled in 597 B.C., he was the last son of David in direct line of succession to rule in Jerusalem, reigning for three months after the death of his father, Jehoiakim, until the city was taken by Nebuchadnezzar (2 Kings 24:8–17). His uncle Zedekiah was placed on the throne as his successor (2 Kings 24:17), although many Judeans continued to consider Jehoiachin the legitimate king. Ezekiel certainly did and makes Jehoiachin's exile the linchpin of the dating of his book. This and the next verse, phrased in the third person, were probably added later by the prophet himself, or an editor, to clarify further the date, author, and location.

1:3 Ezekiel The name means "God strengthens" (cf. Ezek 3:14: "The hand of the LORD [was] strong upon me"). God strengthened Ezekiel for a difficult ministry in the face of rejection. **the priest, the son of Buzi:** Ezekiel came from priestly lineage, which shows itself in his diction, concerns, and themes. His father, Buzi, is not otherwise known. **Chaldeans:** The Hebrew is *Kasdîm*, which is essentially synonymous in the Bible with "Babylonians". Famously, Abraham came from "Ur of the Chaldeans" (Gen 11:28).

1:4–28 Ezekiel's vision of the divine chariot. The mobile throne of God borne on four cherubim is known in Judaism as the *merkavah* ("chariot"). Cherubim are associated with God's presence, especially the divine throne or throne-room (Gen 3:24; Ex 25:18–22; 25:22; 2 Sam 6:2, 22:11; 1 Kings 6:23–35). Four cherubim were depicted in the Holy of Holies: two on the Ark of the Covenant, and two overshadowing the Ark (cf. 1 Kings 8:6–7). This is the likely inspiration for the four cherubim Ezekiel witnesses. Ezekiel beholds the reality represented by the Ark of the Covenant in the Holy of Holies: the Lord God enthroned above the wings of the cherubim (cf. 1 Sam 4:4; 2 Sam 6:2; 2 Kings 19:15; Ps 80:1; 99:1; Is 37:16). This theophany (= an appearance of God) is described using terms and images from other great theophanies at key locations in salvation history: Eden, Ararat, and Sinai. The God who appeared in those places now shows himself to Ezekiel. However, unlike the ark in the Temple, this cherubim-throne of God is highly mobile, born on the wings and wheels of the cherubim, able to visit not only sacred locations (Eden, Ararat, Sinai, Zion) but also profane ones like the river Chebar in Babylon. God's presence has come to visit with Ezekiel and his fellow exiles.

1:4 stormy wind ... great cloud ... fire flashing forth: The imagery resembles the theophany at Mt. Sinai (Ex 19:16–19). Ezekiel is a "new Moses", who beholds the appearance of God. **Gleaming bronze:** Bronze is a symbol of strength, as it is almost as strong as iron; yet, unlike iron, it is suitable for sacred use, such as the altar of sacrifice (Ex 27:2) and the pillars of the Temple (1 Kings 7:15–22). The cherubim represent sacred strength.

1:5 four living creatures: These are cherubim, although they will not be explicitly named as such until Ezek 9:3. Their physical characteristics are symbolic of strength and dominion.

1:6 four wings: These connote unrestricted mobility. The cherubim, and the divine presence they bear, can move anywhere.

1:7 Their legs were straight: They do not need to exert themselves to move. **burnished bronze:** See note on 1:4.

1:8 human hands: Suggests great power to manipulate, shape, and control things and the environment.

1:9 wings touched: Like the wings of the cherubim in the Holy of Holies (1 Kings 6:27). **without turning as they went:** I.e., effortlessly.

The beginning of Ezekiel's ministry overlapped the end of that of Jeremiah and the prophet is concerned with the same evils. But his style and matter are very different. Ezekiel was a priest and mainly concerned with the temple worship and the observances of the law. His description of the future temple should be compared with that in Rev 21. Ezekiel performs a great variety of symbolic actions—as did Jeremiah on a smaller scale. Ezekiel's visions make one think of apocalyptic writing, e.g., Daniel and Revelation. He does not enlarge greatly on Messianic themes. He speaks of a new covenant (16:60) and, like Jeremiah, of personal responsibility (chapter 18). Above all, he insists on the need for interior renewal, and thus prepares the way for the teaching of Christ.

*1:5, *four living creatures*: The description recalls the Assyrian *karibu*: statues of animals with human heads guarding the palace at Nineveh. Here these creatures are pressed into the service of Yahweh. They are met again in Rev 4:6–8. The point of the vision is that Yahweh is not tied to Jerusalem and could follow his people into exile.

went. 10 As for the likeness of their faces, each had the face of a man in front;[a] the four had the face of a lion on the right side, the four had the face of an ox on the left side, and the four had the face of an eagle at the back.[b] 11 Such were their faces. And their wings were spread out above; each creature had two wings, each of which touched the wing of another, while two covered their bodies. 12 And each went straight forward; wherever the spirit would go, they went, without turning as they went. 13 In the midst[c] of the living creatures there was something that looked like burning coals of fire, like torches moving back and forth among the living creatures; and the fire was bright, and out of the fire went forth lightning. 14 And the living creatures darted back and forth, like a flash of lightning.

15 Now as I looked at the living creatures, I saw a wheel upon the earth beside the living creatures, one for each of the four of them.[d] 16 As for the appearance of the wheels and their construction: their appearance was like the gleaming of a chrysolite; and the four had the same likeness, their construction being as it were a wheel within a wheel. 17 When they went, they went in any of their four directions[e] without turning as they went. 18 The four wheels had rims and they had spokes;[f] and their rims were full of eyes round about. 19 And when the living creatures went, the wheels went beside them; and when the living creatures rose from the earth, the wheels rose. 20 Wherever the spirit would go, they went, and the wheels rose along with them; for the spirit of the living creatures was in the wheels. 21 When those went, these went; and when those stood, these stood; and when those rose from the earth, the wheels rose along with them; for the spirit of the living creatures was in the wheels.

22 Over the heads of the living creatures there was the likeness of a firmament, shining like crystal,[g] spread out above their heads. 23 And under the firmament their wings were stretched out straight, one toward another; and each creature had two wings covering its body.* 24 And when they went, I heard the sound of their wings like the sound of many waters, like the thunder of the Almighty, a sound of tumult like the sound of a host; when they stood still, they let down their wings. 25 And there came a voice from above the firmament over their heads; when they stood still, they let down their wings.

1:10: Rev 4:7. **1:13:** Rev 4:5. **1:18:** Ezek 10:12; Rev 4:8. **1:24:** Ezek 43:2; Rev 1:15; 14:2; 19:6.

1:10 man ... lion ... ox ... eagle: The lords of various created domains. The lion is the king of wild animals, the ox of domestic animals, the eagle of flying creatures, and man over all living things. The cherubim possess all the powers and authority of the elite creatures of the cosmos. • The four creatures denote the four evangelists. The *man* represents Matthew, who begins his account with human generations; the *lion* indicates Mark, because he opens with crying in the wilderness; the *ox* describes Luke, who starts from sacrifice; and the *eagle* rightly signifies John, because he begins with the divinity of the Word, fixing his eye on the sun like an eagle (St. Gregory the Great, *Homilies on Ezekiel* 1, 4, 1).

1:11 touched the wing of another: See note on 1:9. **two covered their bodies:** A sign of humility in the divine presence. Nakedness could not be exposed in God's presence (Ex 20:26).

1:12 straight forward ... without turning: Effortlessly guided by the Spirit. See also 1:17.

1:13 burning coals ... torches ... fire ... lightning: Recalls previous theophanies in Gen 15:17 (to Abraham), Ex 3:2 (to Moses), Ex 19:16–18 (to Israel), and Is 6:6 (to Isaiah). Fire is a sign of God's presence generally and, particularly, of God's Spirit (Acts 2:2–3; Rev 4:5). God's Spirit moves among the cherubim.

1:15 a wheel ... one for each: The wheels, too, denote mobility. They may seem redundant, since the cherubim have wings, but Ezekiel's visions often have multiple motifs that pound home the same point. The wings may connote the ability to traverse the heavenly realm (spiritual reality), the wheels to traverse the terrestrial realm (physical reality). Despite what many Israelites thought, God's presence can move wherever it will, not being limited to the Jerusalem Temple or any other earthly location, no matter how venerable.

1:16 chrysolite: Vibrant green, gem-quality olivine, a precious stone associated with Eden, the primordial garden-temple (28:13), and reappearing in the heavenly Jerusalem (Rev 21:20). **a wheel within a wheel:** Suggests hypermobility.

1:18 full of eyes: Nothing escapes the notice of the cherubim—they partake, as it were, in the divine omniscience (cf. Ps 11:4).

1:20 spirit ... in the wheels: Not that the souls of the creatures reside in the wheels, the way the human soul is popularly imagined to reside in the "heart"; but rather that the wheels are joined to the creatures as one being, the same spirit animating both creature and wheel.

1:22 firmament: The Hebrew is *raqia'*, a rare and archaic word, recalling the "firmament" of the sky that separated the waters on the second day of creation (Gen 1:6–7). The creation story is marked by Temple-building motifs: the creation is a Temple for the Lord (cf. Ps 78:69). Likewise, this mobile throne is a microcosm, an icon of the universe-as-Temple, with all living things represented in the faces of the cherubim (the lords of all animals) and the presence of the four elements, fire (1:13), earth (1:16), air (1:22), and water (1:24). See essay: *Theology of the Temple* at 2 Chron 5. **shining like crystal:** Resembles the sapphire pavement under the throne of the Lord beheld at Sinai by Moses and the elders (Ex 24:10). Sinai is one of the key reference points for interpreting this vision, linking Ezekiel to the legacy of Moses.

1:23 their wings: See note on 1:11.

1:24 the sound of many waters: Water is the last of the four elements (earth, air, fire, water) to be mentioned as part of the vision of God's throne.

1:25 a voice from above the firmament: While seated on his throne above the wings of the cherubim, God speaks to Ezekiel. The only other human to experience this privilege was Moses (Ex 25:22). This is one of many motifs that mark Ezekiel as a new Moses figure, a "prophet like me" (Deut 18:15).

[a] Cn: Heb lacks *in front*.
[b] Cn: Heb lacks *at the back*.
[c] Gk Old Latin: Heb *And the likeness of*.
[d] Heb *of their faces*.
[e] Heb *on their four sides*.
[f] Cn: Heb uncertain.
[g] Gk: Heb *awesome crystal*.
*1:23: cf. the cherubim over the ark (Ex 25:20–22; 1 Sam 4:4).

The Glory of the Lord

26 And above the firmament over their heads there was the likeness of a throne, in appearance like sapphire;[h] and seated above the likeness of a throne was a likeness as it were of a human form. [27]And upward from what had the appearance of his loins I saw as it were gleaming bronze, like the appearance of fire enclosed round about; and downward from what had the appearance of his loins I saw as it were the appearance of fire, and there was brightness round about him.[i] [28]Like the appearance of the bow that is in the cloud on the day of rain, so was the appearance of the brightness round about.

Such was the appearance of the likeness of the glory of the LORD.* And when I saw it, I fell upon my face, and I heard the voice of one speaking.

2 And he said to me, "Son of man, stand upon your feet, and I will speak with you." [2]And when he spoke to me, the Spirit entered into me and set me upon my feet; and I heard him speaking to me. [3]And he said to me, "Son of man, I send you to the sons of Israel, to a nation[j] of rebels, who have rebelled against me; they and their fathers have transgressed against me to this very day. [4]The people also are impudent and stubborn: I send you to them; and you shall say to them, 'Thus says the Lord GOD.' [5]And whether they hear or refuse to hear (for they are a rebellious house) they will know that there has been a prophet among them. [6]And you, son of man, be not afraid of them, nor be afraid of their words, though briers and thorns are with you and you sit upon scorpions; be not afraid of their words, nor be dismayed at their looks, for they are a rebellious house. [7]And you shall speak my words to them, whether they hear or refuse to hear; for they are a rebellious house.

The Vision of the Scroll

8 "But you, son of man, hear what I say to you; be not rebellious like that rebellious house; open your mouth, and eat what I give you." [9]And when I looked, behold, a hand was stretched out to me, and behold, a written scroll was in it; [10]and he spread it before me; and it had writing on the front and on the back, and there were written on it words of lamentation and mourning and woe.

1:26: Rev 1:13; 4:2. **2:8—3:3:** Rev 5:1; 10:8–10.

1:26 sapphire: The Hebrew is *sappîr*, the same word used to describe the pavement under God's throne on Sinai, beheld by Moses and the elders (Ex 24:10).

1:28 the bow: The rainbow is a sign of God's benevolent presence, calling to mind the theophany to Noah after the flood (Gen 9:13–16). The flood was a re-creation, and the rainbow image here forms part of the cosmic creation imagery of the cherubim chariot-throne. **appearance of the likeness of the glory:** Ezekiel does not claim direct sight of God, but a vision with three layers of mediation: the *appearance* of the *likeness* of the *glory* of the Lord, not the very Lord himself, whom no man can see and live (Ex 33:20). **I fell upon my face:** Prostration is a typical reaction expressing both fear and worship. **the voice of one speaking:** See note on 1:25.

2:2 The Spirit entered into me: Ezekiel makes a substantial contribution to the development of the theology of the Holy Spirit. Note that Ezekiel is passive here; the Spirit strengthens him and raises him. This represents human helplessness without the assistance of divine grace (see Rom 7:18—8:17). See word study: *Spirit* at 37:1.

2:3 rebels, who have rebelled: The Hebrew word *marad* is used for Israel's rebellion against God in the wilderness under Moses (Num 14:9) and during the tenure of Joshua (Josh 22:16–29).

2:4 impudent and stubborn: The call and mission of Moses lie in the background of this passage. Moses was sent to stubborn Pharaoh, who would not listen. By contrast, Ezekiel is sent to the Israelites themselves; but they have become as stubborn as Pharaoh himself once was!

2:5 rebellious house: The Hebrew *bêth-marî*, "house of rebellion", from *marah*, which can mean both bitter (Ex 15:23) and rebellious (Num 20:10, 24; 27:14; Deut 1:26, 43; 9:7, 23–24; 31:27) but in both instances recalls the infidelity of the wilderness wanderings.

2:6 briers and thorns ... scorpions: Traditional symbols of punishment (Gen 3:18; Deut 8:15; Judg 8:7, 16; 1 Kings 12:11, 14; Job 31:40; Is 5:6; 32:13).

2:8 be not rebellious: Recalls the appeal of Joshua and Caleb to Israel in the wilderness (Num 14:9). The prophet is called to be a solitary, faithful remnant of Israel.

2:10 writing on the front and on the back: Scrolls were usually only inscribed on the interior, as writing on the exterior would be smudged and obscured by hands handling the scroll. The double-sided inscription recalls the tablets of the Law

Word Study

Son of Man (2:1)

Ben-'ādām (Heb.): a phrase that can be translated "son of man", "son of Adam", or "son of mankind". Ezekiel is the only figure in the OT consistently called by this title. We are never told what the meaning of this title is, which appears 93 times in the book, or why the Lord uses it to address Ezekiel. It may be that, as God's primary spokesman to his generation, Ezekiel was viewed as a representative for all mankind. Or, that Ezekiel was, in some sense, the successor of the original Adam, inheriting his priestly and prophetic roles. "Son of man" later becomes Jesus' preferred form of self-reference (Mt 16:13, etc.). When he calls himself "the Son of man", Jesus probably intends to evoke Ps 8:4–8 and Dan 7:13–14, where the "son of man" is a cosmic king. But he may also wish to connect himself with Ezekiel. Like Ezekiel, Jesus Christ is both priest and prophet whose mission is to proclaim judgment on Jerusalem and its Temple and inaugurate a new Temple and a new liturgy.

[h] Heb *lapis lazuli.*
[i] Or *it.*
[j] Syr: Heb *nations.*
*1:28, *the glory of the LORD*: The luminous cloud, or shekinah (Ex 24:16), that normally dwelt in the temple.

3 And he said to me, "Son of man, eat what is
offered to you; eat this scroll, and go, speak to
the house of Israel." 2So I opened my mouth, and he
gave me the scroll to eat. 3And he said to me, "Son
of man, eat this scroll that I give you and fill your
stomach with it." Then I ate it; and it was in my
mouth as sweet as honey.

4 And he said to me, "Son of man, go, get you
to the house of Israel, and speak with my words to
them. 5For you are not sent to a people of foreign
speech and a hard language, but to the house of
Israel—6not to many peoples of foreign speech and
a hard language, whose words you cannot understand. Surely, if I sent you to such, they would listen
to you. 7But the house of Israel will not listen to you;
for they are not willing to listen to me; because all
the house of Israel are of a hard forehead and of a
stubborn heart. 8Behold, I have made your face hard
against their faces, and your forehead hard against
their foreheads. 9Like adamant harder than flint have
I made your forehead; fear them not, nor be dismayed
at their looks, for they are a rebellious house."
10Moreover he said to me, "Son of man, all my words
that I shall speak to you receive in your heart, and
hear with your ears. 11And go, get you to the exiles,
to your people, and say to them, 'Thus says the Lord
GOD'; whether they hear or refuse to hear."

Ezekiel at the River Chebar

12 Then the Spirit lifted me up, and as the glory
of the LORD arose[k] from its place, I heard behind
me the sound of a great earthquake; 13it was the
sound of the wings of the living creatures as they
touched one another, and the sound of the wheels
beside them, that sounded like a great earthquake.
14The Spirit lifted me up and took me away, and I
went in bitterness in the heat of my spirit, the hand
of the LORD being strong upon me; 15and I came
to the exiles at Tela'bib, who dwelt by the river
Che'bar.[l] And I sat there overwhelmed among
them seven days.

16 And at the end of seven days, the word of the
LORD came to me: 17"Son of man, I have made you a
watchman for the house of Israel; whenever you hear
a word from my mouth, you shall give them warning
from me. 18If I say to the wicked, 'You shall surely
die,' and you give him no warning, nor speak to warn
the wicked from his wicked way, in order to save
his life, that wicked man shall die in his iniquity;
but his blood I will require at your hand. 19But if
you warn the wicked, and he does not turn from his
wickedness, or from his wicked way, he shall die
in his iniquity; but you will have saved your life.
20Again, if a righteous man turns from his righteousness and commits iniquity, and I lay a stumbling
block before him, he shall die; because you have not
warned him, he shall die for his sin, and his righteous
deeds which he has done shall not be remembered;
but his blood I will require at your hand. 21Neverthe-
less if you warn the righteous man not to sin, and
he does not sin, he shall surely live, because he took
warning; and you will have saved your life."

Ezekiel Bound and Silenced

22 And the hand of the LORD was there upon me;
and he said to me, "Arise, go forth into the plain,[m]

3:16–21: Ezek 33:1–9.

given to Moses (Ex 32:15). Comparison and contrast with the calling and mission of Moses lie behind all of chaps. 1 to 3. **words of lamentation and mourning and woe:** Ezekiel, like Jeremiah, usually prophesies judgment. The hopeful passages of Ezekiel are largely confined to the end of the book: chaps. 34–37 and 40–48.

3:3 eat this scroll: Ezekiel's eating of the scrolls is analogous to the burning coal touching Isaiah's lips (Is 6:7) or the hand of God touching Jeremiah's mouth (Jer 1:9). It signifies God's presence contacting the prophet's organs of speech and the infusion of the divine word into the prophet. **sweet as honey:** The intimate contact with God entailed by being the recipient of divine revelation is, in itself, pleasurable and consoling, even when the message is severe.

3:5 not sent to a people of foreign speech: Moses was sent to Pharaoh, a foreigner, who refused to listen to him. Ezekiel is sent to Israel itself, yet will receive the same response as Moses did from Pharaoh: stubbornness.

3:7 Israel will not listen to you: Every true prophet is rejected by Israel. Predictions of resistance to the prophetic message are typical of prophetic call narratives (cf. Is 6:9–10; Jer 1:17–19; Mt 13:10–15; Acts 7:51–53). **hard forehead … stubborn heart:** Images similar to the "hard heart" of Pharaoh (Ex 9:34–35).

3:8 your face hard against their faces: Similar to Jeremiah (Jer 1:18–19).

3:9 adamant: The Hebrew is *shamîr*, a very rare noun (only here and Zech 7:12) for a kind of hard rock, similar to flint.

3:10 hear with your ears: A reference to Isaiah's call vision (Is 6:10).

3:12 the Spirit lifted me: The conclusion of Ezekiel's call vision, at the end of which the prophet is left alone among the exiles by the Chebar canal (3:15). **a great earthquake:** Reminiscent of Sinai (Ex 19:18). The same God who appeared to Moses has now called Ezekiel.

3:14 the hand of the LORD being strong: A key verse for understanding the life and mission of Ezekiel, whose name means "God strengthens." The hand of the Lord being strong upon the prophet can mean both that the prophet is empowered with divine strength and also that he is crushed or overwhelmed by the divine presence. Both senses are probably intended.

3:15 Telabib: Not the city of Tel-Aviv in modern Israel, but a small town near Nippur in Babylonia that was probably destroyed during the Babylonian conquest of the region and then resettled with Judeans.

3:16–21 Ezekiel is responsible for proclaiming the divine message, and as long as he does so, he will not be responsible for the lives of his hearers. This theme is reiterated at greater length in chap. 33.

3:22–27 A kind of recapitulation of Ezekiel's initial call, with further specification: Ezekiel will be confined to his house and silenced except for when God wishes to issue an oracle to the people.

[k] Cn: Heb *blessed be the glory of the* LORD.

[l] Heb *Chebar, and to where they dwelt.* Another reading is *Chebar, and I sat where they sat.*

[m] Or *valley.*

and there I will speak with you." 23So I arose and
went forth into the plain;[m] and behold, the glory of
the LORD stood there, like the glory which I had seen
by the river Che′bar; and I fell on my face. 24But the
Spirit entered into me, and set me upon my feet; and
he spoke with me and said to me, "Go, shut yourself
within your house. 25And you, O son of man, behold,
cords will be placed upon you, and you shall be
bound with them, so that you cannot go out among
the people; 26and I will make your tongue cleave
to the roof of your mouth, so that you shall be mute
and unable to reprove them; for they are a rebellious
house. 27But when I speak with you, I will open your
mouth, and you shall say to them, 'Thus says the
Lord GOD'; he that will hear, let him hear; and he
that will refuse to hear, let him refuse; for they are a
rebellious house.

A Brick: The Siege of Jerusalem Portrayed

4 "And you, O son of man, take a brick and lay
it before you, and portray upon it a city, even
Jerusalem; 2and put siegeworks against it, and build
a siege wall against it, and cast up a mound against
it; set camps also against it, and plant battering
rams against it round about. 3And take an iron
plate, and place it as an iron wall between you and
the city; and set your face toward it, and let it be in a
state of siege, and press the siege against it. This is
a sign for the house of Israel.

4 "Then lie upon your left side, and I will lay the
punishment of the house of Israel upon you;[n] for the
number of the days that you lie upon it, you shall
bear their punishment. 5For I assign to you a number
of days, three hundred and ninety days, equal to the
number of the years of their punishment; so long
shall you bear the punishment of the house of Israel.
6And when you have completed these, you shall lie
down a second time, but on your right side, and bear
the punishment of the house of Judah; forty days I
assign you, a day for each year. 7And you shall set
your face toward the siege of Jerusalem, with your
arm bared; and you shall prophesy against the city.
8And behold, I will put cords upon you, so that you
cannot turn from one side to the other, till you have
completed the days of your siege.

9 "And you, take wheat and barley, beans and
lentils, millet and spelt, and put them into a single
vessel, and make bread of them. During the number
of days that you lie upon your side, three hundred
and ninety days, you shall eat it. 10And the food
which you eat shall be by weight, twenty shekels
a day; once a day you shall eat it. 11And water you
shall drink by measure, the sixth part of a hin;
once a day you shall drink. 12And you shall eat it
as a barley cake, baking it in their sight on human
dung." 13And the LORD said, "Thus shall the people
of Israel eat their bread unclean, among the nations
where I will drive them." 14Then I said, "Ah, Lord
GOD! behold, I have never defiled myself; from my
youth up till now I have never eaten what died of
itself or was torn by beasts, nor has foul flesh come
into my mouth." 15Then he said to me, "See, I will
let you have cow's dung instead of human dung, on
which you may prepare your bread." 16Moreover he
said to me, "Son of man, behold, I will break the staff
of bread in Jerusalem; they shall eat bread by weight
and with fearfulness; and they shall drink water by
measure and in dismay. 17I will do this that they
may lack bread and water, and look at one another
in dismay, and waste away under their punishment.

3:26 tongue cleave ... your mouth: His tongue will be unable to move. This recalls the slowness "of speech and of tongue" (Heb., *kebad lashôn*) of Moses in Ex 4:10, only Ezekiel's speech impediment is divinely imposed.

4:1—5:17 In chaps. 4–5, Ezekiel performs three prophetic sign-acts, i.e., public actions or activities that have almost the character of a performance and communicate to the onlookers a theological message. Many of the prophets performed sign-acts (e.g., 1 Kings 11:29–39). Arguably, Jesus does as well, e.g., the cursing of the fig tree (Mk 11:12–14) and the cleansing of the Temple (Mk 11:15–19).

4:1 take a brick and lay it before you: God instructs Ezekiel to build a scale model of Jerusalem and to act out a siege of the city in miniature.

4:4 lie upon your left side: In Israel, directions were taken facing east, so north was "left" and south was "right". Apparently, the prophet lies on the left for the sins of the Northern Kingdom of Israel and on the right for the sins of southern Judah. The significance and origins of the numbers 390 (4:5) and 40 (4:6) are a mystery. They may be a New Exodus motif, as they total the number of years of Israel's exile in Egypt (430 years according to Ex 12:40–41). The Greek LXX, however, reads 150 instead of 390. At least we can be certain that the guilt of northern Israel is presented as more severe. The principle that one day in the life of a man is equivalent to one year in the life of a nation is found in Num 14:34 and also lies behind the forty days of the Lord's temptation (Mt 4:1–2), a recapitulation of Israel's forty years in the desert. The prophet most likely does not lie motionless 24 hours a day, but perhaps lies on his side in public several hours each day to make the point.

4:9 wheat and barley, beans and lentils, millet and spelt: This was siege bread, made when starving citizens did not have enough of any one grain to make a loaf, so they combined all their food stuffs to bake one last meal. The taste and texture were unpleasant. In this sign-act, Ezekiel prophesies that Jerusalem will be reduced to terrible suffering in an upcoming siege.

4:10 twenty shekels a day: About eight ounces.

4:11 sixth part of a hin: About two-thirds of a quart.

4:12 human dung: Animal dung was a common fuel, but not human dung, which was just as disgusting to the ancients as it is to moderns.

4:14 I have never defiled myself: Ezekiel insists he has followed the Mosaic food laws, quoting or alluding to Lev 7:18, 19:7, and especially 22:8.

4:15 cow's dung: A common fuel source, not so offensive as human dung.

4:16 I will break the staff of bread: This passage reuses language from the covenant curses of Lev 26:26, 39 and the covenant blessing of Deut 8:9. Due to sin, the covenantal curses are being triggered and the blessings inverted.

---

[m] Or *valley.*

[n] Cn: Heb *you shall lay . . . upon it.*

A Sharp Sword

5 "And you, O son of man, take a sharp sword; use it as a barber's razor and pass it over your head and your beard; then take balances for weighing, and divide the hair. [2]A third part you shall burn in the fire in the midst of the city, when the days of the siege are completed; and a third part you shall take and strike with the sword round about the city; and a third part you shall scatter to the wind, and I will unsheathe the sword after them. [3]And you shall take from these a small number, and bind them in the skirts of your robe. [4]And of these again you shall take some, and cast them into the fire, and burn them in the fire; from there a fire will come forth into all the house of Israel. [5]Thus says the Lord GOD: This is Jerusalem; I have set her in the center of the nations, with countries round about her. [6]And she has wickedly rebelled against my ordinances[o] more than the nations, and against my statutes more than the countries round about her, by rejecting my ordinances and not walking in my statutes. [7]Therefore thus says the Lord GOD: Because you are more turbulent than the nations that are round about you, and have not walked in my statutes or kept my ordinances, but have acted[p] according to the ordinances of the nations that are round about you; [8]therefore thus says the Lord GOD: Behold, I, even I, am against you; and I will execute judgments in the midst of you in the sight of the nations. [9]And because of all your abominations I will do with you what I have never yet done, and the like of which I will never do again. [10]Therefore fathers shall eat their sons in the midst of you, and sons shall eat their fathers; and I will execute judgments on you, and any of you who survive I will scatter to all the winds. [11]Wherefore, as I live, says the Lord GOD, surely, because you have defiled my sanctuary with all your detestable things and with all your abominations, therefore I will cut you down;[q] my eye will not spare, and I will have no pity. [12]A third part of you shall die of pestilence and be consumed with famine in the midst of you; a third part shall fall by the sword round about you; and a third part I will scatter to all the winds and will unsheathe the sword after them.

13 "Thus shall my anger spend itself, and I will vent my fury upon them and satisfy myself; and they shall know that I, the LORD, have spoken in my jealousy, when I spend my fury upon them. [14]Moreover I will make you a desolation and an object of reproach among the nations round about you and in the sight of all that pass by. [15]You shall be[r] a reproach and a taunt, a warning and a horror, to the nations round about you, when I execute judgments on you in anger and fury, and with furious chastisements—I, the LORD, have spoken—[16]when I loose against you[s] my deadly arrows of famine, arrows for destruction, which I will loose to destroy you, and when I bring more and more famine upon you, and break your staff of bread. [17]I will send famine and wild beasts against you, and they will rob you of your children; pestilence and blood shall pass through you; and I will bring the sword upon you. I, the LORD, have spoken."

Judgment against Idolatrous Israel

6 The word of the LORD came to me: [2]"Son of man, set your face toward the mountains of Israel, and prophesy against them, [3]and say, You mountains of Israel, hear the word of the Lord GOD! Thus says the Lord GOD to the mountains and the hills, to the ravines and the valleys: Behold, I, even I, will bring a sword upon you, and I will destroy your high places. [4]Your altars shall become desolate, and your incense altars shall be broken; and I will cast down

---

5:1–17 In this sign-act, Ezekiel dramatizes in outlandish fashion the various fates that await the inhabitants of Jerusalem: many will die in the privations of the siege; others will be slaughtered by the invading enemy; still others will be driven into exile. A very small number will survive as a remnant, but even some of these will die in the subsequent turmoil.

5:1 take a sharp sword ... razor: The sword was a symbol of warfare. Shaving was sometimes imposed on prisoners or captives as a sign of humiliation. **the hair:** Represents the people of Jerusalem.

5:2 A third part: This does not mean that exactly a third of the people will experience each fate, but rather that one of the three subsequent fates will befall most of the inhabitants of the city.

5:6 rejecting my ordinances and not walking in my statutes: As predicted in Lev 26:43, whose diction Ezekiel reuses, along with Lev 18:4 and 20:23. The point is, Israel in general and Jerusalem in particular have flagrantly disobeyed the Mosaic Law and must experience the covenant curses.

5:10 fathers shall eat their sons ... sons shall eat their fathers: The idea that parents will be reduced to eating their children to stay alive in siege conditions is found in both biblical and ancient Near Eastern curse literature (cf. Lev 26:29; Deut 28:53–57), but the idea of children eating their own parents was so horrific only Ezekiel mentions it.

5:16 my deadly arrows of famine: Images of judgment taken from Deut 32:23, 42 and Lev 26:22–26. Ezekiel is like an executor implementing the "last will and testament" of Moses upon Israel for its covenant infidelity.

6:1–14 Two more oracles (6:1–10 and 6:11–14) continue to expound and explicate the meaning of the sign-act described in 5:1–4.

6:3 mountains ... hills ... ravines ... valleys: In ancient Near Eastern religion, all notable geographic features like mountains and hills were associated with a deity or deities thought to inhabit the site. These deities were called upon as witnesses in covenant documents to hear and enforce the terms of commitment between human parties. Here, Ezekiel makes creative adaptation of this motif. The geographic features of the land of Israel are called as witnesses to the execution of the curses Israel has triggered by breaking its covenant with God.

---

[o] Or *changed my ordinances into wickedness.*
[p] Another reading is *and have not acted.*
[q] Another reading is *I will withdraw.*
[r] Gk Syr Vg Tg: Heb *And it shall be.*
[s] Heb *them.*

your slain before your idols. [5]And I will lay the dead
bodies of the people of Israel before their idols; and
I will scatter your bones round about your altars.
[6]Wherever you dwell your cities shall be waste and
your high places ruined, so that your altars will be
waste and ruined,[t] your idols broken and destroyed,
your incense altars cut down, and your works wiped
out. [7]And the slain shall fall in the midst of you, and
you shall know that I am the LORD.

8 "Yet I will leave some of you alive. When you
have among the nations some who escape the sword,
and when you are scattered through the countries,
[9]then those of you who escape will remember me
among the nations where they are carried captive,
when I have broken[u] their wanton heart which has
departed from me, and blinded their eyes which
turn wantonly after their idols; and they will be
loathsome in their own sight for the evils which
they have committed, for all their abominations.
[10]And they shall know that I am the LORD; I have
not said in vain that I would do this evil to them."

11 Thus says the Lord GOD: "Clap your hands,
and stamp your foot, and say, Alas! because of all
the evil abominations of the house of Israel; for they
shall fall by the sword, by famine, and by pestilence.
[12]He that is far off shall die of pestilence; and he that
is near shall fall by the sword; and he that is left
and is preserved shall die of famine. Thus I will
spend my fury upon them. [13]And you shall know
that I am the LORD, when their slain lie among their
idols round about their altars, upon every high hill,
on all the mountain tops, under every green tree,
and under every leafy oak, wherever they offered
pleasing odor to all their idols. [14]And I will stretch
out my hand against them, and make the land
desolate and waste, throughout all their habitations,
from the wilderness to Riblah.[v] Then they will
know that I am the LORD."

Impending Doom

7 The word of the LORD came to me: [2]"And you, O
son of man, thus says the Lord GOD to the land
of Israel: An end! The end has come upon the four
corners of the land. [3]Now the end is upon you, and I
will let loose my anger upon you, and will judge you
according to your ways; and I will punish you for all
your abominations. [4]And my eye will not spare you,
nor will I have pity; but I will punish you for your
ways, while your abominations are in your midst.
Then you will know that I am the LORD.

5 "Thus says the Lord GOD: Disaster after disaster! Behold, it comes. [6]An end has come, the end
has come; it has awakened against you. Behold, it
comes. [7]Your doom[w] has come to you, O inhabitant
of the land; the time has come, the day is near, a
day of tumult, and not of joyful shouting upon the
mountains. [8]Now I will soon pour out my wrath
upon you, and spend my anger against you, and
judge you according to your ways; and I will punish
you for all your abominations. [9]And my eye will
not spare, nor will I have pity; I will punish you
according to your ways, while your abominations
are in your midst. Then you will know that I am the
LORD, who strike.

10 "Behold, the day! Behold, it comes! Your
doom[w] has come, injustice[x] has blossomed, pride
has budded. [11]Violence has grown up into a rod of
wickedness; none of them shall remain, nor their
abundance, nor their wealth; neither shall there be
preeminence among them.[y] [12]The time has come,
the day draws near. Let not the buyer rejoice,
nor the seller mourn, for wrath[z] is upon all their

6:9: Ezek 20:43; 36:31. **7:2:** Rev 7:1; 20:8.

6:5 scatter your bones round about your altars: Even in paganism, human bones would render sacred sites unclean and unusable.

6:6 high places ruined: Hills and mountains were preferred sites for sanctuaries or temples to local deities. See word study: *High Places* at 2 Kings 23:5.

6:13 upon every high hill . . . under every green tree: A shorthand reference to pagan practice in Deuteronomy (Deut 12:2) as well as in the historical books influenced by Deuteronomy (1 Kings 14:23; 2 Kings 16:4; 17:10).

6:14 from the wilderness to Riblah: The whole land of Israel, from the south to the north. The wilderness (Heb., *midbar*) refers to the desert that marks the southern boundary of Judah; Riblah is a town in Hamath, the region north of Galilee.

7:1–27 It is hard to know whether this chapter is one long oracle or several individual ones on the same theme, but the distinction is trivial. The message is obvious: Unmitigated destruction awaits Israel and Jerusalem as punishment for their sins.

7:2 four corners of the land: Literally, "four wings" (Heb., *kenaphîm*). The image is from tailoring, when a rectangular garment with four corners or "wings" would be laid out on a table for cutting.

7:6 An end has come: The influence of Amos 8:1–3 can be felt throughout this chapter. Amos saw a basket of summer "figs" (Heb. *qayîṣ*) that indicated the "end" (Heb. *qêṣ*) had come.

7:10 Behold, the day! Behold, it comes!: Ezekiel echoes Zeph 1:14–16. A generation earlier, Zephaniah had warned that the "day of the LORD"—a typical term for a feast day or holy day—was coming, but it would not bring rejoicing but doom and judgment. **injustice has blossomed:** Literally, "the staff has blossomed", a reference to the blossoming and fruiting of Aaron's staff in Num 17:8, whose Hebrew wording Ezekiel creatively reuses. The blossoming of Aaron's staff was an omen of blessing, but now the blossoming staff is a "rod of wickedness" (7:11) that will bring violent judgment on the land. Ezekiel frequently takes positive images and language from the Pentateuch and inverts it in messages of judgment to his contemporaries.

[t] Syr Vg Tg: Heb *and be made guilty*.
[u] Syr Vg Tg: Heb *I have been broken*.
[v] Another reading is *Diblah*.
[w] The meaning of the Hebrew word is uncertain.
[x] Or *the rod*.
[y] The Hebrew of verse 11 is uncertain.
[z] Cn: Heb *vision*.

multitude. [13]For the seller shall not return to what he has sold, while they live. For wrath is upon all their multitude; it shall not turn back; and because of his iniquity, none can maintain his life.[a]

14 "They have blown the trumpet and made all ready; but none goes to battle, for my wrath is upon all their multitude. [15]The sword is without, pestilence and famine are within; he that is in the field dies by the sword; and him that is in the city famine and pestilence devour. [16]And if any survivors escape, they will be on the mountains, like doves of the valleys, all of them moaning, every one over his iniquity. [17]All hands are feeble, and all knees weak as water. [18]They clothe themselves with sackcloth, and horror covers them; shame is upon all faces, and baldness on all their heads. [19]They cast their silver into the streets, and their gold is like an unclean thing; their silver and gold are not able to deliver them in the day of the wrath of the LORD; they cannot satisfy their hunger or fill their stomachs with it. For it was the stumbling block of their iniquity. [20]Their[b] beautiful ornament they used for vainglory, and they made their abominable images and their detestable things of it; therefore I will make it an unclean thing to them. [21]And I will give it into the hands of foreigners for a prey, and to the wicked of the earth for a spoil; and they shall profane it. [22]I will turn my face from them, that they may profane my precious[c] place; robbers shall enter and profane it, [23]and make a desolation.[d]

"Because the land is full of bloody crimes and the city is full of violence, [24]I will bring the worst of the nations to take possession of their houses; I will put an end to their proud might, and their holy places shall be profaned. [25]When anguish comes, they will seek peace, but there shall be none. [26]Disaster comes upon disaster, rumor follows rumor; they seek a vision from the prophet, but the law perishes from the priest, and counsel from the elders. [27]The king mourns, the prince is wrapped in despair, and the hands of the people of the land are palsied by terror. According to their way I will do to them, and according to their own judgments I will judge them; and they shall know that I am the LORD."

Vision of Abominations in the Temple

8 In the sixth year, in the sixth month, on the fifth day of the month, as I sat in my house, with the elders of Judah sitting before me, the hand of the Lord GOD fell there upon me. [2]Then I beheld a form that had the appearance of a man;[e] below what appeared to be his loins it was fire, and above his loins it was like the appearance of brightness, like gleaming bronze. [3]He put forth the form of a hand, and took me by a lock of my head; and the Spirit lifted me up between earth and heaven, and brought me in visions of God to Jerusalem, to the entrance of the gateway of the inner court that faces north, where was the seat of the image of jealousy, which provokes to jealousy. [4]And behold, the glory of the God of Israel was there, like the vision that I saw in the plain.

5 Then he said to me, "Son of man, lift up your eyes now in the direction of the north." So I lifted

---

7:13 the seller shall not return to what he has sold: A reference to the Jubilee Year laws of Lev 25:10–55, according to which property could not be sold permanently, but would return to the owner or his family within 50 years. In the coming destruction, all the functions of Israelite society will cease.

7:15 sword ... pestilence ... famine: A traditional triad of curses, very common in Jeremiah and Ezekiel, possibly inspired by the enumeration of covenantal curses in Lev 26:25–26, a passage to which Ezekiel often alludes.

7:16 like doves ... moaning: Doves tend to gather in flocks where they communicate with mournful-sounding calls.

7:17 knees weak as water: Literally, "knees running with water", referring to men wetting themselves from fear.

7:20 Their beautiful ornament ... vainglory: In one sense, a reference to the Temple is intended here. The idea of Israel using its holy and beautiful gifts from God for the profane worship of idols will be developed more fully in chap. 16.

7:22 my precious place: The Jerusalem Temple.

7:26 the prophet ... the priest ... the elders: The failure of the leadership classes of Israel. Prophets delivered divine revelation; priests were supposed to be experts in sacred law; and elders were supposed to be fonts of wisdom from their long experience of life.

7:27 According to their way I will do to them: Ezekiel often describes God in terms of wrath, but in the final analysis, what Israel receives is poetically just: the violence and injustice it practices on the poor and vulnerable come back upon its own head.

8:1 sixth year ... sixth month ... fifth day: Probably September 18, 592 B.C. The last date notice was in 1:1, probably August 7, 593 B.C. A formal recording of the date signals a major new section of the book. In this case, it introduces a long vision that will extend to the end of chap. 11 (see 11:24–25). **elders of Judah sitting before me:** An indication that, despite the predictions that his message would be ignored or rejected, Ezekiel does receive a certain amount of respect from his contemporaries.

8:2 the appearance of a man: Ezekiel is careful not to assert that it *is* a man. God is appearing to the prophet in images he can comprehend. Note the visual similarities to the vision of the divine chariot in chaps. 1–3.

8:3 in visions of God to Jerusalem: Ezekiel is physically in Babylon but is transported in a visionary state to Jerusalem. **image of jealousy:** Apparently an idol stood at this place in the Temple. It may be similar to the image of the goddess Asherah (= Juno or Hera) set up by King Manasseh in the sanctuary (see 2 Kings 21:7; cf. 2 Chron 33:7, 15).

8:4 the vision that I saw in the plain: The opening vision of chaps. 1–3. The divine chariot of God's presence appears again. Ezekiel is resuming the exposition of themes introduced at the beginning of the book.

---

[a] Heb obscure.
[b] Syr Symmachus: Heb *Its.*
[c] Or *secret.*
[d] Cn: Heb *make the chain.*
[e] Gk: Heb *fire.*

up my eyes toward the north, and behold, north of
the altar gate, in the entrance, was this image
of jealousy. 6And he said to me, "Son of man, do
you see what they are doing, the great abominations
that the house of Israel are committing here, to drive
me far from my sanctuary? But you will see still
greater abominations."
7 And he brought me to the door of the court; and
when I looked, behold, there was a hole in the wall.
8Then said he to me, "Son of man, dig in the wall";
and when I dug in the wall, behold, there was a
door. 9And he said to me, "Go in, and see the vile
abominations that they are committing here." 10So
I went in and saw; and there, portrayed upon the
wall round about, were all kinds of creeping things,
and loathsome beasts, and all the idols of the house
of Israel. 11And before them stood seventy men of
the elders of the house of Israel, with Ja-azani'ah the
son of Sha'phan standing among them. Each had
his censer in his hand, and the smoke of the cloud
of incense went up. 12Then he said to me, "Son of
man, have you seen what the elders of the house of
Israel are doing in the dark, every man in his room[f]
of pictures? For they say, 'The LORD does not see us,
the LORD has forsaken the land.'" 13He said also to
me, "You will see still greater abominations which
they commit."
14 Then he brought me to the entrance of the
north gate of the house of the LORD; and behold,
there sat women weeping for Tammuz.* 15Then he
said to me, "Have you seen this, O son of man? You
will see still greater abominations than these."
16 And he brought me into the inner court of
the house of the LORD; and behold, at the door
of the temple of the LORD, between the porch and
the altar, were about twenty-five men, with their
backs to the temple of the LORD, and their faces
toward the east, worshiping the sun toward the
east. 17Then he said to me, "Have you seen this,
O son of man? Is it too slight a thing for the house
of Judah to commit the abominations which they
commit here, that they should fill the land with
violence, and provoke me further to anger? Behold,
they put the branch to their nose. 18Therefore I will
deal in wrath; my eye will not spare, nor will I have
pity; and though they cry in my ears with a loud
voice, I will not hear them."

Vision of the Executioners

9 Then he cried in my ears with a loud voice,
saying, "Draw near, you executioners of the
city, each with his destroying weapon in his hand."
2And behold, six men came from the direction of
the upper gate, which faces north, every man with
his weapon for slaughter in his hand, and with
them was a man clothed in linen, with a writing
case at his side. And they went in and stood beside
the bronze altar.
3 Now the glory of the God of Israel had gone
up from the cherubim on which it rested to the
threshold of the house; and he called to the man
clothed in linen, who had the writing case at his
side. 4And the LORD said to him, "Go through the
city, through Jerusalem, and put a mark upon

9:4, 6: 1 Pet 4:17; Rev 7:3; 9:4; 14:1.

8:10 creeping things ... loathsome beasts: The language intentionally recalls the prohibition of idolatry in Deut 4:15–19.

8:11 seventy men of the elders: It was traditional for Israel's national ruling council to be composed of seventy elders (Ex 24:1, 9; Num 11:16, 24). The meaning is that the entire leadership of Israel is secretly involved in this illicit worship. **Ja-azaniah the son of Shaphan**: Presumably an important public figure. Shaphan was the royal scribe (2 Kings 22:3; cf. Jer 29:3; 36:12), so this was an influential family. **the cloud of incense:** Incense was reserved for the holiest acts of worship in the Temple, so the elders of Israel are offering the highest form of worship to images of creatures.

8:12 room of pictures: Implies that the leading citizens reserved rooms in their homes for private devotion to pagan deities.

8:14 weeping for Tammuz: Mesopotamian religion honored the demigod Dumuzi as lord of abundance. He was thought to die and descend to the underworld at the end of spring, provoking his worshipers, women in particular, to mourn for him. This pagan cult practice had been imported to Israel.

8:16 between the porch and the altar: A place with a high degree of sanctity (Joel 2:17). **about twenty-five men:** A round number. Ezekiel has a penchant for the number 25, which is half the Jubilee cycle of fifty years. **backs to the temple:** A sign of contempt by those who have turned away from the Lord. **worshiping the sun:** Having their backs to the Temple means they are facing east, toward the rising sun. All ancient Near Eastern societies worshiped the sun or a sun-god in some form. The sun was the chief deity of the Egyptians (Amun-Ra or Amon-Re). The Mesopotamians called him *Shamash*, and the Greeks worshiped the sun-god Apollo. Manasseh promoted the sun-cult within Israel (2 Kings 23:11–12), though it is explicitly forbidden in Deut 4:19 and 17:2–5.

8:17 they put the branch to their nose: Meaning obscure, but the context suggests this is an idiom or gesture for insulting another person, in this case, God himself.

9:2 six men: Probably angels of judgment. Six is a number of ill omen in the Bible. Alternatively, if the angelic scribe is included with the six, we have seven total, a number of completion and divinity. **a man clothed in linen:** Linen is the clothing of the priesthood, and a writing case the mark of a professional scribe. There is an association of priests with angels in the later books of the Old Testament and in Second Temple literature and the Dead Sea Scrolls. The priests of Israel, as ministers of worship, are viewed as earthly counterparts to the angels of God who serve in the heavenly sanctuary.

9:4 put a mark upon the foreheads: Literally, "put a *tav* upon the foreheads." The *tav* was the last letter of the Hebrew alphabet, phonetically equivalent to the English "t". In the old Hebrew script used prior to the Babylonian Exile, it was written either as an *X* or a simple cross (+). This shape

[f] Gk Syr Vg Tg: Heb *rooms*.

*8:14, *weeping for Tammuz*: A vegetation god known as Adonis to the Phoenicians. He was supposed to die in the summer and come to life again in the spring. Women wept at the time of his departure to the underworld.

the foreheads of the men who sigh and groan over
all the abominations that are committed in it." 5And
to the others he said in my hearing, "Pass through
the city after him, and kill; your eye shall not spare,
and you shall show no pity; 6slay old men outright,
young men and maidens, little children and women,
but touch no one upon whom is the mark. And begin
at my sanctuary." So they began with the elders
who were before the house. 7Then he said to them,
"Defile the house, and fill the courts with the slain.
Go forth." So they went forth, and killed in the city.
8And while they were killing, and I was left alone, I
fell upon my face, and cried, "Ah, Lord GOD! will you
destroy all that remains of Israel in the outpouring
of your wrath upon Jerusalem?"
9 Then he said to me, "The guilt of the house of
Israel and Judah is exceedingly great; the land is
full of blood, and the city full of injustice; for they
say, 'The LORD has forsaken the land, and the LORD
does not see.' 10As for me, my eye will not spare,
nor will I have pity, but I will repay their deeds
upon their heads."
11 And behold, the man clothed in linen, with the
writing case at his side, brought back word, saying,
"I have done as you commanded me."

Divine Glory over the Cherubim

10 Then I looked, and behold, on the firmament
that was over the heads of the cherubim there
appeared above them something like a sapphire,
in form resembling a throne. 2And he said to the
man clothed in linen, "Go in among the whirling
wheels underneath the cherubim; fill your hands
with burning coals from between the cherubim, and
scatter them over the city."
And he went in before my eyes. 3Now the cherubim were standing on the south side of the house,
when the man went in; and a cloud filled the inner
court. 4And the glory of the LORD went up from
the cherubim to the threshold of the house; and the
house was filled with the cloud, and the court was
full of the brightness of the glory of the LORD. 5And
the sound of the wings of the cherubim was heard as
far as the outer court, like the voice of God Almighty
when he speaks.
6 And when he commanded the man clothed in
linen, "Take fire from between the whirling wheels,
from between the cherubim," he went in and stood
beside a wheel. 7And a cherub stretched forth his
hand from between the cherubim to the fire that was
between the cherubim, and took some of it, and put
it into the hands of the man clothed in linen, who
took it and went out. 8The cherubim appeared to
have the form of a human hand under their wings.
9 And I looked, and behold, there were four wheels
beside the cherubim, one beside each cherub; and
the appearance of the wheels was like sparkling
chrysolite. 10And as for their appearance, the four
had the same likeness, as if a wheel were within a
wheel. 11When they went, they went in any of their
four directions[g] without turning as they went, but in
whatever direction the front wheel faced the others
followed without turning as they went. 12And[h] their
rims, and their spokes,[i] and the wheels were full of
eyes round about—the wheels that the four of them
had. 13As for the wheels, they were called in my
hearing the whirling wheels. 14And every one had
four faces: the first face was the face of the cherub, and
the second face was the face of a man, and the third
the face of a lion, and the fourth the face of an eagle.

10:1: Rev 4:2. **10:2:** Rev 8:5. **10:12:** Ezek 1:18; Rev 4:8. **10:14:** Ezek 1:10; Rev 4:7.

is still partially represented in the Latin capital *T* and lowercase *t*, which derive ultimately from the same ancient Semitic alphabet the Israelites employed. • Early Christian commentators saw great significance in the fact that the cross on the forehead marked those saved from destruction, and the motif has had a long afterlife in Christian piety (CCC 1296). See note on Rev 7:3. • We should sign ourselves with the seal of Baptism when we pray. We should make the sign of the cross on our foreheads, as on the day of our Baptism, as it is written in Ezekiel. We should not lower our hand to our mouth or beard but lift it to our forehead and sing in our heart that we have signed ourselves with the seal (St. Horsiesi, *Regulations* 7, 7).

9:6 touch no one upon whom is the mark: The vision resembles the original Passover, in which the angel of Lord went throughout Egypt, striking every household that did not have the door marked with the blood of the lamb (Ex 12:21–28). Only now it is the people of Israel, and not the Egyptians, who fall under judgment. This is one of many inversions of motifs from the Pentateuch that we find in Ezekiel.

9:10 I will repay their deeds: The wrath of God is not arbitrary, but the violence and injustice perpetrated by the Israelites come back upon them.

10:1 cherubim: In chaps. 1–3, these living creatures are never identified, but here they are explicitly called cherubim. For comments on their appearance, see the notes on chaps. 1–3. **like a sapphire ... resembling a throne:** See the notes on 1:22–26.

10:2 burning coals from between the cherubim: It is assumed that there is an altar continually burning incense before the presence of the Lord, as also implied in Is 6:6. This was represented by the altar of incense in the Jerusalem Temple.

10:3 a cloud filled the inner court: Recalling the cloud of the Lord's presence that indwelt the Tabernacle and the Solomonic Temple at its dedication (Ex 40:34–35; 1 Kings 8:10–11).

10:9–17 The description is almost identical to 1:4–21.

10:9 chrysolite: See note on 1:16.

10:14 four faces: Curiously, the description of faces from 1:10 is repeated, only the face of the ox (or bull) is replaced here with the "face of the cherub". The reason for this is obscure. From 10:22, we see that the prophet's intention was to describe an identical appearance, so perhaps there is textual corruption in the Hebrew.

[g] Heb *on their four sides.*
[h] Gk: Heb *And their whole body and.*
[i] Heb *spokes and their wings.*

15 And the cherubim mounted up. These were the living creatures that I saw by the river Che′bar. [16]And when the cherubim went, the wheels went beside them; and when the cherubim lifted up their wings to mount up from the earth, the wheels did not turn from beside them. [17]When they stood still, these stood still, and when they mounted up, these mounted up with them; for the spirit of the living creatures[j] was in them.

18 Then the glory of the LORD went forth from the threshold of the house, and stood over the cherubim. [19]And the cherubim lifted up their wings and mounted up from the earth in my sight as they went forth, with the wheels beside them; and they stood at the door of the east gate of the house of the LORD; and the glory of the God of Israel was over them.

20 These were the living creatures that I saw underneath the God of Israel by the river Che′bar; and I knew that they were cherubim. [21]Each had four faces, and each four wings, and underneath their wings the semblance of human hands. [22]And as for the likeness of their faces, they were the very faces whose appearance I had seen by the river Che′bar. They went every one straight forward.

Judgment against the Wicked Counselors

11 The Spirit lifted me up, and brought me to the east gate of the house of the LORD, which faces east. And behold, at the door of the gateway there were twenty-five men; and I saw among them Ja-azani′ah the son of Azzur, and Pelati′ah the son of Bena′iah, princes of the people. [2]And he said to me, "Son of man, these are the men who devise iniquity and who give wicked counsel in this city; [3]who say, 'The time is not near[k] to build houses; this city is the caldron, and we are the flesh.' [4]Therefore prophesy against them, prophesy, O son of man."

5 And the Spirit of the LORD fell upon me, and he said to me, "Say, Thus says the LORD: So you think, O house of Israel; for I know the things that come into your mind. [6]You have multiplied your slain in this city, and have filled its streets with the slain. [7]Therefore thus says the Lord GOD: Your slain whom you have laid in the midst of it, they are the flesh, and this city is the caldron; but you shall be brought forth out of the midst of it. [8]You have feared the sword; and I will bring the sword upon you, says the Lord GOD. [9]And I will bring you forth out of the midst of it, and give you into the hands of foreigners, and execute judgments upon you. [10]You shall fall by the sword; I will judge you at the border of Israel; and you shall know that I am the LORD. [11]This city shall not be your caldron, nor shall you be the flesh in the midst of it; I will judge you at the border of Israel; [12]and you shall know that I am the LORD; for you have not walked in my statutes, nor executed my ordinances, but have acted according to the ordinances of the nations that are round about you."

13 And it came to pass, while I was prophesying, that Pelati′ah the son of Bena′iah died. Then I fell down upon my face, and cried with a loud voice, and said, "Ah, Lord GOD! will you make a full end of the remnant of Israel?"

God Will Restore Israel

14 And the word of the LORD came to me: [15]"Son of man, your brethren, even your brethren, your fellow exiles,[l] the whole house of Israel, all of them, are those of whom the inhabitants of Jerusalem have said, 'They have gone far from the LORD; to us this land is given for a possession.' [16]Therefore say, 'Thus says the Lord GOD: Though I removed them far off among the nations, and though I scattered them

---

10:18 the glory of the LORD went forth: Ezekiel is witnessing God's presence departing from the Jerusalem Temple and moving to be with the exiles in Babylon. This is an ominous sign of the imminent destruction of the Temple. Once Israel and the Temple have been restored and reestablished, the Lord will return through the same eastern gate from which he departed (10:19, 43:1–2, 4).

11:1 twenty-five men: Presumably the same group of idolaters identified in 8:16. **Ja-azaniah the son of Azzur:** Not the same as Ja-azaniah son of Shaphan. The name Ja-azaniah means "may the LORD hear (my plea)" or "The LORD hears (my plea)" and can be found in 2 Kings 25:23; Jer 35:3, and on various *bullae* or seal impressions recovered from ancient Jerusalem. **son of Azzur, and Pelatiah the son of Benaiah:** Known public figures mentioned elsewhere in Scriptures from this time period. For Azzur, see Jer 28:1; Pelatiah, 1 Chron 3:21; Neh 10:22. Multiple Benaiahs are mentioned in 1–2 Chronicles and Ezra.

11:3 the time is not near to build houses: The probable meaning is: "No need to build houses as we can take over those of the deported exiles." **this city is the caldron, and we are the flesh:** I.e., we are like choice morsels in a pot filled with food, enjoying the plenty round about us.

11:7 Your slain ... are the flesh, and this city is the caldron: God changes what the wealthy meant as a positive metaphor into an image of death and injustice. **you shall be brought forth out of the midst of it:** The wealthy of the city thought they would be as happy in Jerusalem as chunks of meat cozily simmering in a stew, but they would in fact be pulled from the "pot" and thrown out.

11:12 you have not walked in my statutes ... ordinances: As predicted in Lev 26:43.

11:15 They have gone far ... to us this land is given: This states explicitly the attitude expressed more figuratively in 11:3. Those Jerusalemites left behind when the Babylonians exiled a large part of the population in 597 B.C. considered themselves as blessed by God to inherit the land and the deportees as accursed.

11:16 I have been a sanctuary to them: A major theme of Ezekiel is that God has accompanied the Israelites who have been exiled, and he will bring them back to the land one day and fulfill his covenant promises to them. In fact, it will largely be the descendants of the exile of 597 B.C. who repopulate the land of Judah and Jerusalem beginning in the 530s B.C. Jesus himself descends from these exiles (Mt 1:1–17; Lk 3:23–38).

---

[j] Or *of life.*
[k] Or *Is not the time near...?*
[l] Gk Syr: Heb *men of your kindred.*

among the countries, yet I have been a sanctuary to them for a while[m] in the countries where they have gone.' [17]Therefore say, 'Thus says the Lord GOD: I will gather you from the peoples, and assemble you out of the countries where you have been scattered, and I will give you the land of Israel.' [18]And when they come there, they will remove from it all its detestable things and all its abominations. [19]And I will give them one[n] heart, and put a new spirit within them; I will take the stony heart out of their flesh and give them a heart of flesh, [20]that they may walk in my statutes and keep my ordinances and obey them; and they shall be my people, and I will be their God. [21]But as for those[o] whose heart goes after their detestable things and their abominations, I will repay their deeds upon their own heads, says the Lord GOD."

22 Then the cherubim lifted up their wings, with the wheels beside them; and the glory of the God of Israel was over them. [23]And the glory of the LORD went up from the midst of the city, and stood upon the mountain which is on the east side of the city. [24]And the Spirit lifted me up and brought me in the vision by the Spirit of God into Chalde'a, to the exiles. Then the vision that I had seen went up from me. [25]And I told the exiles all the things that the LORD had showed me.

Judah's Captivity Portrayed

12 The word of the LORD came to me: [2]"Son of man, you dwell in the midst of a rebellious house, who have eyes to see, but see not, who have ears to hear, but hear not; [3]for they are a rebellious house. Therefore, son of man, prepare for yourself an exile's baggage, and go into exile by day in their sight; you shall go like an exile from your place to another place in their sight. Perhaps they will understand, though[p] they are a rebellious house. [4]You shall bring out your baggage by day in their sight, as baggage for exile; and you shall go forth yourself at evening in their sight, as men do who must go into exile. [5]Dig through the wall in their sight, and go[q] out through it. [6]In their sight you shall lift the baggage upon your shoulder, and carry it out in the dark; you shall cover your face, that you may not see the land; for I have made you a sign for the house of Israel."

7 And I did as I was commanded. I brought out my baggage by day, as baggage for exile, and in the evening I dug through the wall with my own hands; I went forth in the dark, carrying my outfit upon my shoulder in their sight.

8 In the morning the word of the LORD came to me: [9]"Son of man, has not the house of Israel, the rebellious house, said to you, 'What are you doing?' [10]Say to them, 'Thus says the Lord GOD: This oracle concerns the prince in Jerusalem and all the house of Israel who are in it.'[r] [11]Say, 'I am a sign for you: as I have done, so shall it be done to them; they shall go into exile, into captivity.' [12]And the prince who is among them shall lift his baggage upon his shoulder in the dark, and shall go forth; he[s] shall

11:19: Ezek 18:31; 36:26; 2 Cor 3:3. **12:2:** Mk 8:18.

11:17 I will gather you from the peoples: Scholars refer to this as the "Second Exodus" or "New Exodus" theme that is found in all the major prophets, Ezekiel being no exception. See essay: *The New Exodus in Isaiah* at Is 42.

11:19 I will give them one heart ... a new spirit: This theme will be developed further in 36:26–27, where the near context associates this gift of a new heart and spirit with a sprinkling "of clean water" that will forgive sins (36:25) (CCC 715).

11:20 they shall be my people, and I will be their God: This kind of phrase is called a "covenant formula", an explicit statement of the kind of relationship being established by means of an oath and covenant. It may be modeled on a statement in the ancient Israelite rite of marriage, when the bridegroom would declare: "You shall be my wife, and I shall be your husband."

11:23 mountain ... on the east side of the city: The Mount of Olives. This vision of Ezekiel is just one of many reasons why the Mount of Olives figured so prominently in Jewish and early Christian end-times beliefs. It was believed that God's presence would return along the same path by which it departed. Thus, God would reenter the Temple from the east (43:1–2), coming from the Mount of Olives (see Zech 14:4). Compare the accounts of the triumphal entry (Mt 21:1–11, etc.).

11:24 into Chaldea, to the exiles: Ezekiel never physically traveled to Jerusalem and back. Everything from chaps. 8–11 has been a vision, while his body has remained in Chaldea, i.e., Babylonia.

11:25 I told the exiles: The end of the vision and narrative that began in 8:1.

12:1 The word of the LORD came: God commands Ezekiel to perform another sign-act, this time to act like a person being exiled from his city as a foreshadowing of the exile of the population of Jerusalem that would take place in 586 B.C.

12:2 eyes to see, but see not,... ears to hear, but hear not: A familiar motif in the prophets. Compare Is 6:9–10, and Jesus' refrain "He who has ears to hear, let him hear" and similar phrases concerning eyes (Mt 11:15; 13:16; Mk 4:9, 23; 8:18; Lk 8:8; 10:23; 14:35; Jn 12:40).

12:4 as men do who must go into exile: I.e., naked. In the ancient Near East, exiles were typically taken away naked, in order to prevent them from making any effective resistance to their captors and to humiliate them. This practice was so common that the Hebrew verb "to exile [someone]" is actually a form of the verb meaning "to reveal or unclothe".

12:6 you shall cover your face, that you may not see the land: Foreshadowing the blinding of King Zedekiah, who was blinded by the Babylonians after witnessing the execution of his sons and then taken into exile (2 Kings 25:7).

12:12 the prince who is among them: King Zedekiah, whom Nebuchadnezzar, king of Babylon, had appointed king of Judah in place of his nephew Jehoiachin, when Jehoiachin

[m] Or *in small measure.*
[n] Another reading is *a new.*
[o] Cn: Heb *To the heart of their detestable things and their abominations their heart goes.*
[p] Or *will see that.*
[q] Gk Syr Vg Tg: Heb *bring.*
[r] Heb *in the midst of them.*
[s] Gk Syr: Heb *they.*

dig through the wall and go[t] out through it; he shall cover his face, that he may not see the land with his eyes. 13And I will spread my net over him, and he shall be taken in my snare; and I will bring him to Babylon in the land of the Chalde'ans, yet he shall not see it; and he shall die there. 14And I will scatter toward every wind all who are round about him, his helpers[u] and all his troops; and I will unsheathe the sword after them. 15And they shall know that I am the LORD, when I disperse them among the nations and scatter them through the countries. 16But I will let a few of them escape from the sword, from famine and pestilence, that they may confess all their abominations among the nations where they go, and may know that I am the LORD."

Judgment Will Not Be Delayed

17 Moreover the word of the LORD came to me: 18"Son of man, eat your bread with quaking, and drink water with trembling and with fearfulness; 19and say of the people of the land, Thus says the Lord GOD concerning the inhabitants of Jerusalem in the land of Israel: They shall eat their bread with fearfulness, and drink water in dismay, because their land will be stripped of all it contains, on account of the violence of all those who dwell in it. 20And the inhabited cities shall be laid waste, and the land shall become a desolation; and you shall know that I am the LORD."

21 And the word of the LORD came to me: 22"Son of man, what is this proverb that you have about the land of Israel, saying, 'The days grow long, and every vision comes to nothing'? 23Tell them therefore, 'Thus says the Lord GOD: I will put an end to this proverb, and they shall no more use it as a proverb in Israel.' But say to them, The days are at hand, and the fulfilment[v] of every vision. 24For there shall be no more any false vision or flattering divination within the house of Israel. 25But I the LORD will speak the word which I will speak, and it will be performed. It will no longer be delayed, but in your days, O rebellious house, I will speak the word and perform it, says the Lord GOD."

26Again the word of the LORD came to me: 27"Son of man, behold, they of the house of Israel say, 'The vision that he sees is for many days hence, and he prophesies of times far off.' 28Therefore say to them, Thus says the Lord GOD: None of my words will be delayed any longer, but the word which I speak will be performed, says the Lord GOD."

False Prophets Condemned

13 The word of the LORD came to me: 2"Son of man, prophesy against the prophets of Israel, prophesy[w] and say to those who prophesy out of their own minds: 'Hear the word of the LORD!' 3Thus says the Lord GOD, Woe to the foolish prophets who follow their own spirit, and have seen nothing! 4Your prophets have been like foxes among ruins, O Israel. 5You have not gone up into the breaches, or built up a wall for the house of Israel, that it might stand in battle in the day of the LORD. 6They have spoken falsehood and divined a lie; they say, 'Says the LORD,' when the LORD has not sent them, and yet they expect him to fulfil their word. 7Have you not seen a delusive vision, and uttered a lying divination, whenever you have said, 'Says the LORD,' although I have not spoken?"

8 Therefore thus says the Lord God: "Because you have uttered delusions and seen lies, therefore behold, I am against you, says the Lord GOD. 9My hand will be against the prophets who see delusive visions and who give lying divinations; they shall not be in the council of my people, nor be enrolled

---

was exiled in 597 B.C. Many Judeans did not recognize a nephew-to-uncle succession imposed by a foreign conqueror as legitimate and continued to view Jehoiachin and his heirs as heads of the royal house.

12:13 Babylon ... he shall not see it: Zedekiah's blinding by Nebuchadnezzar is predicted (2 Kings 25:7).

12:14 I will scatter ... unsheathe the sword after them: An apt description of the fall of Jerusalem in 586 B.C., known to us from Jeremiah's writings (Jer 39:1–9).

12:18 eat your bread with quaking: God gives Ezekiel another sign-act to perform. Presumably Ezekiel eats food in a public place in an exaggeratedly fearful manner.

12:22 days grow long, and every vision comes to nothing: Means "time is passing, yet what the prophets promised has not come true." This proverb was probably inspired by the preaching of the false prophets, who insisted the time of judgment and exile would be short (cf. Jer 29:1–9).

12:23 The days are at hand: The Judeans thought the positive visions of the false prophets were being delayed, but in actuality, the disastrous judgment of the true prophets was going to be fulfilled shortly.

12:27 he prophesies of times far off: It was not uncommon for prophets to speak of the distant future. Many spoke in hidden ways of the Messiah, who would not come for centuries. But in this instance, Ezekiel's prophecies of doom would be fulfilled within a few years of his proclamation of them, in 586 B.C.

13:1–23 In this chapter, the prophet calls down judgment on two classes of public deceivers: male prophets (13:1–16) and female mediums (13:17–23).

13:3 foolish prophets: Prophets could exercise great public influence, and it is natural that the role should attract counterfeits who sought to profit from it. False prophecy was a scourge of ancient Israelite society, roundly criticized by the biblical prophets (Is 9:15; Jer 14:14; 23:14, 25–26; 29:8; Lam 2:14; Zech 13:3–4; 1 Kings 22:22–23).

13:4 foxes among ruins: Or "jackals among ruins". Jackals were common scavengers in defeated cities, where they would feed on the bodies of the dead. The false prophets are taking advantage of the collapse of Judah and Jerusalem rather than strengthening their contemporaries.

13:5 built up a wall: Probably a reference to the reinforcement of the defensive walls of Jerusalem that preceded the revolts of 597 B.C. and 587 B.C.

---

[t] Gk Syr Tg: Heb *bring*.
[u] Gk Syr Tg: Heb *his help*.
[v] Heb *word*.
[w] Gk: Heb *who prophesy*.

in the register of the house of Israel, nor shall they enter the land of Israel; and you shall know that I am the Lord God. [10]Because, yes, because they have misled my people, saying, 'Peace,' when there is no peace; and because, when the people build a wall, these prophets daub it with whitewash; [11]say to those who daub it with whitewash that it shall fall! There will be a deluge of rain,[x] great hailstones will fall, and a stormy wind break out; [12]and when the wall falls, will it not be said to you, 'Where is the daubing with which you daubed it?' [13]Therefore thus says the Lord God: I will make a stormy wind break out in my wrath; and there shall be a deluge of rain in my anger, and great hailstones in wrath to destroy it. [14]And I will break down the wall that you have daubed with whitewash, and bring it down to the ground, so that its foundation will be laid bare; when it falls, you shall perish in the midst of it; and you shall know that I am the Lord. [15]Thus will I spend my wrath upon the wall, and upon those who have daubed it with whitewash; and I will say to you, The wall is no more, nor those who daubed it, [16]the prophets of Israel who prophesied concerning Jerusalem and saw visions of peace for her, when there was no peace, says the Lord God.

17 "And you, son of man, set your face against the daughters of your people, who prophesy out of their own minds; prophesy against them [18]and say, Thus says the Lord God: Woe to the women who sew magic bands upon all wrists, and make veils for the heads of persons of every stature, in the hunt for souls! Will you hunt down souls belonging to my people, and keep other souls alive for your profit? [19]You have profaned me among my people for handfuls of barley and for pieces of bread, putting to death persons who should not die and keeping alive persons who should not live, by your lies to my people, who listen to lies.

20 "Wherefore thus says the Lord God: Behold, I am against your magic bands with which you hunt the souls,[y] and I will tear them from your arms; and I will let the souls that you hunt go free[z] like birds. [21]Your veils also I will tear off, and deliver my people out of your hand, and they shall be no more in your hand as prey; and you shall know that I am the Lord. [22]Because you have disheartened the righteous falsely, although I have not disheartened him, and you have encouraged the wicked, that he should not turn from his wicked way to save his life; [23]therefore you shall no more see delusive visions nor practice divination; I will deliver my people out of your hand. Then you will know that I am the Lord."

Idolatry Condemned

14 Then came certain of the elders of Israel to me; and sat before me. [2]And the word of the Lord came to me: [3]"Son of man, these men have taken their idols into their hearts, and set the stumbling block of their iniquity before their faces; should I let myself be inquired of at all by them? [4]Therefore speak to them, and say to them, Thus says the Lord God: Any man of the house of Israel who takes his idols into his heart and sets the stumbling block of his iniquity before his face, and yet comes to the prophet, I the Lord will answer him myself[a] because of the multitude of his idols, [5]that I may lay hold of the hearts of the house of Israel, who are all estranged from me through their idols.

6 "Therefore say to the house of Israel, Thus says the Lord God: Repent and turn away from your idols; and turn away your faces from all your abominations. [7]For any one of the house of Israel, or of the strangers that sojourn in Israel, who separates himself from me, taking his idols into his heart and putting the stumbling block of his iniquity before his face, and yet comes to a prophet to inquire for himself of me, I the Lord will answer him myself; [8]and I will set my face against that man, I will make him a sign and a byword and cut him off from the midst of my people; and you shall know that I am the Lord. [9]And if the prophet be deceived

---

13:10 people build a wall ... prophets daub it with whitewash: Probably referring to the populace building up the defensive walls of Jerusalem in preparation for an ill-advised and disastrous revolt against Babylon, while the false prophets add a veneer of religious sanction and credibility to this foolish endeavor by predicting the Lord's favor on the revolt.

13:18 women who sew magic bands: It is not known exactly what these women were doing or how these magic bands and veils were thought to operate. Apparently, it was a voodoo-like practice in which the bands and veils were thought to protect the wearer and/or call down a curse on enemies.

13:19 handfuls of barley ... pieces of bread: It seems the women who made the "magic" articles sold them for food. **putting to death ... keeping alive:** It is not clear that persons were actually killed or saved by these bands and veils, but the women selling them made such promises.

13:22 disheartened the righteous ... encouraged the wicked: Righteous persons were being placed under illicit curses, and wicked persons were being falsely encouraged to seek salvation in magic rather than in repentance.

14:1 the elders of Israel: Leading men of the exiles came to inquire of the Lord from Ezekiel, yet they continued to worship other gods by the veneration of idols in private.

14:4 I the Lord will answer him myself: In other words, the Lord will judge that man directly and personally—also in 14:7.

14:9 I, the Lord, have deceived that prophet: Ezekiel uses startlingly direct language to emphasize that the deception of the false prophets is guided by God's providential hand as a means of punishment to the house of Israel. Romans 1:18–32 reveals that God's "wrath" against those who choose other things in preference to him is to "give them up" to their own choices and desire: He "gave them up to a base mind" (1:28). So the false prophets, who pursue prophecy as a means to

[x] Heb *rain and you.*
[y] Gk Syr: Heb *souls for birds.*
[z] Cn: Heb *the souls.*
[a] Cn Compare Tg: Heb uncertain.

and speak a word, I, the LORD, have deceived that prophet, and I will stretch out my hand against him, and will destroy him from the midst of my people Israel. 10 And they shall bear their punishment—the punishment of the prophet and the punishment of the inquirer shall be alike—11 that the house of Israel may go no more astray from me, nor defile themselves any more with all their transgressions, but that they may be my people and I may be their God, says the Lord GOD."

12 * And the word of the LORD came to me: 13 "Son of man, when a land sins against me by acting faithlessly, and I stretch out my hand against it, and break its staff of bread and send famine upon it, and cut off from it man and beast, 14 even if these three men, Noah, Daniel,† and Job, were in it, they would deliver but their own lives by their righteousness, says the Lord GOD. 15 If I cause wild beasts to pass through the land, and they ravage it, and it be made desolate, so that no man may pass through because of the beasts; 16 even if these three men were in it, as I live, says the Lord GOD, they would deliver neither sons nor daughters; they alone would be delivered, but the land would be desolate. 17 Or if I bring a sword upon that land, and say, Let a sword go through the land; and I cut off from it man and beast; 18 though these three men were in it, as I live, says the Lord GOD, they would deliver neither sons nor daughters, but they alone would be delivered. 19 Or if I send a pestilence into that land, and pour out my wrath upon it with blood, to cut off from it man and beast; 20 even if Noah, Daniel, and Job were in it, as I live, says the Lord GOD, they would deliver neither son nor daughter; they would deliver but their own lives by their righteousness.

21 "For thus says the Lord GOD: How much more when I send upon Jerusalem my four sore acts of judgment, sword, famine, evil beasts, and pestilence, to cut off from it man and beast! 22 Yet, if there should be left in it any survivors to lead out sons and daughters, when they come forth to you, and you see their ways and their doings, you will be consoled for the evil that I have brought upon Jerusalem, for all that I have brought upon it. 23 They will console you, when you see their ways and their doings; and you shall know that I have not done without cause all that I have done in it, says the Lord GOD."

The Useless Vine

15 And the word of the LORD came to me: 2 "Son of man, how does the wood of the vine surpass any wood, the vine branch which is among the trees of the forest? 3 Is wood taken from it to make anything? Do men take a peg from it to hang any vessel on? 4 Behold, it is given to the fire for fuel; when the fire has consumed both ends of it, and the middle of it is charred, is it useful for anything? 5 Behold, when it was whole, it was used for nothing; how much less, when the fire has consumed it and it is charred, can it ever be used for anything! 6 Therefore thus says the Lord GOD: Like

14:21: Rev 6:8.

make a living rather than a true calling from God, are handed over to the deceptions they seek as a just punishment for themselves and their hearers.

14:10 punishment of the prophet ... the inquirer ... alike: Inquirers are persons who seek out the services of the false prophets, paying them to gain insight into the future for their own advantage. Both prophet and inquirer seek an easy way around the challenging message of repentance from the true prophets, and thus they end up sharing the fate of those who turn away from God.

14:12–23 In this oracle, God insists that even if three great heroes of faith—Noah, Daniel, and Job—were in a land that turns away from him, they would not save that land. The background here is Gen 18, in which Abraham elicits from God a promise not to judge Sodom and Gomorrah for the sake of ten righteous (Gen 18:32). Although Ezekiel mentions fewer righteous—just three—they make up for numbers by the fame of their holiness.

14:13 break its staff of bread: The covenant curse found in Lev 26:26. Language from the covenant curses of Lev 26 is laced through the oracle.

*14:12–23: The Lord stresses individual responsibility rather than collective responsibility. It had been taken for granted that some just men would have to suffer in a group or city with the guilty majority.

†14:14, *Daniel*: It is possible that this refers to Danel, an ancient Phoenician sage known to us from the Ras Shamra literature. It is unlikely that Ezekiel would have been speaking of Daniel the prophet as the other names in this passage are both of more ancient personages. Moreover, the spelling of the name in the book of Ezekiel is different from the spelling used in the book of Daniel.

14:14 Noah, Daniel, and Job: Men renowned for righteousness. Israel is so far gone, not even great saints can save them. Noah and Job were famous heroes of faith from Israel's hoary past (CCC 58). Daniel was a contemporary of Ezekiel who was taken to Babylon as a hostage already in 605 B.C., but quickly distinguished himself within the Babylonian court according to Dan 1–2. Some commentators argue that a contemporary such as Daniel does not fit among ancient heroes like Noah and Job and seek to identify "Daniel" here with Dan'el, the maternal grandfather of Methuselah known in late Jewish tradition (*Jubilees* 4, 20) or the legendary King Dan'el mentioned in an ancient Canaanite source as a ruler famous for justice and righteousness. (Indeed, the name in Ezekiel is spelled consonantally *dn'l* rather than *dny'l* as in the Book of Daniel.) Yet, it seems unlikely that Ezekiel's readership could have been expected to recognize a reference to these more obscure Dan'el's rather than the famous Daniel remembered in the biblical tradition. The slight difference in spelling may be an insignificant variant.

14:21 sword, famine, evil beasts, and pestilence: Covenant curses. All four are mentioned in close proximity in Lev 26:22–26 and elsewhere throughout Lev 26:14–45. Similar chastisements are mentioned in Deut 28:15–68.

15:2 the wood of the vine ... among the trees of the forest: The metaphor of Israel as a cultivated vine can be found in some famous, older Scriptures: Ps 80:8–19 and Is 5:1–7. However, as so often, Ezekiel inverts this traditional image. Jerusalem is not a cultivated grape vine but a nuisance vine from the forest with no economic worth.

the wood of the vine among the trees of the forest, which I have given to the fire for fuel, so will I give up the inhabitants of Jerusalem. 7And I will set my face against them; though they escape from the fire, the fire shall yet consume them; and you will know that I am the LORD, when I set my face against them. 8And I will make the land desolate, because they have acted faithlessly, says the Lord GOD."

God's Unfaithful Bride

16 Again the word of the LORD came to me: 2"Son of man, make known to Jerusalem her abominations, 3and say, Thus says the Lord GOD to Jerusalem: Your origin and your birth are of the land of the Canaanites; your father was an Am′orite, and your mother a Hit′tite. 4And as for your birth, on the day you were born your navel string was not cut, nor were you washed with water to cleanse you, nor rubbed with salt, nor swathed with bands. 5No eye pitied you, to do any of these things to you out of compassion for you; but you were cast out on the open field, for you were abhorred, on the day that you were born.

6 "And when I passed by you, and saw you weltering in your blood, I said to you in your blood, 'Live, 7and grow up[b] like a plant of the field.' And you grew up and became tall and arrived at full maidenhood;[c] your breasts were formed, and your hair had grown; yet you were naked and bare.

8 "When I passed by you again and looked upon you, behold, you were at the age for love; and I spread my skirt over you, and covered your nakedness: yes, I pledged myself to you and entered into a covenant with you, says the Lord GOD, and you became mine. 9Then I bathed you with water and washed off your blood from you, and anointed you with oil. 10I clothed you also with embroidered cloth and shod you with leather, I wrapped you in fine linen and covered you with silk. 11And I decked you with ornaments, and put bracelets on your arms, and a chain on your neck. 12And I put a ring on your nose, and earrings in your ears, and a beautiful crown upon your head. 13Thus you were decked with gold and silver; and your clothing was of fine linen, and silk, and embroidered cloth; you ate fine flour and honey and oil. You grew exceedingly beautiful, and came to regal estate. 14And your renown went forth among the nations because of your beauty, for it was perfect through the splendor which I had bestowed upon you, says the Lord GOD.

15 "But you trusted in your beauty, and played the harlot because of your renown, and lavished your harlotries on any passer-by. 16You took some of your garments, and made for yourself gaily decked shrines, and on them played the harlot; the like has never been, nor ever shall be. 17You also took your fair jewels of my gold and of my silver, which I had given you, and made for yourself images of men, and with them played the harlot; 18and you took your embroidered garments to cover them, and set my oil and my incense before them. 19Also my bread which I gave you—I fed you with fine flour and oil and honey—you set before them for a pleasing odor, says the Lord GOD.[d] 20And you

16:3: Ezek 16:45.

16:1–63 One of two allegories of Israel-as-unfaithful-wife found in Ezekiel, the other being chap. 23. Both are so unrelenting and graphic as to have provoked the ancient rabbis and inspired restrictions on who was allowed to read them. These passages of Ezekiel take their place with the Song of Songs, Hos 1–3, Is 54, and a handful of other prophetic oracles to establish a theological paradigm of Israel as the bride of God and the covenantal relationship between them as having the character of a spousal commitment. The repercussions continue to be felt in the New Testament, as Jesus is understood as the Bridegroom King of the People of God (CCC 219, 1611).

16:3 Thus says the Lord GOD to Jerusalem: Jerusalem originally was a city of no consequence to the Israelites, but after David conquered it and made it his capital in 2 Sam 5 (ca. 1004 B.C.), the city grew into the spiritual and social heart of the entire nation. **origin and ... birth are of the land of the Canaanites:** Jerusalem was the last Canaanite enclave in the Promised Land to be conquered (2 Sam 5:6–10). The previous inhabitants were a Canaanite tribe known as the Jebusites, and for some time the city was known as Jebus (see Josh 18:28). **your father was an Amorite:** A wordplay on a traditional Israelite recitation of faith that began, "A wandering Aramean was my father ..." (Deut 26:5). The word "Aramean" (Heb., *ʾrmy*) and "Amorite" (Heb., *ʾmry*) differ only by the swapping of two letters. However, the *Arameans* were the ancestral stock of the patriarchs (Gen 25:20), whereas the *Amorites* were roughly synonymous with the despised Canaanites who occupied the land (Amos 2:9–10). Ezekiel is again emphasizing Jerusalem's long-held ties to Canaanite culture, as the last major Canaanite city to fall to the Israelites. **your mother a Hittite:** Canaanites, Hittites, and Amorites are all three mentioned in one breath on numerous occasions as the first three of the nations inhabiting the Promised Land (Ex 3:17; 13:5; 33:2, etc.). Some theorize that the Jebusites who inhabited pre-Davidic Jerusalem were a branch of the Hittites. There may be here also a reference to Bathsheba, wife of Uriah the Hittite, who became the mother of the royal dynasty through Solomon.

16:8 I spread my skirt over you: A traditional sign of betrothal (cf. Ruth 3:9). **entered into a covenant with you:** Possibly a distant flashback to the founding of the Mosaic covenant, but more likely an allusion to the Davidic covenant, which included the choice of Zion/Jerusalem as the seat of the sanctuary and the kingdom (see Ps 132:11–18).

16:11 I decked you with ornaments: The Lord dressed Jerusalem as a queen. The apparel reflects the growth of the city's wealth as a royal capital.

16:19 fine flour and oil: Used for the grain offering of the Temple. **a pleasing odor:** A technical term in the priestly literature of the Bible for certain kinds of sacrificial offerings. The Temple cult enriched Jerusalem, but it took its wealth and used it to subsidize pagan worship as well, beginning already in the days of Solomon (1 Kings 11:5–8).

[b] Gk Syr: Heb *I made you a myriad.*
[c] Cn: Heb *ornament of ornaments.*
[d] Syr: Heb *and it was, says the Lord GOD.*

took your sons and your daughters, whom you had
borne to me, and these you sacrificed to them to be
devoured. Were your harlotries so small a matter
21that you slaughtered my children and delivered
them up as an offering by fire to them? 22And in all
your abominations and your harlotries you did not
remember the days of your youth, when you were
naked and bare, weltering in your blood.

23 "And after all your wickedness (woe, woe
to you! says the Lord GOD), 24you built yourself a
vaulted chamber, and made yourself a lofty place
in every square; 25at the head of every street you
built your lofty place and prostituted your beauty,
offering yourself to any passer-by, and multiplying
your harlotry. 26You also played the harlot with
the Egyptians, your lustful neighbors, multiplying
your harlotry, to provoke me to anger. 27Behold,
therefore, I stretched out my hand against you, and
diminished your allotted portion, and delivered
you to the greed of your enemies, the daughters of
the Philis'tines, who were ashamed of your lewd
behavior. 28You played the harlot also with the
Assyrians, because you were insatiable; yes, you
played the harlot with them, and still you were not
satisfied. 29You multiplied your harlotry also with
the trading land of Chalde'a; and even with this you
were not satisfied.

30 "How lovesick is your heart, says the Lord
GOD, seeing you did all these things, the deeds of
a brazen harlot; 31building your vaulted chamber
at the head of every street, and making your lofty
place in every square. Yet you were not like a harlot,
because you scorned hire. 32Adulterous wife, who
receives strangers instead of her husband! 33Men
give gifts to all harlots; but you gave your gifts to all
your lovers, bribing them to come to you from every
side for your harlotries. 34So you were different from
other women in your harlotries: none solicited you
to play the harlot; and you gave hire, while no hire
was given to you; therefore you were different.

35 "Wherefore, O harlot, hear the word of the
LORD: 36Thus says the Lord GOD, Because your
shame was laid bare and your nakedness uncovered
in your harlotries with your lovers, and because
of all your idols, and because of the blood of your
children that you gave to them, 37therefore, behold,
I will gather all your lovers, with whom you took
pleasure, all those you loved and all those you
loathed; I will gather them against you from every
side, and will uncover your nakedness to them, that
they may see all your nakedness. 38And I will judge
you as women who break wedlock and shed blood
are judged, and bring upon you the blood of wrath
and jealousy. 39And I will give you into the hand of
your lovers, and they shall throw down your vaulted
chamber and break down your lofty places; they
shall strip you of your clothes and take your fair
jewels, and leave you naked and bare. 40They shall
bring up a host against you, and they shall stone
you and cut you to pieces with their swords. 41And
they shall burn your houses and execute judgments
upon you in the sight of many women; I will make
you stop playing the harlot, and you shall also give
hire no more. 42So will I satisfy my fury on you, and
my jealousy shall depart from you; I will be calm,
and will no more be angry. 43Because you have
not remembered the days of your youth, but have
enraged me with all these things; therefore, behold,
I will repay your deeds upon your head, says the
Lord GOD.

"Have you not committed lewdness in addition
to all your abominations? 44Behold, every one who
uses proverbs will use this proverb about you, 'Like
mother, like daughter.' 45You are the daughter of
your mother, who loathed her husband and her
children; and you are the sister of your sisters, who
loathed their husbands and their children. Your
mother was a Hit'tite and your father an Am'orite.
46And your elder sister is Samar'ia, who lived with
her daughters to the north of you; and your younger

16:45: Ezek 16:3.

16:21 you slaughtered my children: Referring to the infanticidal sacrifices offered to the pagan god Molech (and possibly other gods) in the valley of Hinnom, directly southwest of Jerusalem (2 Kings 23:10; 2 Chron 28:3; 33:6; Jer 7:31–32; 32:35). Ezekiel's contemporary Jeremiah also roundly criticizes this practice, which foreshadows the modern abortion movement.

16:24 in every square: Describes the proliferation of pagan shrines in Jerusalem.

16:26 played the harlot with the Egyptians: Political and religious alliances with the Egyptians (Is 30:2–3; 36:6; Jer 37:5; etc.). Israelite royal iconography from at least the time of King Hezekiah onward shows strong Egyptian influence.

16:28 played the harlot ... Assyrians: Refers to political and religious alliances with Assyria, as in 2 Kings 16:7–18.

16:29 harlotry ... Chaldea: Refers to political and religious alliances with Babylon (2 Kings 20:12–18; 2 Chron 32:31). King Josiah also allied himself with Babylon against Egypt, leading to his death (2 Kings 23:29–30).

16:33 gifts to all your lovers: Judah paid the tribute of a vassal kingdom to Egypt, Assyria, and Babylon at various times.

16:37 I ... will uncover your nakedness: In the ancient Near East, if a wife divorced her husband, the custom was for the husband to remove publicly from the wife the clothing he had provided for her, as a sign of the dissolution of the bond.

16:39 I will give you into the hand of your lovers: Emphasizing a theological theme, strongly articulated by the Apostle Paul (Rom 1:18–28), that those who choose against God are "punished" by being given what they have chosen. To choose what is not God ends up being its own punishment.

16:43 I will repay your deeds: God's judgments are just. The culture of violence practiced by the Judeans, in particular their violence to children through sacrifice to pagan deities, comes back upon themselves.

16:45 Your mother was a Hittite ... father an Amorite: See note on 16:3.

16:46 your elder sister is Samaria: Samaria became the capital of the Northern Kingdom of Israel, which broke from the house of David at the beginning of the reign of Rehoboam (1 Kings 12) ca. 930 B.C. and was destroyed by the Assyrians ca. 722 B.C. It is unclear why Samaria is considered the "older"

sister, who lived to the south of you, is Sodom
with her daughters. 47Yet you were not content
to walk in their ways, or do according to their
abominations; within a very little time you were
more corrupt than they in all your ways. 48As I
live, says the Lord GOD, your sister Sodom and
her daughters have not done as you and your
daughters have done. 49Behold, this was the guilt
of your sister Sodom: she and her daughters had
pride, surfeit of food, and prosperous ease, but did
not aid the poor and needy. 50They were haughty,
and did abominable things before me; therefore I
removed them, when I saw it. 51Samar'ia has not
committed half your sins; you have committed
more abominations than they, and have made your
sisters appear righteous by all the abominations
which you have committed. 52Bear your disgrace,
you also, for you have made judgment favorable
to your sisters; because of your sins in which you
acted more abominably than they, they are more in
the right than you. So be ashamed, you also, and
bear your disgrace, for you have made your sisters
appear righteous.

53 "I will restore their fortunes, both the fortunes
of Sodom and her daughters, and the fortunes of
Samar'ia and her daughters, and I will restore your
own fortunes in the midst of them, 54that you may
bear your disgrace and be ashamed of all that you
have done, becoming a consolation to them. 55As
for your sisters, Sodom and her daughters shall
return to their former estate, and Samar'ia and her
daughters shall return to their former estate; and
you and your daughters shall return to your former
estate. 56Was not your sister Sodom a byword in
your mouth in the day of your pride, 57before your
wickedness was uncovered? Now you have become
like her[e] an object of reproach for the daughters of
E'dom[f] and all her neighbors, and for the daughters
of the Philis'tines, those round about who despise
you. 58You bear the penalty of your lewdness and
your abominations, says the LORD.

The Everlasting Covenant

59 "Yes, thus says the Lord GOD: I will deal with
you as you have done, who have despised the oath
in breaking the covenant, 60yet I will remember my
covenant with you in the days of your youth, and
I will establish with you an everlasting covenant.
61Then you will remember your ways, and be
ashamed when I[g] take your sisters, both your elder
and your younger, and give them to you as daughters,
but not on account of the covenant with you. 62I will
establish my covenant with you, and you shall know
that I am the LORD, 63that you may remember and
be confounded, and never open your mouth again
because of your shame, when I forgive you all that
you have done, says the Lord GOD."

Two Eagles and the Vine

17 The word of the LORD came to me: *2"Son of
man, propound a riddle, and speak an allegory

sister. **with her daughters:** Smaller villages in the region around a large city were considered "daughter" settlements of the "mother" city, in Greek *metropolis* from *mater-polis,* "mother city". **Sodom:** A populous and wealthy city not far from the north end of the Dead Sea, on the eastern (modern Jordanian) side of the Jordan River. Sodom was notoriously wicked and destroyed by divine judgment in the time of Abraham (Gen 18–19). It is probably to be identified with Tell-El-Hammam, a site currently being excavated by archaeologists that was destroyed by an aerial heat blast in the second millennium B.C. Ezekiel is being very provocative by identifying Jerusalem with Sodom, but Isaiah already did so in a previous generation (Is 1:7–11).

16:49 did not aid the poor and needy: This omission on the part of the Sodomites is not highlighted in the description of the sins of the city in Gen 19:1–29.

16:50 did abominable things: Such as attempting to sexually assault its visitors (Gen 19:5).

16:51 made your sisters appear righteous: Jerusalem has sinned more grievously than her notorious sister cities. There is no evidence that the Samarians or Sodomites practiced child sacrifice, for instance.

16:57 the daughters of Edom: The Edomites occupied the desert highlands on Judah's southern border. They gloated over the destruction of Jerusalem in 586 B.C., prompting the prophecies of Obadiah (Obad 1–21). **the daughters of the Philistines:** The Philistines were a seafaring people probably related to the ancient Greeks and Cretans. They occupied a chain of cities along the Mediterranean coast of Palestine that cut Judah off from access to the sea. The Philistines were a thorn in the side of Judah until about 605 B.C. when Nebuchadnezzar exiled a large number of them to Babylon. There was still a remnant population left, however, who took the opportunity to abuse the Judean population after the defeats of 597 B.C. and 586 B.C. (cf. 25:15–16).

16:59 despised the oath in breaking the covenant: A covenant is the extension of kinship (a family bond) by means of an oath. The oath can be verbal or ritual. Here, the "covenant" is probably the Davidic covenant by which Jerusalem/Zion came to have a special place as the Temple-city and dwelling of God on earth.

16:60 my covenant with you in the days of your youth: If Ezekiel is maintaining a consistent frame of reference, then this is also the covenant of David. However, if he is shifting the frame and understanding Jerusalem as the whole nation by metonymy, perhaps this covenant "of your youth" is the Mosaic or even the Abrahamic covenant. **an everlasting covenant:** Translates the Hebrew *berît ʿôlam.* This is the reality that Jeremiah describes as a "new covenant" (Jer 31:31). Ezekiel prefers the terms "everlasting covenant" and "covenant of peace".

16:61 I take your sisters . . . and give . . . as daughters: In the future, Samaria and Sodom will be dependent cities of a realm ruled by Jerusalem. **not on account of the covenant with you:** Perhaps meaning "not as a reward for your faithfulness to the covenant".

17:1–24 The prophet launches into yet another allegorical description of Jerusalem's relationship to God, this time using the imagery of tall trees and an eagle perched in them, rather than the strongly erotic imagery of the previous chapter.

[e] Cn: Heb uncertain.
[f] Another reading is *Aram.*
[g] Syr: Heb *you.*
*17:2–24: The Messiah, a shoot from the stump of Jesse. Cf. Is 11:1, and also the parable of the mustard seed (Mt 13:31–32).

to the house of Israel; [3]say, Thus says the Lord GOD: A great eagle with great wings and long pinions, rich in plumage of many colors, came to Lebanon and took the top of the cedar; [4]he broke off the topmost of its young twigs and carried it to a land of trade, and set it in a city of merchants. [5]Then he took of the seed of the land and planted it in fertile soil; he placed it beside abundant waters. He set it like a willow twig, [6]and it sprouted and became a low spreading vine, and its branches turned toward him, and its roots remained where it stood. So it became a vine, and brought forth branches and put forth foliage.

7 "But there was another great eagle with great wings and much plumage; and behold, this vine bent its roots toward him, and shot forth its branches toward him that he might water it. From the bed where it was planted [8]he transplanted it[h] to good soil by abundant waters, that it might bring forth branches, and bear fruit, and become a noble vine. [9]Say, Thus says the Lord GOD: Will it thrive? Will he not pull up its roots and cut off its branches,[i] so that all its fresh sprouting leaves wither? It will not take a strong arm or many people to pull it from its roots. [10]Behold, when it is transplanted, will it thrive? Will it not utterly wither when the east wind strikes it—wither away on the bed where it grew?"

11 Then the word of the LORD came to me: [12]"Say now to the rebellious house, Do you not know what these things mean? Tell them, Behold, the king of Babylon came to Jerusalem, and took her king and her princes and brought them to him to Babylon. [13]And he took one of the royal offspring and made a covenant with him, putting him under oath. (The chief men of the land he had taken away, [14]that the kingdom might be humble and not lift itself up, and that by keeping his covenant it might stand.) [15]But he rebelled against him by sending ambassadors to Egypt, that they might give him horses and a large army. Will he succeed? Can a man escape who does such things? Can he break the covenant and yet escape? [16]As I live, says the Lord GOD, surely in the place where the king dwells who made him king, whose oath he despised, and whose covenant with him he broke, in Babylon he shall die. [17]Pharaoh with his mighty army and great company will not help him in war, when mounds are cast up and siege walls built to cut off many lives. [18]Because he despised the oath and broke the covenant, because he gave his hand and yet did all these things, he shall not escape. [19]Therefore thus says the Lord GOD: As I live, surely my oath which he despised, and my covenant which he broke, I will repay upon his head. [20]I will spread my net over him, and he shall be taken in my snare, and I will bring him to Babylon and enter into judgment with him there for the treason he has committed against me. [21]And all the pick[j] of his troops shall fall by the sword, and the survivors shall be scattered to every wind; and you shall know that I, the LORD, have spoken."

22 Thus says the Lord GOD: "I myself will take a sprig from the lofty top of the cedar, and will set it out; I will break off from the topmost of its young twigs a tender one, and I myself will plant it upon a high and lofty mountain; [23]on the mountain height of Israel will I plant it, that it may bring forth boughs and bear fruit, and become a noble cedar; and under it will dwell all kinds of beasts;[k] in the shade of its branches birds of every sort will nest. [24]And all the trees of the field shall know that I the LORD bring low the high tree, and make high the low tree, dry up the green tree, and make the dry tree flourish. I the LORD have spoken, and I will do it."

Each Will Be Judged by His Own Conduct

18 The word of the LORD came to me again: [2]"What do you mean by repeating this proverb concerning the land of Israel, 'The fathers have eaten sour grapes, and the children's teeth are set on edge'? [3]As I live, says the Lord GOD, this proverb shall no more be used by you in Israel.

17:23: Ezek 31:6; Mt 13:32; Mk 4:32; Lk 13:19. **18:2:** Jer 31:29.

17:3 A great eagle: Nebuchadnezzar II "the Great" of Babylon (r. 605–562 B.C.), who subjugates Judah as a vassal kingdom in 605 B.C. and captures Jerusalem in 597 B.C. and 586 B.C., exiling the better part of the population both times and destroying the city and Temple the second time.

17:4 the topmost of its young twigs: The royal house, in particular, the young king Jehoiachin, exiled in 597 B.C. **a land of trade ... a city of merchants:** A clear reference to Chaldea/Babylon.

17:5 He took of the seed of the land and planted it: Nebuchadnezzar establishes Zedekiah, Jehoiachin's uncle, as king.

17:7 another great eagle: The Pharaoh of Egypt. **this vine bent its roots toward him:** Zedekiah seeks the patronage of Egypt rather than Babylon.

17:8 transplanted it: Judah shifts loyalty and tribute payments to Egypt.

17:11–21 These verses describe the events of 597 B.C. and succeeding years, in which Nebuchadnezzar II exiles King Jehoiachin and replaces him with Zedekiah, who subsequently is disloyal and seeks the support of Egypt for a revolt.

17:22 I myself will take a sprig: What follows is an allegorical messianic prophecy. God himself will choose a descendant of the house of David (a "twig") and establish him in Jerusalem (the "mountain height of Israel"), where his dynasty and kingdom will flourish. • Jesus likely alludes to this prophecy in his parable of the Mustard Seed (Mt 13:31–32).

18:2 The fathers have eaten sour grapes, and the children's teeth are set on edge: Meaning, "The previous generation sinned, and the present generation is paying the price." Ezekiel's contemporaries (wrongly) embrace a kind of theological fatalism in which one's destiny is fixed by the actions of one's parents or even one's own actions earlier in life and in which destiny cannot be changed for good or ill.

[h] Cn: Heb *it was transplanted.*
[i] Cn: Heb *fruit.*
[j] Another reading is *fugitives.*
[k] Gk: Heb lacks *all kinds of beasts.*

[4]Behold, all souls are mine; the soul of the father as
well as the soul of the son is mine: the soul that sins
shall die.
5 "If a man is righteous and does what is lawful
and right—[6]if he does not eat upon the mountains
or lift up his eyes to the idols of the house of Israel,
does not defile his neighbor's wife or approach a
woman in her time of impurity, [7]does not oppress
any one, but restores to the debtor his pledge,
commits no robbery, gives his bread to the hungry
and covers the naked with a garment, [8]does not lend
at interest or take any increase, withholds his hand
from iniquity, executes true justice between man
and man, [9]walks in my statutes, and is careful to
observe my ordinances[l]—he is righteous, he shall
surely live, says the Lord GOD.
10 "If he begets a son who is a robber, a shedder
of blood,[m] [11]who does none of these duties, but eats
upon the mountains, defiles his neighbor's wife,
[12]oppresses the poor and needy, commits robbery,
does not restore the pledge, lifts up his eyes to the
idols, commits abomination, [13]lends at interest, and
takes increase; shall he then live? He shall not live.
He has done all these abominable things; he shall
surely die; his blood shall be upon himself.
14 "But if this man begets a son who sees all the
sins which his father has done, and fears, and does
not do likewise, [15]who does not eat upon the mountains or lift up his eyes to the idols of the house of
Israel, does not defile his neighbor's wife, [16]does
not wrong any one, exacts no pledge, commits no
robbery, but gives his bread to the hungry and covers
the naked with a garment, [17]withholds his hand from
iniquity,[n] takes no interest or increase, observes my
ordinances, and walks in my statutes; he shall not
die for his father's iniquity; he shall surely live. [18]As
for his father, because he practiced extortion, robbed
his brother, and did what is not good among his
people, behold, he shall die for his iniquity.
19 "Yet you say, 'Why should not the son suffer
for the iniquity of the father?' When the son has
done what is lawful and right, and has been careful
to observe all my statutes, he shall surely live. [20]The
soul that sins shall die. The son shall not suffer
for the iniquity of the father, nor the father suffer
for the iniquity of the son; the righteousness of the
righteous shall be upon himself, and the wickedness
of the wicked shall be upon himself.
21 "But if a wicked man turns away from all
his sins which he has committed and keeps all my
statutes and does what is lawful and right, he shall
surely live; he shall not die. [22]None of the transgressions which he has committed shall be remembered
against him; for the righteousness which he has
done he shall live. [23]Havc I any pleasure in the
death of the wicked, says the Lord GOD, and not
rather that he should turn from his way and live?
[24]But when a righteous man turns away from his
righteousness and commits iniquity and does the
same abominable things that the wicked man does,
shall he live? None of the righteous deeds which he
has done shall be remembered; for the treachery of
which he is guilty and the sin he has committed, he
shall die.

18:4: Ezek 18:20. **18:20:** Ezek 18:4. **18:23:** Ezek 18:32; 33:11.

18:4 the soul that sins shall die: Everyone will receive punishment or reward from God for his own actions, and not for those of others. Reflecting on this in light of Christ, we can affirm that our temporal suffering or prosperity in this life often is tied to the actions of those around us, but at the particular judgment, we will be held to account only for our own actions.

18:6–9 The sins and violations listed in this passage are largely taken from the second half of Leviticus (chaps. 17–27), a unit scholars call the "Holiness Code". Ezekiel often uses the same technical terms and phrases found in Leviticus, as we would expect for a priest. Occasionally, he draws on the laws and language of Deuteronomy as well.

18:6 if he does not eat upon the mountains: I.e., participate in the worship at the "high places"—hilltop shrines where the Israelites offer sacrifice either to pagan deities or illicitly to the Lord. Most of the sacrificial animal is consumed by the worshiper, thus this illicit worship is described as "eating upon the mountains". **approach a woman in her time of impurity:** According to Mosaic Law, a woman was ritually unclean during menstruation and thus legally unfit to engage in marital relations (Lev 15:19–31). Intercourse during this time was uncomfortable for the wife and unable to result in conception, so the only reason for it was to satisfy the husband's desire. Thus, it was not only a ritual violation but a selfish imposition of a husband toward his wife.

18:7 restores to the debtor his pledge: The poor borrow small amounts of money or goods and leave personal items—like garments—as collateral (Ex 22:25). It is cruel to refuse to return these "pledges" when the impoverished person needs them.

18:8 does not lend at interest: In the subsistence economy that characterizes ancient Israel, charging interest is forbidden, as all Israelites are to treat each other as family members and not as sources of profit (Lev 25:35–38).

18:12 abomination: The Hebrew term *tô'êvah*, "abomination", is reserved for very offensive sins that can only be committed intentionally and with flagrant disregard for the Lord and his Law, e.g., perverted sexual acts (Lev 18:22), the sacrifice of children (Deut 12:31), and idolatry (Deut 7:25).

18:13 his blood shall be upon himself: An idiom meaning he will be responsible for his own wrongdoing, suffering the appropriate punishment.

18:19 Why should not the son suffer . . . ?: Strange as it seems to modern sensibilities, the ancient Israelites (and other ancient peoples) consider it just that children suffer for their parents' sins.

18:23 Have I any pleasure in the death of the wicked . . . ?: The prophet corrects a misconception entertained by many in ancient and modern times that the God of Israel enjoys punishing the wicked. Rather, the punishment of the wicked is either **(1)** intended to provoke their repentance and rehabilitation, or else **(2)** demanded by the nature of justice. As the Guardian of perfect justice, God cannot simply overlook injustice without a corrective response; at the same time, he takes no delight in taking the lives of his creatures (Wis 1:13).

[l] Gk: Heb *has kept my ordinances, to deal truly.*
[m] Heb *blood, and he does any one of these things.*
[n] Gk: Heb *the poor.*

25 "Yet you say, 'The way of the Lord is not just.'
Hear now, O house of Israel: Is my way not just? Is it
not your ways that are not just? 26When a righteous
man turns away from his righteousness and
commits iniquity, he shall die for it; for the iniquity
which he has committed he shall die. 27Again, when
a wicked man turns away from the wickedness he
has committed and does what is lawful and right,
he shall save his life. 28Because he considered and
turned away from all the transgressions which he
had committed, he shall surely live, he shall not die.
29Yet the house of Israel says, 'The way of the Lord
is not just.' O house of Israel, are my ways not just?
Is it not your ways that are not just?

30 "Therefore I will judge you, O house of Israel,
every one according to his ways, says the Lord GOD.
Repent and turn from all your transgressions, lest
iniquity be your ruin.[o] 31Cast away from you all the
transgressions which you have committed against
me, and get yourselves a new heart and a new spirit!
Why will you die, O house of Israel? 32For I have no
pleasure in the death of any one, says the Lord GOD;
so turn, and live."

A Lamentation for Israel

19 And you, take up a lamentation for the
princes of Israel, 2and say:

What a lioness was your mother among lions!
She lurked in the midst of young lions,
rearing her whelps.
3And she brought up one of her whelps;
he became a young lion,
and he learned to catch prey;
he devoured men.
4The nations sounded an alarm against him;
he was taken in their pit;
and they brought him with hooks
to the land of Egypt.
5When she saw that she was baffled,[p]
that her hope was lost,
she took another of her whelps and made him
a young lion.
6He prowled among the lions;
he became a young lion,
and he learned to catch prey;
he devoured men.
7And he ravaged their strongholds,[q]
and laid waste their cities;
and the land was appalled and all who were
in it
at the sound of his roaring.
8Then the nations set against him
snares[r] on every side;
they spread their net over him;
he was taken in their pit.
9With hooks they put him in a cage,
and brought him to the king of Babylon;
they brought him into custody,
that his voice should no more be heard
upon the mountains of Israel.

10Your mother was like a vine in a vineyard[s]
transplanted by the water,
fruitful and full of branches
by reason of abundant water.
11Its strongest stem became
a ruler's scepter;
it towered aloft
among the thick boughs;
it was seen in its height
with the mass of its branches.

18:31: Ezek 11:19; 36:26. **18:32:** Ezek 18:23; 33:11.

18:25 The way of the Lord is not just: Ezekiel upholds and develops the principle of each person being punished for his own sin, and not those of his ancestors, as articulated already by Moses (Deut 24:16). The idea that God "[visits] the iniquity of the fathers upon the children to the third and fourth generation of those who hate me" (Ex 20:5; cf. 34:7; Num 14:18; Deut 5:9) should be understood as God permitting successive generations to imitate and repeat the sins of their forebears, thus continuing to provoke divine judgment. See note on 18:2.

18:32 For I have no pleasure in the death of any one: According to Paul, God "desires all men to be saved and to come to the knowledge of the truth" (1 Tim 2:4). Yet God will force no one to choose him, who is perfect truth and love. Men can reject God, who is the source of all life; but the inevitable consequence of rejecting the source of life is death, which has both a physical-temporal and a spiritual-eternal dimension. See note on 18:23.

[o] Or *so that they shall not be a stumbling block of iniquity to you.*
[p] Heb *had waited.*
[q] Tg Compare Theodotion: Heb *knew his widows.*
[r] Cn: Heb *from the provinces.*
[s] Cn: Heb *in your blood.*

19:1 a lamentation for the princes: A "lamentation" (Heb., *qînah*) is a well-established poetic genre with certain typical patterns and structures. This lamentation is an allegory, in which the "lioness" is the dynasty of David, and the "young lions" represent Davidic kings who rebelled against and were deposed by the kings of Egypt and Babylon.

19:3 one of her whelps: Seems to be a combined symbol of King Josiah and his son Jehoahaz.

19:4 with hooks to the land of Egypt: Josiah is a mighty warrior king who is conquered by Pharaoh (2 Kings 23:29–30) and whose son Jehoahaz is taken into exile in Egypt (2 Kings 23:31–34).

19:5 another of her whelps: This second young lion also seems to be a combined symbol of King Jehoiakim, who rebels against Nebuchadnezzar, king of Babylon, but dies before being captured, and his son Jehoiachin, who is taken into Babylonian Exile in his stead (2 Kings 23:36–24:15).

19:10 like a vine in a vineyard: The prophet abruptly introduces a different allegory, in which the royal Davidic dynasty is no longer a lion but a vine. The image of either Israel or the royal house as a vine or vineyard occurs in many places in Scripture (Ps 80:8–14; Is 5:1–7; 27:2; Jer 2:21; 6:9; Hos 10:1; 14:6; Mt 20:1–16; 21:28–43; Jn 15:1–5).

12But the vine was plucked up in fury,
cast down to the ground;
the east wind dried it up;
its fruit was stripped off,
its strong stem was withered;
the fire consumed it.
13Now it is transplanted in the wilderness,
in a dry and thirsty land.
14And fire has gone out from its stem,
has consumed its branches and fruit,
so that there remains in it no strong stem,
no scepter for a ruler.

This is a lamentation, and has become a lamentation.

Israel's Continuing Rebellion

20 In the seventh year, in the fifth month, on the tenth day of the month, certain of the elders of Israel came to inquire of the LORD, and sat before me. 2And the word of the LORD came to me: 3"Son of man, speak to the elders of Israel, and say to them, Thus says the Lord GOD, Is it to inquire of me that you come? As I live, says the Lord GOD, I will not be inquired of by you. 4Will you judge them, son of man, will you judge them? Then let them know the abominations of their fathers, 5and say to them, Thus says the Lord GOD: On the day when I chose Israel, I swore to the seed of the house of Jacob, making myself known to them in the land of Egypt, I swore to them, saying, I am the LORD your God. 6On that day I swore to them that I would bring them out of the land of Egypt into a land that I had searched out for them, a land flowing with milk and honey, the most glorious of all lands. 7And I said to them, Cast away the detestable things your eyes feast on, every one of you, and do not defile yourselves with the idols of Egypt; I am the LORD your God. 8But they rebelled against me and would not listen to me; they did not every man cast away the detestable things their eyes feasted on, nor did they forsake the idols of Egypt.

"Then I thought I would pour out my wrath upon them and spend my anger against them in the midst of the land of Egypt. 9But I acted for the sake of my name, that it should not be profaned in the sight of the nations among whom they dwelt, in whose sight I made myself known to them in bringing them out of the land of Egypt. 10So I led them out of the land of Egypt and brought them into the wilderness. 11I gave them my statutes and showed them my ordinances, by whose observance man shall live. 12Moreover I gave them my sabbaths, as a sign between me and them, that they might know that I the LORD sanctify them. 13But the house of Israel rebelled against me in the wilderness; they did not walk in my statutes but rejected my ordinances, by whose observance man shall live; and my sabbaths they greatly profaned.

"Then I thought I would pour out my wrath upon them in the wilderness, to make a full end of them. 14But I acted for the sake of my name, that it should not be profaned in the sight of the nations, in whose sight I had brought them out. 15Moreover I swore to them in the wilderness that I would not bring them into the land which I had given them, a land flowing with milk and honey, the most glorious of all lands, 16because they rejected my ordinances and did not walk in my statutes, and profaned my sabbaths; for their heart went after their idols. 17Nevertheless my eye spared them, and I did not destroy them or make a full end of them in the wilderness.

19:13 transplanted in the wilderness: Ezekiel speaks of the royal house of David, which has been exiled with its head, King Jehoiachin, to Babylon. Archaeological records indicate that regular rations were supplied to King Jehoiachin and his sons while they were in Babylonian Exile (cf. 2 Kings 25:27–30).

20:1 seventh year ... fifth month ... tenth day: Most likely August 14, 591 B.C. **the elders of Israel came to inquire:** Ezekiel has a conflicted relationship with his contemporary Israelites. On the one hand, his messages are largely ignored or opposed. On the other hand, some even among the leadership of the people regard him as God's spokesman.

20:4 the abominations of their fathers: What follows, up through 20:32, is a famous retelling of the history of Israel that emphasizes Israel's rebellions against God at every crucial juncture.

20:5–9 The first stage of Ezekiel's retelling of Israel's history is God's self-revelation to Israel in Egypt. This would correspond to Ex 3–11.

20:7 Do not defile yourselves with the idols of Egypt: According to Ezekiel, God exhorts Israelites to abandon idolatry while they are still in Egypt, yet they refuse. This is not explicitly recorded in the Book of Exodus, but nonetheless the Book of Joshua does imply that, despite the miracles of the Exodus (Josh 24:16–18), the Israelites continue to serve idols until the end of Joshua's life (Josh 24:23).

20:10–14 The second stage of Ezekiel's retelling extends from the Exodus proper to the year Israel spent at Sinai, corresponding to Ex 19—Num 10.

20:11 I gave them ... statues ... ordinances: The lawgiving at Sinai, primarily Ex 20–24.

20:12 my sabbaths: The Sabbath is revealed to Israel as part of the Ten Commandments (Ex 20:8–11). It could be, however, that by "sabbaths" Ezekiel means the whole sabbatical system of time, including holy sabbath years (see Lev 25) (CCC 2168–73).

20:13 Israel rebelled: Primarily by worshiping the golden calf (Ex 32:1–6). **I thought I would pour out my wrath:** Ezekiel seems to have in mind the incident of Ex 32:7–14, where wrathful judgment on Israel is averted only by Moses' intercession.

20:14 for the sake of my name: See Ex 32:11–14 and CCC 2811–12.

20:15–17 The third stage of Ezekiel's retelling of Israel's history covers the time of wandering and rebellion of the first generation in the wilderness, corresponding roughly to Num 11–14.

20:15 I would not bring them into the land: This is recorded in the wake of the rebellion after the report of the 12 spies in Num 14:20–23.

20:17 my eye spared them: See Num 14:13–20.

18 "And I said to their children in the wilderness,
Do not walk in the statutes of your fathers, nor
observe their ordinances, nor defile yourselves with
their idols. 19 I the LORD am your God; walk in my
statutes, and be careful to observe my ordinances,
20 and hallow my sabbaths that they may be a sign
between me and you, that you may know that I
the LORD am your God. 21 But the children rebelled
against me; they did not walk in my statutes, and
were not careful to observe my ordinances, by
whose observance man shall live; they profaned my
sabbaths.

"Then I thought I would pour out my wrath
upon them and spend my anger against them in the
wilderness. 22 But I withheld my hand, and acted for
the sake of my name, that it should not be profaned
in the sight of the nations, in whose sight I had
brought them out. 23 Moreover I swore to them in
the wilderness that I would scatter them among the
nations and disperse them through the countries,
24 because they had not executed my ordinances,
but had rejected my statutes and profaned my
sabbaths, and their eyes were set on their fathers'
idols. 25 Moreover I gave them statutes that were not

20:18–22 The fourth stage of Ezekiel's retelling covers the rise of the second generation of Israel in the wilderness, corresponding to Num 15–36.

20:21 The children rebelled against me: The quintessential rebellion of the *second* generation in the wilderness is found in Num 25:1–15, where—in an incident reminiscent of the golden calf apostasy—the young men of Israel engage in fornication with the women of Moab as part of the worship of a local deity. The first generation is almost completely gone by this time, as we find out from the census of Num 26.

20:23–26 The fifth stage of Ezekiel's retelling of Israel's history fast-forwards into the Book of Deuteronomy. The Lord's promise to scatter his people among the nations can be found in Deut 4:27; 32:26; the sworn oath of God, in Deut 32:40. Deuteronomy records Moses' final speeches and lawgiving on the plains of Moab shortly before his death.

20:25–26 For the meaning of these difficult verses, see essay: *What Laws Were Not Good?*

20:25 statutes that were not good: The laws of Deuteronomy, which were delivered to the second generation in the wilderness, after their rebellion at Peor (Num 25:1–15; Deut 4:3–4). The statutes of Deuteronomy were "not good" in the sense that some were imperfect laws given as divine concessions for Israel's "hardness of heart" (e.g., the divorce permission in Deut 24:1–4; cf. Mt 19:7–8). They were "ordinances by which they could not have life" in the sense that the laws of Deuteronomy were tied to fearsome curses (Deut 27:14–26; 28:15–68) plus the promise that Israel would violate the laws and trigger the curses (Deut 31:16–22; 32:1–43).

What Laws Were Not Good?

Ezekiel 20:25–26 is a difficult passage of Scripture that has long puzzled scholars. A very literal translation reads as follows:

> [25]*Moreover, I gave them laws that were not good and rules by which they could not live:* [26]*When they set aside every first issue of the womb, I defiled them by their very gifts—that I might render them desolate, that they might know that I am the* LORD.

Contemporary scholarship often infers from these verses that ancient Israelites sacrificed their first-born sons to the Lord, a murderous practice that God is thought to have allowed or commanded. However, this disturbing interpretation is not supported by the text or by what we know of ancient Israelite society. To be sure, wicked Israelites did sacrifice their children to the Ammonite god Molech (1 Kings 11:7; 2 Kings 23:10; Jer 32:35), to the Canaanite god Baal (Jer 19:5), and to other deities as well (Ps 106:37–38; Ezek 20:31; 23:37, 39). However, there is no evidence that *first-born children* were singled out for this practice, and it is highly unlikely that they were. The only record of a first-born being sacrificed is 2 Kings 3:27, where a foreign king, pressed hard in battle, resorts to appeasing his god through such a desperate measure. The incident is recorded in Scripture because it was shocking and unique, not because it was a common practice among the Gentiles, much less in Israel. Furthermore, although the Old Testament is keenly aware of the horrors of child sacrifice (Lev 18:21; 20:2–5; Deut 18:10; 2 Kings 16:3; 17:17; 21:6; 2 Chron 28:3; 33:6; Ezek 16:20–21; 20:31), it never says these young victims were offered to the Lord. In fact, the prophet Jeremiah emphatically denies that they were (Jer 19:5; 32:35).

If, then, Ezek 20:25–26 is not about child sacrifice, what are these verses talking about? Context is key. In Ezek 20, the prophet is rehearsing the narrative of salvation history recorded in the Pentateuch, and by 20:25 he is at the point of describing the giving of the Law to the second generation of Israelites that grew up in the wilderness after their parents escaped from Egypt (20:18–21). The rebellion of the children mentioned in 20:21 is probably the Baal of Peor episode in Num 25, which was primarily the moral failure of the second generation (cf. Num 26:64–65) and has many parallels with the golden calf debacle of Ex 32, the epic failure of their parents, the first generation. The reference in 20:23–24 to swearing an oath to scatter Israel among the nations corresponds to Deut 4:26–27, where Moses swears an oath that God will scatter Israel among the nations if it breaks the covenant. Therefore, 20:25–26 stand in the context of the Book of Deuteronomy, in which the Law of God was regiven to the second generation in the wilderness. When Ezekiel refers to "laws that were not good", he is talking about laws found in Deuteronomy.

(*continued on next page*)

good and ordinances by which they could not have life; [26]and I defiled them through their very gifts in making them offer by fire all their first-born, that I might horrify them; I did it that they might know that I am the LORD.

27 "Therefore, son of man, speak to the house of Israel and say to them, Thus says the Lord GOD: In this again your fathers blasphemed me, by dealing treacherously with me. [28]For when I had brought them into the land which I swore to give them, then wherever they saw any high hill or any leafy tree, there they offered their sacrifices and presented the provocation of their offering; there they sent up their soothing odors, and there they poured out their drink offerings. [29](I said to them, What is the high place to which you go? So its name is called Ba'mah[t] to this day.) [30]Wherefore say to the house of Israel, Thus says the Lord GOD: Will you defile yourselves after the manner of your fathers and go astray after their detestable things? [31]When you offer your gifts and sacrifice your sons by fire, you defile yourselves with all your idols to this day. And shall I be inquired of by you, O house of Israel? As I live, says the Lord GOD, I will not be inquired of by you.

32 "What is in your mind shall never happen—the thought, 'Let us be like the nations, like the tribes of the countries, and worship wood and stone.'

God Will Restore Israel

33 "As I live, says the Lord GOD, surely with a mighty hand and an outstretched arm, and with wrath poured out, I will be king over you. [34]I will bring you out from the peoples and gather you out of the countries where you are scattered, with a mighty hand and an outstretched arm, and with wrath poured out; [35]and I will bring you into the wilderness of the peoples, and there I will enter into judgment with you face to face. [36]As I entered into judgment with your fathers in the wilderness of the land of Egypt, so I will

20:26 offer by fire: The phrase "by fire" is not in the Hebrew. Its inclusion in the RSV2CE reflects a misunderstanding on the part of interpreters and translators that God mandated the sacrifice of human infants by incineration, which is emphatically denied by Jeremiah (Jer 19:5; 32:35). **their first-born:** Refers to first-born animals, not first-born Israelites. Prior to the laws of Deuteronomy, the Israelites were required to offer all the firstlings of their livestock as a sacrifice to God (Ex 13:2–15; 34:19). Deuteronomy relaxed this requirement by permitting firstling animals (which are holy) to be sold for money and allowing non-firstling animals (which are profane) to be offered in their place, even though this was expressly forbidden in earlier legislation (Num 18:17). Ezekiel, a devout priest sensitive to the meaning of the liturgy, recognizes that Deuteronomy institutionalizes practices that would have been considered profane by the standards of holiness found in Exodus, Leviticus, and Numbers.

20:27–31 In the sixth and last stage of Ezekiel's retelling of Israel's history, he describes how the people continue to practice idolatry even after entering the Promised Land. There are many examples of such behavior in the Book of Judges, but the prophet may have in mind here the entire period in which Israel is settled in the land, because in every generation from the Judges to the Exile, there are examples of idolatry.

20:28 any high hill or any leafy tree: Moses expressly commanded Israel to destroy the illicit shrines that were established in these places (Deut 12:2).

20:29 called Bamah to this day: A play on words. The Hebrew for "high place" is *bamah*, the Hebrew *mah* means "what", and the Hebrew *ba'* means "go". Thus, "What [*mah*] is the high place [*bamah*] to which you go [*ba'*]? So its name is called *Bamah* to this day." See word study: *High Places* at 2 Kings 23:5.

20:31 sacrifice your sons by fire: Literally, "offer your sons by fire". "Fire" is in the Hebrew text, and here indeed the prophet is describing child sacrifice offered to Molech and other deities in the valley of Hinnom. But no ancient Near Eastern deity demanded the sacrifice of first-born children, and so 20:26 cannot refer to this practice.

20:34 I will bring you out: Ezekiel foresees a kind of second Exodus. In the original Exodus, God brought his people out of Egypt into the desert of Sinai, where he entered into a covenant relationship with them that involved a sifting out of rebels and evildoers, who died by plague at Sinai and through the wilderness wanderings. In the future, God will again bring Israel out of the lands where they sojourn, into the desert, and will purify them once again.

[t] That is *High Place*.

What Laws Were Not Good? (*continued*)

Why would Ezekiel describe Deuteronomy in this way? A careful reading of the Pentateuch shows that the ritual and moral standards of Deuteronomy are lower than the standards given at Mt. Sinai. Ezekiel mentions an example of this in 20:26: "I defiled them through their very gifts in making them offer ... all their first-born." This is a reference to the offering of firstlings, the first male offspring of any domestic animal (Ex 13:12, 15; 34:19, Num 3:12; 18:15). Prior to Deuteronomy, God's Law stated that first-born animals could not be redeemed or exchanged; these animals were considered holy and had to be sacrificed to God (Num 18:17; cf. Lev 27:26). Deuteronomy, by contrast, permitted the firstlings to be sold for a price and even allowed non-first-born animals to be purchased and offered in their place (Deut 14:22–26). As a priest, Ezekiel is well aware that this is a lower ritual standard, and, according to the principles stated prior to Deuteronomy (i.e., Num 18:17; Lev 27:26), it could be considered a profanation. Thus, Ezek 20 amounts to a sensitive reading of the Pentateuchal narrative, which understands the inferior laws given to Israel in Deuteronomy as a mysterious punishment from God for the constant rebellions of Israel during the journey from Egypt to the Promised Land.

enter into judgment with you, says the Lord GOD. 37I
will make you pass under the rod, and I will let you
go in by number.[u] 38I will purge out the rebels from
among you, and those who transgress against me; I
will bring them out of the land where they sojourn,
but they shall not enter the land of Israel. Then you
will know that I am the LORD.
39 "As for you, O house of Israel, thus says the
Lord GOD: Go serve every one of you his idols, now
and hereafter, if you will not listen to me; but my
holy name you shall no more profane with your
gifts and your idols.
40 "For on my holy mountain, the mountain
height of Israel, says the Lord GOD, there all the
house of Israel, all of them, shall serve me in the land;
there I will accept them, and there I will require your
contributions and the choicest of your gifts, with all
your sacred offerings. 41As a pleasing odor I will
accept you, when I bring you out from the peoples,
and gather you out of the countries where you have
been scattered; and I will manifest my holiness among
you in the sight of the nations. 42And you shall know
that I am the LORD, when I bring you into the land
of Israel, the country which I swore to give to your
fathers. 43And there you shall remember your ways
and all the doings with which you have polluted
yourselves; and you shall loathe yourselves for all
the evils that you have committed. 44And you shall
know that I am the LORD, when I deal with you for
my name's sake, not according to your evil ways, nor
according to your corrupt doings, O house of Israel,
says the Lord GOD."

A Prophecy against the Negeb

45 [v] And the word of the LORD came to me:
46"Son of man, set your face toward the south,
preach against the south, and prophesy against the
forest land in the Neg'eb; 47say to the forest of the
Neg'eb, Hear the word of the LORD: Thus says
the Lord GOD, Behold, I will kindle a fire in you,
and it shall devour every green tree in you and
every dry tree; the blazing flame shall not be
quenched, and all faces from south to north shall be
scorched by it. 48All flesh shall see that I the LORD
have kindled it; it shall not be quenched." 49Then I
said, "Ah, Lord GOD! they are saying of me, 'Is he not
a maker of allegories?' "

The Sharpened Sword Unsheathed

21 [w]The word of the LORD came to me: 2"Son
of man, set your face toward Jerusalem and
preach against the sanctuaries; prophesy against
the land of Israel 3and say to the land of Israel, Thus
says the LORD: Behold, I am against you, and will
draw forth my sword out of its sheath, and will cut
off from you both righteous and wicked. 4Because
I will cut off from you both righteous and wicked,
therefore my sword shall go out of its sheath against
all flesh from south to north; 5and all flesh shall
know that I the LORD have drawn my sword out
of its sheath; it shall not be sheathed again. 6Sigh
therefore, son of man; sigh with breaking heart and
bitter grief before their eyes. 7And when they say to
you, 'Why do you sigh?' you shall say, 'Because of
the tidings. When it comes, every heart will melt and
all hands will be feeble, every spirit will faint and all
knees will be weak as water. Behold, it comes and it
will be fulfilled,' " says the Lord GOD.
8 And the word of the LORD came to me: 9"Son of
man, prophesy and say, Thus says the Lord, Say:
A sword, a sword is sharpened
and also polished,
10sharpened for slaughter,
polished to flash like lightning!

20:41: Eph 5:2; Phil 4:18. **20:43:** Ezek 6:9; 36:31.

20:37 pass under the rod: Probably an image from shepherding, as a shepherd would use his rod to help count the sheep that passed one-by-one into or out of the sheepfold.

20:40 my holy mountain: Mt. Zion. Having recounted Israel's past in six stages, the prophet now gives a more hopeful vision of Israel's future, gathered around Jerusalem in true worship. **there all the house of Israel ... shall serve me:** In this verse, Ezekiel uses language reminiscent of Deut 12:5–7, the command to establish a single licit shrine in the Promised Land, where the "name" of the Lord could dwell. Especially noticeable is the triple repetition of Heb. *sham*, "there", found only in these two passages of the Old Testament. Ezekiel's point is that, in the future, Jerusalem will become firmly established as the central place of worship that Moses envisioned and commanded.

20:41 a pleasing odor: A technical term for an acceptable sacrifice in the parts of the Old Testament concerned with priesthood and the liturgy.

20:45 the south ... the forest land in the Negeb: Probably poetic references to Jerusalem. Jerusalem was not central, but toward the south of the traditional territory of Israel. It was close to the Negeb—the southern desert—but situated on the well-watered ridgeline, and it was forested.

20:49 Is he not a maker of allegories?: Ezekiel's listeners think he is speaking in riddles about distant events, when in fact the judgments he describes will be fulfilled soon.

21:1–7 This is the beginning of three oracles linked together by the image of the sword of judgment, each beginning with the same announcement ("the word of the LORD came to me"). The second oracle is 21:8–17, and the third 21:18–32.

21:2 set your face toward Jerusalem: The poetic descriptions of Jerusalem as the "forest land in the Negeb" were not interpreted properly by his listeners (20:49), so now the prophet is explicit. **preach against the sanctuaries:** Emphasizing the illicit religious practice of Israel. There should have been only one sanctuary, the Temple, but Israel made numerous shrines, both to worship other gods and also to worship the Lord in an unlawful manner.

21:10 the rod: An instrument of wood used in judicial punishment. Criminals were assigned a certain number of strokes with the rod for non-capital crimes. Israel has not repented in response to the moderate punishments God has sent, but rather has increased its crimes, so now the punishment is the "sword"—the armies of Babylon.

---

[u] Gk: Heb *bring you into the bond of the covenant.*
[v] Ch 21:1 in Heb.
[w] Ch 21:6 in Heb.

Or do we make mirth? You have despised the rod,
my son, with everything of wood. 11So the sword
is given to be polished, that it may be handled; it is
sharpened and polished to be given into the hand
of the slayer. 12Cry and wail, son of man, for it is
against my people; it is against all the princes of
Israel; they are delivered over to the sword with my
people. Strike therefore upon your thigh. 13For it
will not be a testing—what could it do if you despise
the rod?" says the Lord GOD.

14 "Prophesy therefore, son of man; clap your
hands and let the sword come down twice, yes,
thrice, the sword for those to be slain; it is the sword
for the great slaughter, which encompasses them,
15that their hearts may melt, and many fall at all
their gates. I have given the glittering sword; ah! it is
made like lightning, it is polished[x] for slaughter.
16Cut sharply to right[y] and left where your edge
is directed. 17I also will clap my hands, and I will
satisfy my fury; I the LORD have spoken."

18 The word of the LORD came to me again: 19"Son
of man, mark two ways for the sword of the king
of Babylon to come; both of them shall come forth
from the same land. And make a signpost, make it
at the head of the way to a city; 20mark a way for
the sword to come to Rabbah of the Am'monites
and to Judah and to[z] Jerusalem the fortified. 21For
the king of Babylon stands at the parting of the
way, at the head of the two ways, to use divination;
he shakes the arrows, he consults the teraphim, he
looks at the liver. 22Into his right hand comes the
lot for Jerusalem,[a] to open the mouth with a cry,[b]
to lift up the voice with shouting, to set battering
rams against the gates, to cast up mounds, to build
siege towers. 23But to them it will seem like a false
divination; they have sworn solemn oaths; but he
brings their guilt to remembrance, that they may
be captured.

24 "Therefore thus says the Lord GOD: Because
you have made your guilt to be remembered, in
that your transgressions are uncovered, so that
in all your doings your sins appear—because you
have come to remembrance, you shall be taken in
them.[c] 25And you, O unhallowed wicked one, prince
of Israel, whose day has come, the time of your final
punishment, 26thus says the Lord GOD: Remove the
turban, and take off the crown; things shall not
remain as they are; exalt that which is low, and
abase that which is high. 27A ruin, ruin, ruin I will
make it; there shall not be even a trace[d] of it until
he comes whose right it is; and to him I will give it.

28 "And you, son of man, prophesy, and say,
Thus says the Lord GOD concerning the Am'monites, and concerning their reproach; say, A sword,
a sword is drawn for the slaughter, it is polished to
glitter[e] and to flash like lightning—29while they
see for you false visions, while they make up lies
for you—to be laid on the necks of the unhallowed
wicked, whose day has come, the time of their final
punishment. 30Return it to its sheath. In the place
where you were created, in the land of your origin, I
will judge you. 31And I will pour out my indignation
upon you; I will blow upon you with the fire of my
wrath; and I will deliver you into the hands of brutal
men, skilful to destroy. 32You shall be fuel for the
fire; your blood shall be in the midst of the land;
you shall be no more remembered; for I the LORD
have spoken."

21:28–32: Ezek 25:1–7; Jer 49:1–6; Amos 1:13–15; Zeph 2:8–11.

21:19 two ways for the sword: Refers to the fact that Nebuchadnezzar is consulting oracles from his gods to determine whether to attack Jerusalem or Ammon, both of which are the capitals of rebellious vassal states in his empire. Ammon is the center of a small kingdom east and north of Jerusalem. The modern capital of the state of Jordan, Amman, is built over ancient Ammon.

21:20 mark a way for the sword: Presumably the prophet does this in figure, perhaps by drawing a map on the ground in public.

21:21 shakes the arrows, he consults the teraphim, he looks at the liver: Forms of ancient divination. Arrows were shaken and thrown on the ground, and their pattern interpreted by priests or other diviners. The teraphim were usually household idols, perhaps the personal idols of the king. Inspecting the livers of sacrificed animals was a well-developed pseudoscience called *extispicy* in the classical world. Many marked clay models of livers that were used in training diviners have been unearthed by archaeologists.

21:22 the lot for Jerusalem: The prophet predicts that Nebuchadnezzar's divination will identify Jerusalem as his first target.

21:23 will seem like a false divination: The inhabitants of Jerusalem will not recognize that Nebuchadnezzar's assault on their city has been ordained by God. **they have sworn solemn oaths:** The leaders of Israel have sworn oaths, either in the name of the Lord or in that of other gods, which they believe will protect them.

21:25 O unhallowed wicked one: King Zedekiah, the uncle of the exiled King Jehoiachin. Zedekiah was the last reigning king of the line of David in Jerusalem. He is sympathetic to the prophet Jeremiah yet permits Jeremiah to be persecuted and does not heed his advice (see Jer 27–39).

21:27 A ruin, ruin, ruin I will make it: That is, the dignity of the royal house. **until he comes whose right it is:** Any visible signs of the royal house of David will disappear until the promised heir of the house appears. This is a messianic prophecy. Later Ezekiel will speak of "my servant David" who is to come, i.e., a righteous descendant of David who will rule once more over the people of Israel. This is why the Gospels of Matthew and Luke place emphasis on Jesus' Davidic lineage (Mt 1:1–17; Lk 3:23–38).

---

[x] Tg: Heb *wrapped up*.
[y] Gk Syr Vg: Heb *right, set*.
[z] Gk Syr: Heb *in*.
[a] Heb *Jerusalem, to set battering rams*.
[b] Gk: Heb *with slaughter*.
[c] Gk: Heb *with the hand*.
[d] Cn: Heb *not even this*.
[e] Cn: Heb *to contain*.

The Sins of Jerusalem

22 Moreover the word of the LORD came to me,
saying, 2“And you, son of man, will you judge,
will you judge the bloody city? Then declare to her
all her abominable deeds. 3You shall say, Thus says
the Lord GOD: A city that sheds blood in the midst
of her, that her time may come, and that makes idols
to defile herself! 4You have become guilty by the
blood which you have shed, and defiled by the idols
which you have made; and you have brought your
day near, the appointed time[f] of your years has
come. Therefore I have made you a reproach to the
nations, and a mocking to all the countries. 5Those
who are near and those who are far from you will
mock you, you infamous one, full of tumult.
6 “Behold, the princes of Israel in you, every one
according to his power, have been bent on shedding
blood. 7Father and mother are treated with contempt
in you; the sojourner suffers extortion in your midst;
the fatherless and the widow are wronged in you.
8You have despised my holy things, and profaned
my sabbaths. 9There are men in you who slander
to shed blood, and men in you who eat upon the
mountains; men commit lewdness in your midst.
10In you men uncover their fathers’ nakedness;
in you they humble women who are unclean in
their impurity. 11One commits abomination with
his neighbor’s wife; another lewdly defiles his
daughter-in-law; another in you defiles his sister,
his father’s daughter. 12In you men take bribes to
shed blood; you take interest and increase and make
gain of your neighbors by extortion; and you have
forgotten me, says the Lord GOD.
13 “Behold, therefore, I strike my hands together
at the dishonest gain which you have made, and at
the blood which has been in the midst of you. 14Can
your courage endure, or can your hands be strong, in
the days that I shall deal with you? I the LORD have
spoken, and I will do it. 15I will scatter you among
the nations and disperse you through the countries,
and I will consume your filthiness out of you. 16And
I[g] shall be profaned through you in the sight of the
nations; and you shall know that I am the LORD.”
17 And the word of the LORD came to me: 18“Son
of man, the house of Israel has become dross to me;
all of them, silver[h] and bronze and tin and iron and
lead in the furnace, have become dross. 19Therefore
thus says the Lord GOD: Because you have all
become dross, therefore, behold, I will gather you
into the midst of Jerusalem. 20As men gather silver
and bronze and iron and lead and tin into a furnace,
to blow the fire upon it in order to melt it; so I will
gather you in my anger and in my wrath, and I
will put you in and melt you. 21I will gather you
and blow upon you with the fire of my wrath, and
you shall be melted in the midst of it. 22As silver is
melted in a furnace, so you shall be melted in the
midst of it; and you shall know that I the LORD have
poured out my wrath upon you.”
23 And the word of the LORD came to me: 24“Son
of man, say to her, You are a land that is not
cleansed, or rained upon in the day of indignation.
25Her princes[i] in the midst of her are like a roaring
lion tearing the prey; they have devoured human
lives; they have taken treasure and precious things;
they have made many widows in the midst of her.
26Her priests have done violence to my law and
have profaned my holy things; they have made
no distinction between the holy and the common,
neither have they taught the difference between the

22:1–16 An oracle in which Ezekiel rebukes Jerusalem for multiple violations of God’s law, especially bloodshed.

22:7–12 A representative list of violations of the Mosaic Law. It includes treating parents **with contempt** (Deut 27:16); the **extortion** and wrongful treatment of sojourners, orphans, and widows (Ex 22:21–22; Deut 14:29; 16:11); profaning the Lord’s **sabbaths** (Lev 19:30); slandering to **shed blood** (Lev 19:16); eating sacrifices on **the mountains** (Deut 12:2, 1 Kings 14:23); committing **lewdness** (Lev 18:17; 19:29; 20:14); uncovering their **fathers’ nakedness** (Lev 18:7); humbling (= forcing oneself upon) women **in their impurity** (Lev 18:19); adultery against a **neighbor’s wife** (Lev 20:10); defiling one’s **daughter-in-law** (Lev 18:15) and **father’s daughter** (Lev 18:9, 11); taking **bribes to shed blood** (Deut 27:25); and collecting **interest** (Lev 25:36, cf. Deut 23:19–20).

22:12 gain . . . by extortion: The Hebrew word translated here “extortion” occurs as a verb in the prohibitions of Lev 19:13 and Deut 24:14 (translated “oppress”). **forgotten me:** The greatest and most fundamental sin, because it is the root of all the others and itself a violation of the greatest commandment, “You shall love the LORD your God . . .” (Deut 6:5).

22:13 strike my hands together: An overt gesture of disapproval in the ancient Near East, something like booing and hissing in modern culture.

22:15 scatter you among the nations: In fulfillment of the covenant curses in Lev 26:33; Deut 4:27; 28:64. Ezekiel combines terms borrowed from both Leviticus and Deuteronomy.

22:17–22 The prophet introduces a new oracle, this one marked by the motif of metalworking and smelting.

22:18 dross: The mass of impurities isolated and removed from molten metal during smelting. They had no economic value and were discarded as worthless.

22:21 blow upon you: An image from metalworking. In order to raise the temperature of furnaces for smelting, additional air was blown into the furnace using bellows.

22:23–31 The third oracle of this chapter focuses on the corruption of three classes of leadership in Israelite society: princes, priests, and prophets.

22:26 the holy and the common . . . the unclean and the clean: Priests were obliged to teach the people about the two axes of distinction on which the Israelite ritual system was based. One axis was “holy vs. common”: holy things were imbued with the divine presence, whereas common ones were not. The other axis was “clean vs. unclean”: clean things had the potential to become holy (sanctified), whereas unclean things did not. The Book of Leviticus teaches the distinction between clean and unclean in Lev 11–15, and between holy and common in Lev 17–25.

---

[f] Two Mss Gk Syr Vg Tg: Heb *until.*

[g] Gk Syr Vg: Heb *you.*

[h] Transposed from the end of the verse. Compare verse 20.

[i] Gk: Heb *a conspiracy of her prophets.*

unclean and the clean, and they have disregarded
my sabbaths, so that I am profaned among them.
27 Her princes in the midst of her are like wolves
tearing the prey, shedding blood, destroying lives to
get dishonest gain. 28 And her prophets have daubed
for them with whitewash, seeing false visions and
making up lies for them, saying, 'Thus says the
Lord GOD,' when the LORD has not spoken. 29 The
people of the land have practiced extortion and
committed robbery; they have oppressed the poor
and needy, and have extorted from the sojourner
without redress. 30 And I sought for a man among
them who should build up the wall and stand in
the breach before me for the land, that I should
not destroy it; but I found none. 31 Therefore I have
poured out my indignation upon them; I have
consumed them with the fire of my wrath; their way
have I repaid upon their heads, says the Lord GOD."

Oholah and Oholibah

23 The word of the LORD came to me: 2 "Son of
man, there were two women, the daughters
of one mother; 3 they played the harlot in Egypt; they
played the harlot in their youth; there their breasts
were pressed and their virgin bosoms handled.
4 Oho'lah was the name of the elder and Ohol'ibah
the name of her sister. They became mine, and they
bore sons and daughters. As for their names, Oholah
is Samar'ia, and Oholibah is Jerusalem.

5 "Oho'lah played the harlot while she was
mine; and she doted on her lovers the Assyrians,
6 warriors clothed in purple, governors and
commanders, all of them desirable young men,
horsemen riding on horses. 7 She bestowed her
harlotries upon them, the choicest men of Assyria
all of them; and she defiled herself with all the idols
of every one on whom she doted. 8 She did not give
up her harlotry which she had practiced since her
days in Egypt; for in her youth men had lain with
her and handled her virgin bosom and poured
out their lust upon her. 9 Therefore I delivered
her into the hands of her lovers, into the hands
of the Assyrians, upon whom she doted. 10 These
uncovered her nakedness; they seized her sons and
her daughters; and her they slew with the sword;
and she became a byword among women, when
judgment had been executed upon her.

11 "Her sister Ohol'ibah saw this, yet she was
more corrupt than she in her doting and in her
harlotry, which was worse than that of her sister.
12 She doted upon the Assyrians, governors and
commanders, warriors clothed in full armor, horsemen riding on horses, all of them desirable young
men. 13 And I saw that she was defiled; they both
took the same way. 14 But she carried her harlotry
further; she saw men portrayed upon the wall, the
images of the Chalde'ans portrayed in vermilion,
15 with belts around their waists, with flowing
turbans on their heads, all of them looking like
officers, a picture of Babylonians whose native land
was Chalde'a. 16 When she saw them she doted upon
them, and sent messengers to them in Chalde'a.
17 And the Babylonians came to her into the bed of
love, and they defiled her with their lust; and after
she was polluted by them, she turned from them
in disgust. 18 When she carried on her harlotry so
openly and flaunted her nakedness, I turned in
disgust from her, as I had turned from her sister.

22:28 daubed ... whitewash: A metaphor. Just as whitewash—an inexpensive form of paint made with lime and water—can mask over imperfections in a wall, so the prophets cover over the serious moral failures of Israel with false, optimistic prophecies.

22:29 extortion ... robbery: An abbreviated version of the longer list of crimes in 22:6-12.

22:30 stand in the breach: An image from siege warfare. Attacking armies will breach (break down) the defensive walls, but heroic defenders will "stand in the breach" and prevent the enemy from entering the city. God is coming against Jerusalem in judgment, yet actively seeks someone to "stand in the breach" by interceding for the people and finds no one. Moses performed this intercessory role when Israel endangered itself in the wilderness wanderings (Ex 32:11-14; Num 14:13-20).

23:1-49 Chapter 23 is a graphic allegory of Samaria and Jerusalem as adulterous wives of the Lord. Much like the Catholic author Flannery O'Connor, Ezekiel's mission is to shock his contemporaries out of their complacency. This chapter is closely connected in theme, imagery, and message to chap. 16, which portrays Jerusalem and Samaria as sisters of the infamously immoral Sodom. • Ezekiel's picture of Samaria and Jerusalem as sisters who commit outrageous sexual sin may be influenced by the narrative of the two daughters of Lot (Gen 19:30-38), who, after of the destruction of immoral Sodom, had relations with their father in order to conceive sons, Moab and Ammon. It may not be accidental, then, that Ammon (25:1-7) and Moab (25:8-10) head the list of Ezekiel's "Oracles against the Nations" only a chapter later. Thus, Ezekiel's prophecies reflect themes and motifs from the Pentateuch.

23:4 Oholah: Can be understood as Hebrew for "her [own] tent." Samaria had its own sanctuary or place of worship (= tent) that was not authorized by God. **Oholibah:** Can be understood as Hebrew for "my tent is in her", referring to the fact that God's legitimate Temple is located in Jerusalem.

23:5 her lovers the Assyrians: Northern Israel, whose capital was Samaria, became a vassal state of the Assyrian Empire in order to gain its protection, but ultimately the relationship between the two states became antagonistic, and the Assyrians destroyed Israel in 722 B.C., exiling much of the population.

23:10 slew with the sword: Much of the population of Samaria was slain in the conquest of the city. Ezekiel moves back and forth between the allegory and the reality it represents, which can be disconcerting for modern readers.

23:12 doted upon the Assyrians: Judah, too, went through a phase in which it sought Assyrian patronage (2 Kings 16:10-15).

23:14 the Chaldeans: After the fall of Assyria, the kingdom of Judah allied itself with the Babylonians. King Josiah died trying to prevent Pharaoh from coming to the aid of the Assyrians against the Babylonians—in other words, in an effort to assist Babylonian dominance.

23:17 turned from them in disgust: Josiah's successors became frustrated with Babylonian suzerainty and rebelled repeatedly, hoping for Egyptian assistance.

[19]Yet she increased her harlotry, remembering the
days of her youth, when she played the harlot in
the land of Egypt [20]and doted upon her paramours
there, whose members were like those of donkeys,
and whose issue was like that of horses. [21]Thus you
longed for the lewdness of your youth, when the
Egyptians[j] handled your bosom and pressed[k] your
young breasts."

22 Therefore, O Ohol'ibah, thus says the Lord
God: "Behold, I will rouse against you your lovers
from whom you turned in disgust, and I will bring
them against you from every side: [23]the Babylonians
and all the Chalde'ans, Pe'kod and Shoa and Koa, and
all the Assyrians with them, desirable young men,
governors and commanders all of them, officers and
warriors,[l] all of them riding on horses. [24]And they
shall come against you from the north[m] with chariots
and wagons and a host of peoples; they shall set
themselves against you on every side with buckler,
shield, and helmet, and I will commit the judgment
to them, and they shall judge you according to
their judgments. [25]And I will direct my indignation
against you, that they may deal with you in fury.
They shall cut off your nose and your ears, and your
survivors shall fall by the sword. They shall seize
your sons and your daughters, and your survivors
shall be devoured by fire. [26]They shall also strip
you of your clothes and take away your fine jewels.
[27]Thus I will put an end to your lewdness and your
harlotry brought from the land of Egypt; so that
you shall not lift up your eyes to the Egyptians or
remember them any more. [28]For thus says the Lord
God: Behold, I will deliver you into the hands of those
whom you hate, into the hands of those from whom
you turned in disgust; [29]and they shall deal with you
in hatred, and take away all the fruit of your labor,
and leave you naked and bare, and the nakedness
of your harlotry shall be uncovered. Your lewdness
and your harlotry [30]have brought this upon you,
because you played the harlot with the nations, and
polluted yourself with their idols. [31]You have gone
the way of your sister; therefore I will give her cup
into your hand. [32]Thus says the Lord God:

"You shall drink your sister's cup
which is deep and large;
you shall be laughed at and held in derision,
for it contains much;
[33]you will be filled with drunkenness and sorrow.
A cup of horror and desolation,
is the cup of your sister Samar'ia;
[34]you shall drink it and drain it out,
and pluck out your hair,[n]
and tear your breasts;
for I have spoken, says the Lord God. [35]Therefore
thus says the Lord God: Because you have forgotten
me and cast me behind your back, therefore bear the
consequences of your lewdness and harlotry."

36 The Lord said to me: "Son of man, will you
judge Oho'lah and Ohol'ibah? Then declare to them
their abominable deeds. [37]For they have committed
adultery, and blood is upon their hands; with their
idols they have committed adultery; and they have
even offered up to them for food the sons whom they
had borne to me. [38]Moreover this they have done to
me: they have defiled my sanctuary on the same day
and profaned my sabbaths. [39]For when they had
slaughtered their children in sacrifice to their idols,
on the same day they came into my sanctuary to
profane it. And behold, this is what they did in my
house. [40]They even sent for men to come from far,
to whom a messenger was sent, and behold, they
came. For them you bathed yourself, painted your
eyes, and decked yourself with ornaments; [41]you sat
upon a stately couch, with a table spread before it
on which you had placed my incense and my oil.
[42]The sound of a carefree multitude was with her;
and with men of the common sort drunkards[o] were
brought from the wilderness; and they put bracelets upon the hands of the women, and beautiful
crowns upon their heads.

43 "Then I said, Do not men now commit
adultery[p] when they practice harlotry with her?
[44]For they have gone in to her, as men go in to a
harlot. Thus they went in to Oho'lah and to Ohol'-
ibah to commit lewdness.[q] [45]But righteous men
shall pass judgment on them with the sentence of

23:23 Pekod and Shoa and Koa, and all the Assyrians: Pekod was a Syrian tribe allied to the Babylonians; presumably Shoa and Koa were similar tribes. The Assyrians mentioned here probably refer to the Assyrian soldiers who were forcibly incorporated into the Babylonian army.

23:27 you shall not lift up your eyes to the Egyptians: For the last several decades of the existence of the kingdom of Judah, the Judeans followed a pro-Egyptian policy, attempting to extricate themselves from the Babylonian empire and ally themselves with Egypt.

23:37 offered up ... sons whom they had borne: Referring to the practice of child sacrifice to Molech and other deities in the valley of Hinnom (Gehenna), against which Ezekiel inveighs repeatedly.

23:39 on the same day they came into my sanctuary: The ancient Israelites would worship Molech through child sacrifice and then go to the Temple to worship the Lord as well. This brought corpse contamination into the Jerusalem Temple.

23:42 The sound of a carefree multitude was with her: The Hebrew of this verse is very difficult to understand and translate. There may be copying errors in the ancient manuscripts. Nonetheless, the general sense is clear that Jerusalem is like a wealthy woman of low morals, hosting a hedonistic feast with unsavory persons joining in.

[j] Two Mss: Heb *from Egypt.*
[k] Cn: Heb *for the sake of.*
[l] Compare verses 6 and 12: Heb *called.*
[m] Gk: The meaning of the Hebrew word is unknown.
[n] Compare Syr: Heb *gnaw its sherds.*
[o] Heb uncertain.
[p] Compare Gk: Heb obscure.
[q] Gk: Heb *a woman of lewdness.*

adulteresses, and with the sentence of women that
shed blood; because they are adulteresses, and
blood is upon their hands."
46 For thus says the Lord GOD: "Bring up a host
against them, and make them an object of terror
and a spoil. 47And the host shall stone them and
dispatch them with their swords; they shall slay
their sons and their daughters, and burn up their
houses. 48Thus will I put an end to lewdness in the
land, that all women may take warning and not
commit lewdness as you have done. 49And your
lewdness shall be repaid upon you, and you shall
bear the penalty for your sinful idolatry; and you
shall know that I am the Lord GOD."

The Boiling Pot

24 In the ninth year, in the tenth month, on the
tenth day of the month, the word of the LORD
came to me: 2"Son of man, write down the name of
this day, this very day. The king of Babylon has
laid siege to Jerusalem this very day. 3And utter an
allegory to the rebellious house and say to them,
Thus says the Lord GOD:

Set on the pot, set it on,
pour in water also;
4put in it the pieces of flesh,
all the good pieces, the thigh and the shoulder;
fill it with choice bones.
5Take the choicest one of the flock,
pile the logs[r] under it;
boil its pieces,[s]
seethe[t] also its bones in it.

6 "Therefore thus says the Lord GOD: Woe to the
bloody city, to the pot whose rust is in it, and whose
rust has not gone out of it! Take out of it piece after
piece, without making any choice.[u] 7For the blood
she has shed is still in the midst of her; she put it on
the bare rock, she did not pour it upon the ground
to cover it with dust. 8To rouse my wrath, to take
vengeance, I have set on the bare rock the blood
she has shed, that it may not be covered. 9Therefore
thus says the Lord GOD: Woe to the bloody city! I
also will make the pile great. 10Heap on the logs,
kindle the fire, boil well the flesh, and empty out
the broth,[v] and let the bones be burned up. 11Then
set it empty upon the coals, that it may become hot,
and its copper may burn, that its filthiness may
be melted in it, its rust consumed. 12In vain I have
wearied myself;[w] its thick rust does not go out of it
by fire. 13Its rust is your filthy lewdness. Because I
would have cleansed you and you were not cleansed
from your filthiness, you shall not be cleansed any
more till I have satisfied my fury upon you. 14I the
LORD have spoken; it shall come to pass, I will do it;
I will not go back, I will not spare, I will not repent;
according to your ways and your doings I will judge
you, says the Lord GOD."

Ezekiel's Wife Dies

15 Also the word of the LORD came to me: 16"Son
of man, behold, I am about to take the delight of your
eyes away from you at a stroke; yet you shall not
mourn or weep nor shall your tears run down. 17Sigh,
but not aloud; make no mourning for the dead. Bind
on your turban, and put your shoes on your feet; do
not cover your lips, nor eat the bread of mourners."[x]
18So I spoke to the people in the morning, and at
evening my wife died. And on the next morning I
did as I was commanded.
19 And the people said to me, "Will you not
tell us what these things mean for us, that you are
acting thus?" 20Then I said to them, "The word of
the LORD came to me: 21'Say to the house of Israel,
Thus says the Lord GOD: Behold, I will profane my
sanctuary, the pride of your power, the delight of
your eyes, and the desire of your soul; and your sons
and your daughters whom you left behind shall fall
by the sword. 22And you shall do as I have done;
you shall not cover your lips, nor eat the bread of
mourners.[x] 23Your turbans shall be on your heads
and your shoes on your feet; you shall not mourn
or weep, but you shall pine away in your iniquities
and groan to one another. 24Thus shall Ezek'iel be
to you a sign; according to all that he has done you

24:1 ninth year ... tenth month ... tenth day: Ca. January 15, 588. Cf. 2 Kings 25:1.

24:3 the pot: The prophet returns to an image employed earlier in the book (11:3–11), in which the elite of Jerusalem likened themselves to choice morsels simmering in a rich stew. Ezekiel turns this image into one of judgment and develops it at great length.

24:7 she did not pour ... cover it with dust: The blood of animals was to be covered, not left exposed, according to the Mosaic Law (Lev 17:13, Deut 15:23). The idea is that the inhabitants of Jerusalem have not even attempted to be discreet about their crimes but have sinned blatantly and obviously.

24:11 its copper may burn: Ancient Israelite cooking pots were made of copper or a copper alloy (bronze). Copper does not rust, but Ezekiel is mixing his imagery.

24:15 the delight of your eyes: Ezekiel's wife.

24:17 Bind on your turban, and put your shoes on: Ancient mourning rituals included sitting with bare head and bare feet, with one's face partially covered. Friends and relatives would bring food: this was the "bread of mourners". God commands Ezekiel to participate in none of these rituals.

24:19 Will you not tell us ...?: Ezekiel's contemporaries are puzzled as to why he does not mourn in the usual fashion.

24:21 I will profane my sanctuary: The Temple is the pride and delight of the people of Jerusalem, as Ezekiel's wife was to him.

24:22 you shall not cover your lips: Being an oppressed people in exile, the Israelites will not have the freedom to mourn for the Temple and the city as otherwise they would have.

[r] Compare verse 10: Heb *the bones.*
[s] Two Mss: Heb *its boilings.*
[t] Cn: Heb *its bones seethe.*
[u] Heb *no lot has fallen upon it.*
[v] Compare Gk: Heb *mix the spices.*
[w] Cn: Heb uncertain.
[x] Vg Tg: Heb *men.*

shall do. When this comes, then you will know that
I am the Lord God.'
25 "And you, son of man, on the day when I take
from them their stronghold, their joy and glory, the
delight of their eyes and their heart's desire, and also
their sons and daughters, 26on that day a fugitive
will come to you to report to you the news. 27On
that day your mouth will be opened to the fugitive,
and you shall speak and be no longer mute. So you
will be a sign to them; and they will know that I am
the Lord."

Prophecy against the Ammonites

25 The word of the Lord came to me: 2"Son
of man, set your face toward the Am'monites, and prophesy against them. 3Say to the
Am'monites, Hear the word of the Lord God: Thus
says the Lord God, Because you said, 'Aha!' over my
sanctuary when it was profaned, and over the land
of Israel when it was made desolate, and over the
house of Judah when it went into exile; 4therefore I
am handing you over to the people of the East for
a possession, and they shall set their encampments
among you and make their dwellings in your midst;
they shall eat your fruit, and they shall drink your
milk. 5I will make Rabbah a pasture for camels and
the cities of the Am'monites[y] a fold for flocks. Then
you will know that I am the Lord. 6For thus says the
Lord God: Because you have clapped your hands and
stamped your feet and rejoiced with all the malice
within you against the land of Israel, 7therefore,
behold, I have stretched out my hand against you,
and will hand you over as spoil to the nations; and I
will cut you off from the peoples and will make you
perish out of the countries; I will destroy you. Then
you will know that I am the Lord.

Prophecy against Moab

8 "Thus says the Lord God: Because Moab[z]
said, Behold, the house of Judah is like all the
other nations, 9therefore I will lay open the flank
of Moab from the cities[a] on its frontier, the glory
of the country, Beth-jesh'imoth, Ba'al-me'on, and
Kir'iatha'im. 10I will give it along with the Am'monites to the people of the East as a possession, that
it[b] may be remembered no more among the nations,
11and I will execute judgments upon Moab. Then
they will know that I am the Lord.

Prophecy against Edom

12 "Thus says the Lord God: Because E'dom
acted revengefully against the house of Judah and
has grievously offended in taking vengeance upon
them, 13therefore thus says the Lord God, I will
stretch out my hand against E'dom, and cut off
from it man and beast; and I will make it desolate;

25:1–7: Ezek 21:28–32; Jer 49:1–6; Amos 1:13–15; Zeph 2:8–11. **25:8–11:** Is 15–16; 25:10–12; Jer 48; Amos 2:1–3; Zeph 2:8–11. **25:12–14:** Ezek 35; Is 34; 63:1–6; Jer 49:7–22; Amos 1:11–12; Obad; Mal 1:2–5.

24:27 Your mouth will be opened ... and be no longer mute: A supernatural dumbness—the exact workings of which are difficult to understand—was imposed on Ezekiel at the beginning of his prophetic ministry (3:25–27). After the fall of Jerusalem, however, this inability to speak will be removed.

25:1—32:32 Ezekiel's oracles against the nations. Between the announcement of the siege of Jerusalem in chap. 24 and the announcement of the fall of Jerusalem in chap. 33, we have a lengthy section of the book devoted to oracles of judgment on the nations around Israel. These oracles may all have been revealed to Ezekiel in this time period, or else they may have been gathered together and inserted in this place in the book for thematic coherence. The development moves roughly from the less significant nations to the more significant. Chapter 25 covers the four small nations Ammon, Moab, Edom, and Philistia. Tyre, the capital of a seafaring empire, dominates chaps. 26–28; and Egypt, a perennial world power, occupies chaps. 29–32.

25:2 the Ammonites: Ammon was a small nation east of the Jordan River and the Dead Sea (in modern Jordan). Its traditional boundaries were the Jabbok River on the north and the Arnon River on the south. The Ammonites descended from Abraham's nephew Lot through relations with his younger daughter (Gen 19:30–38). They were a constant thorn in the side of Israel throughout its history (Deut 23:3). In times of Israelite strength, Ammon was subjugated as a vassal state (2 Sam 12:26–31; 2 Chron 26:8), only to reassert independence when the Israelite monarchies waned (e.g., 2 Kings 24:2). The Ammonite god was Molech (1 Kings 11:7), who was infamous for demanding child sacrifice (Lev 20:2–5).

25:5 Rabbah: The traditional capital of Ammon. The full name was *Rabbath Ammon*, "the multitude of Ammon", probably meaning "the common meeting place of the ethnic group known as Ammon". The capital of modern Jordan, Amman, occupies the site of the ancient city.

25:8 Moab: A sister nation to Ammon, occupying the east bank of the Dead Sea from the Arnon River (Ammon's southern border, Num 21:13) south to the Zered River, which empties into the southern tip of the sea. The Moabites descended from Lot through his older daughter (Gen 19:30–38). Israel usually subjugated Moab (Judg 3:30; 2 Sam 8:2); but at times Moab obtained independence (2 Kings 1:1; 3:4–27). Their god was Chemosh, who was worshiped also by unfaithful Israelites (1 Kings 11:7, 33; 2 Kings 23:13).

25:9 Beth-jeshimoth, Baal-meon, and Kiriathaim: Towns of the ancient tribe of Reuben (Josh 13:17, 19) that lay north of the traditional boundary of Moab (the Arnon River). Mesha, king of Moab, took them over ca. 840 B.C., according to the famous *Mesha Stele* (also called the Moabite Stone). The region of these towns was desirable as rich grazing land for flocks and herds.

25:12 Edom: The Edomites were descendants of Esau, also called Edom (Gen 25:30), Jacob/Israel's brother. They inhabited the desert south of Judah. They were subjugated under David and Solomon (2 Sam 8:13–14; 1 Kings 9:26) but gained independence as Judah's political power waned (2 Kings 8:20–22; 16:6; 2 Chron 28:17). The relationship between Judah and Edom was particularly bitter, and the entire Book of Obadiah is directed against the Edomites.

25:13 Teman even to Dedan: Historic cities of Edom (Jer 25:23; Jer 49:7–8). Job's primary counselor, Eliphaz, was a Temanite. The elders of these cities were renowned for wisdom (Jer 49:7–8; Obad 8). The locations of these ancient cities are unknown.

[y] Cn: Heb lacks *the cities of.*
[z] Gk Old Latin: Heb *Moab and Seir.*
[a] Heb *cities from its cities.*
[b] Cn: Heb *the Ammonites.*

from Te'man even to De'dan they shall fall by the
sword. 14And I will lay my vengeance upon E'dom
by the hand of my people Israel; and they shall do in
Edom according to my anger and according to my
wrath; and they shall know my vengeance, says the
Lord God.

Prophecy against the Philistines

15 "Thus says the Lord God: Because the
Philis'tines acted revengefully and took vengeance
with malice of heart to destroy in never-ending
enmity; 16therefore thus says the Lord God, Behold,
I will stretch out my hand against the Philis'tines,
and I will cut off the Cher'ethites, and destroy the
rest of the seacoast. 17I will execute great vengeance
upon them with wrathful chastisements. Then
they will know that I am the Lord, when I lay my
vengeance upon them."

Prophecy against Tyre

26 *In the eleventh year, on the first day of the
month, the word of the Lord came to me: 2"Son
of man, because Tyre said concerning Jerusalem,
'Aha, the gate of the peoples is broken, it has swung
open to me; I shall be replenished, now that she
is laid waste,' 3therefore thus says the Lord God:
Behold, I am against you, O Tyre, and will bring up
many nations against you, as the sea brings up its
waves. 4They shall destroy the walls of Tyre, and
break down her towers; and I will scrape her soil
from her, and make her a bare rock. 5She shall be in
the midst of the sea a place for the spreading of nets;
for I have spoken, says the Lord God; and she shall
become a spoil to the nations; 6and her daughters on
the mainland shall be slain by the sword. Then they
will know that I am the Lord.

7 "For thus says the Lord God: Behold, I will bring
upon Tyre from the north Nebuchadrez'zar king of
Babylon, king of kings, with horses and chariots, and
with horsemen and a host of many soldiers. 8He will
slay with the sword your daughters on the mainland;
he will set up a siege wall against you, and throw
up a mound against you, and raise a roof of shields
against you. 9He will direct the shock of his battering
rams against your walls, and with his axes he will
break down your towers. 10His horses will be so many
that their dust will cover you; your walls will shake at
the noise of the horsemen and wagons and chariots,
when he enters your gates as one enters a city which
has been breached. 11With the hoofs of his horses he
will trample all your streets; he will slay your people
with the sword; and your mighty pillars will fall to the
ground. 12They will make a spoil of your riches and a
prey of your merchandise; they will break down your
walls and destroy your pleasant houses; your stones
and timber and soil they will cast into the midst of
the waters. 13And I will stop the music of your songs,
and the sound of your lyres shall be heard no more.
14I will make you a bare rock; you shall be a place for
the spreading of nets; you shall never be rebuilt; for I
the Lord have spoken, says the Lord God.

15 "Thus says the Lord God to Tyre: Will not
the islands shake at the sound of your fall, when
the wounded groan, when slaughter is made in the
midst of you? 16Then all the princes of the sea will
step down from their thrones, and remove their
robes, and strip off their embroidered garments;
they will clothe themselves with trembling; they
will sit upon the ground and tremble every moment,
and be appalled at you. 17And they will raise a
lamentation over you, and say to you,

'How you have vanished[c] from the seas,
O city renowned,
that was mighty on the sea,
you and your inhabitants,

25:15–17: Is 14:29–31; Jer 47; Amos 1:6–8; Zeph 2:4–7; Zech 9:5–7. **26:1—28:19:** Is 23; Joel 3:4–8; Amos 1:9–10; Zech 9:3–4. **26:13:** Rev 18:22. **26:16–17:** Rev 18:9–10.

25:15 the Philistines: A seafaring people related to the Greeks, Minoans, and other eastern Mediterranean islanders. They settled in five cities on the southern Mediterranean coast of Israel and were in constant conflict with the Israelites.

25:16 the Cherethites: Cretans, from Crete, a people-group related to the Philistines.

26:1 eleventh year ... first day of the month: The date formula is incomplete as it stands, lacking the number of the month. There is good reason to think some words have dropped out of the manuscripts here. Some scholars reconstruct: "In the twelfth year, the eleventh month, the first day of the month" = February 3, 585 B.C. This was the day Nebuchadnezzar began the siege of Tyre, which would fit the oracle.

26:2 Tyre: A port city on the southern Lebanese coast that served as a major center of the Phoenician seafaring culture. Tyre enjoyed friendly relations with Israel under David and Solomon (2 Sam 5:11; 1 Kings 5:1; 9:11–12), but by the time Jerusalem fell to Nebuchadnezzar in 586 B.C., the Tyrians considered Jerusalem a trade rival and were glad to be rid of it. Tyre's name (Heb. *Ṣôr*) means "Rock", referring to the city's site on a rocky island just off the coast of Lebanon. Nebuchadnezzar besieged the city for 13 years (ca. 585–572 B.C.). Alexander the Great captured and destroyed it in 332 B.C. **I shall be replenished:** Tyre probably hopes to dominate the trade routes to the Dead Sea and Red Sea that Jerusalem formerly controlled.

26:4 bare rock: A play on the meaning of "Tyre", which is one of the words for "rock" in Hebrew.

26:7 Nebuchadrezzar king of Babylon: Tyre had become a vassal state of Babylon in 604 B.C. but was constantly attempting to throw off the Babylonian yoke. In 585 Nebuchadrezzar (= Nebuchadnezzar) arrived and began a 13 year siege of the city. Ancient sources are unclear, but the siege seems to have ended with the exile of the king of Tyre to Babylon, leaving the city itself largely intact.

26:14 bare rock: See note on 26:4.

---

[c] Gk Old Latin Aquila: Heb *vanished, O inhabited one.*

*26: The city of Tyre, in those days an island and one of the richest cities in the East, was regarded as impregnable from the landward side. In this instance the siege lasted thirteen years but remained indecisive, as Nebuchadnezzar had no fleet. We must, therefore, regard the prophet's language here as rhetorical rather than historical; cf. 29:18.

who imposed your terror
on all the mainland![d]
18Now the isles tremble
on the day of your fall;
yes, the isles that are in the sea
are dismayed at your passing.'
19 "For thus says the Lord GOD: When I make
you a city laid waste, like the cities that are not
inhabited, when I bring up the deep over you, and
the great waters cover you, 20then I will thrust you
down with those who descend into the Pit, to the people of old, and I will make you to dwell in the nether
world, among primeval ruins, with those who go
down to the Pit, so that you will not be inhabited or
have a place[e] in the land of the living. 21I will bring
you to a dreadful end, and you shall be no more;
though you be sought for, you will never be found
again, says the Lord GOD."

Lamentation over Tyre

27 The word of the LORD came to me: 2"Now you,
son of man, raise a lamentation over Tyre,
3and say to Tyre, who dwells at the entrance to the
sea, merchant of the peoples on many islands, thus
says the Lord GOD:
"O Tyre, you have said,
'I am perfect in beauty.'
4Your borders are in the heart of the seas;
your builders made perfect your beauty.
5They made all your planks
of fir trees from Se'nir;
they took a cedar from Lebanon
to make a mast for you.
6Of oaks of Ba'shan
they made your oars;
they made your deck of pines
from the coasts of Cyprus,
inlaid with ivory.
7Of fine embroidered linen from Egypt
was your sail,
serving as your ensign;
blue and purple from the coasts of Eli'shah
was your awning.
8The inhabitants of Si'don and Arvad
were your rowers;
skilled men of Ze'mer[f] were in you,
they were your pilots.
9The elders of Ge'bal and her skilled men were
in you,
caulking your seams;
all the ships of the sea with their mariners were
in you,
to barter for your wares.
10 "Persia and Lud and Put were in your army
as your men of war; they hung the shield and helmet in you; they gave you splendor. 11The men of
Arvad and He'lech[g] were upon your walls round
about, and men of Ga'mad were in your towers; they
hung their shields upon your walls round about;
they made perfect your beauty.
12 "Tar'shish trafficked with you because
of your great wealth of every kind; silver, iron,
tin, and lead they exchanged for your wares.
13Ja'van, Tu'bal, and Me'shech traded with you;
they exchanged the persons of men and vessels of
bronze for your merchandise. 14Beth'-togar'mah
exchanged for your wares horses, war horses, and
mules. 15The men of Rhodes[h] traded with you;
many islands were your own special markets, they
brought you in payment ivory tusks and ebony.

27:13: Rev 18:13.

27:2 raise a lamentation: Ezekiel follows the same pattern for dealing with Tyre as he does with Egypt. In both cases, he delivers an oracle against the nation followed by a lament, then an oracle against the nation's king and another lament.

27:4 your builders made perfect your beauty: Tyre is described as if the city were a ship that is beautifully built but then shipwrecked.

27:5 Senir: An ancient name for Mt. Hermon in northern Israel, the highest peak in Israel and the source of fragrant evergreens.

27:6 Bashan: The region east of the northern Jordan and Sea of Galilee, famous for its fine oak trees and timber.

27:7 Elishah: Probably a term for part or all of the island of Cyprus.

27:8 Sidon and Arvad: Sidon was an older Phoenician port city 25 miles north of Tyre on the Lebanese coast. Sidon was actually the mother city of Tyre, but later became eclipsed in wealth and trade by the newer port. Arvad was a lesser-known Phoenician island city another hundred miles farther north along the coast (cf. Gen 10:18; 1 Chron 1:16). **Zemer:** A minor Phoenician city on the north Lebanese coast.

27:9 Gebal: Another name for ancient Byblos, a Phoenician port city located between Tyre and Arvad. Byblos was famous for its trade in papyrus, which it imported from Egypt. For this reason, the city was named from the Greek word *biblos*, meaning "book". The English word "Bible" derives from this word via Latin.

27:10 Lud and Put: Lud is Lydia, a region in central western Asia Minor (modern Turkey), whereas Put is probably Libya. These were allies of Egypt and frequently cooperated with Egypt militarily.

27:11 Arvad: See note on 27:8. **Helech:** Probably Cilicia, the south coastal region of Asia Minor. **Gamad:** Location unknown.

27:12 Tarshish: Probably ancient Tartessus, a Phoenician colony in southwest Spain.

27:13 Javan: The Ionians, i.e., the Greeks. **Tubal:** A landlocked kingdom in central Asia Minor. **Meshech:** Another kingdom in Asia Minor, to the west of Tubal (cf. Gen 10:2).

27:14 Beth-togarmah: A kingdom of northeastern Asia Minor, renowned for horse breeding (cf. Gen 10:3).

27:15 Rhodes: A large Greek island off the southwest coast of Asia Minor. The reading *Rhodes* is taken from the Greek Septuagint (LXX). The Hebrew text (MT) has Dedan here, which seems to be an error since it also occurs below in 27:20.

[d] Cn: Heb *her inhabitants*.
[e] Gk: Heb *I will give beauty*.
[f] Compare Gen 10:18: Heb *your skilled men, O Tyre*.
[g] Or *and your army*.
[h] Gk: Heb *Dedan*.

16 E′dom[i] trafficked with you because of your abundant goods; they exchanged for your wares emeralds,
purple, embroidered work, fine linen, coral, and
agate. 17 Judah and the land of Israel traded with you;
they exchanged for your merchandise wheat, olives
and early figs,[j] honey, oil, and balm. 18 Damascus
trafficked with you for your abundant goods,
because of your great wealth of every kind; wine
of Helbon, and white wool, 19 and wine[k] from U′zal
they exchanged for your wares; wrought iron, cassia,
and calamus were bartered for your merchandise.
20 De′dan traded with you in saddlecloths for riding.
21 Arabia and all the princes of Ke′dar were your
favored dealers in lambs, rams, and goats; in these
they trafficked with you. 22 The traders of Sheba and
Ra′amah traded with you; they exchanged for your
wares the best of all kinds of spices, and all precious
stones, and gold. 23 Haran, Canneh, Eden,[l] Asshur,
and Chil′mad traded with you. 24 These traded
with you in choice garments, in clothes of blue and
embroidered work, and in carpets of colored stuff,
bound with cords and made secure; in these they
traded with you.[m] 25 The ships of Tar′shish traveled
for you with your merchandise.[n]

"So you were filled and heavily laden
in the heart of the seas.
26 Your rowers have brought you out
into the high seas.
The east wind has wrecked you
in the heart of the seas.
27 Your riches, your wares, your merchandise,
your mariners and your pilots,
your caulkers, your dealers in merchandise,
and all your men of war who are in you,
with all your company
that is in your midst,
sink into the heart of the seas
on the day of your ruin.
28 At the sound of the cry of your pilots
the countryside shakes,
29 and down from their ships
come all that handle the oar.
The mariners and all the pilots of the sea
stand on the shore
30 and wail aloud over you,
and cry bitterly.
They cast dust on their heads
and wallow in ashes;
31 they make themselves bald for you,
and put on sackcloth,
and they weep over you in bitterness of soul,
with bitter mourning.
32 In their wailing they raise a lamentation for you,
and lament over you:
'Who was ever destroyed[o] like Tyre
in the midst of the sea?
33 When your wares came from the seas,
you satisfied many peoples;
with your abundant wealth and merchandise
you enriched the kings of the earth.
34 Now you are wrecked by the seas,
in the depths of the waters;
your merchandise and all your crew
have sunk with you.
35 All the inhabitants of the islands
are appalled at you;
and their kings are horribly afraid,
their faces are convulsed.
36 The merchants among the peoples hiss at you;
you have come to a dreadful end
and shall be no more for ever.'"

Ruin of Tyre Foretold

28 The word of the LORD came to me: 2 "Son of
man, say to the prince of Tyre, Thus says the
Lord GOD:

27:27–36: Rev 18:9–19. **28:2:** Dan 11:36; 2 Thess 2:4; Rev 13:5.

27:16 Edom: The Hebrew reads *ʾrm*, Aram, but most scholars think it should be *ʾdm*, Edom. The letters *r* and *d* in Hebrew are written very similarly and easily mistaken for each other.

27:18 Damascus: The traditional capital of Aram (modern Syria), about 60 miles northeast of Galilee. **Helbon:** A small town north of Damascus renowned for its wine.

27:19 Uzal: Probably ancient Izalla, a town in the foothills of Asia Minor renowned for its wine.

27:20 Dedan: An oasis in central Arabia associated at times with the people of Edom.

27:21 Kedar: An Arabian tribe associated with the oasis at Dumah, halfway between the north end of the Persian Gulf and the Gulf of Aqaba.

27:22 Sheba and Raamah: Sheba was an Arabian kingdom in what is now eastern Yemen that grew wealthy from trade between Africa, Arabia, and India. The location of Raamah is unknown, but it is always associated with Sheba in the Bible, so it probably indicates a nearby city or kingdom.

27:23 Haran: Associated with Abraham as an important city in upper Mesopotamia. **Canneh:** Not identified with certainty. **Eden:** Short for Beth-eden, a kingdom located in north-central Syria. **Asshur:** The Hebrew form of Assyria, either the people or the capital city. **Chilmad:** Unidentified and possibly a scribal error.

27:25 Tarshish: See note on 27:12.

28:1–10 The oracle against Tyre (chap. 26) and the lament for its people (chap. 27) is followed with an oracle (28:1–10) and lament (28:11–19) specifically for the king. • The blasphemous things the king of Tyre is described as saying and doing have long been understood in the Christian tradition as reflecting the mind and disposition of Satan when he fell.

28:2 the seat of the gods ... the seas: In ancient paganism, various important gods were imagined as being enthroned upon the waters of the sea (cf. Ps 29:10). The king of Tyre imagines himself a god because his throne is on an island in the middle of the sea.

[i] Another reading is *Aram*.
[j] Cn: Heb *wheat of minnith and pannag*.
[k] Gk: Heb *Vedan and Javan*.
[l] Cn: Heb *Eden the traders of Sheba*.
[m] Cn: Heb *in your market*.
[n] Cn: Heb *your travelers your merchandise*.
[o] Tg Vg: Heb *like silence*.

"Because your heart is proud,
and you have said, 'I am a god,
I sit in the seat of the gods,
in the heart of the seas,'
yet you are but a man, and no god,
though you consider yourself as wise as a god—
3you are indeed wiser than Daniel;
no secret is hidden from you;
4by your wisdom and your understanding
you have gotten wealth for yourself,
and have gathered gold and silver
into your treasuries;
5by your great wisdom in trade
you have increased your wealth,
and your heart has become proud in your wealth—
6therefore thus says the Lord GOD:
"Because you consider yourself
as wise as a god,
7therefore, behold, I will bring strangers upon you,
the most terrible of the nations;
and they shall draw their swords
against the beauty of your wisdom
and defile your splendor.
8They shall thrust you down into the Pit,
and you shall die the death of the slain
in the heart of the seas.
9Will you still say, 'I am a god,'
in the presence of those who slay you,
though you are but a man, and no god,
in the hands of those who wound you?
10You shall die the death of the uncircumcised
by the hand of foreigners;
for I have spoken, says the Lord GOD."

Lamentation over the King of Tyre

11 Moreover the word of the LORD came to me:
12"Son of man, raise a lamentation over the king of
Tyre, and say to him, Thus says the Lord GOD:
"You were the signet of perfection,[p]
full of wisdom
and perfect in beauty.
13You were in Eden, the garden of God;
every precious stone was your covering,
carnelian, topaz, and jasper,
chrysolite, beryl, and onyx,
sapphire,[q] carbuncle, and emerald;
and wrought in gold were your settings
and your engravings.[r]
On the day that you were created
they were prepared.
14With an anointed guardian cherub I placed you;[s]
you were on the holy mountain of God;
in the midst of the stones of fire you walked.
15You were blameless in your ways
from the day you were created,
till iniquity was found in you.
16In the abundance of your trade
you were filled with violence, and you sinned;
so I cast you as a profane thing from the mountain of God,
and the guardian cherub drove you out
from the midst of the stones of fire.
17Your heart was proud because of your beauty;
you corrupted your wisdom for the sake of your splendor.
I cast you to the ground;
I exposed you before kings,
to feast their eyes on you.

28:3 Daniel: See note on 14:14.

28:10 the death of the uncircumcised: The Tyrians, like most peoples of the ancient Near East, practiced circumcision, which was considered a sign of culture and civilization—similar to shaving in early modern Europe. Thus, an uncircumcised person was a barbarian. Ezekiel condemns the king of Tyre to die like an uncivilized foreigner.

28:11–19 The king of Tyre is described in this lamentation as if he were originally one of the guardian cherubim in the garden of Eden, before losing God's favor. This passage has been understood to reflect the downfall of Satan. See note on 28:1–10 (CCC 391–95). • The devil is the author of sin and the father of the wicked. Of his own free will, he went from being a high angel and God's good servant to becoming Satan, meaning "adversary". These are not my teachings but those of the prophet Ezekiel in his lamentation (St. Cyril of Jerusalem, *Catechesis* 2, 4).

28:12 the signet of perfection: A signet was usually a ring used to impress the final seal on a document or other object. Thus, this has the sense: "you are the pinnacle of perfection."

28:13 Eden, the garden of God: One of only two passages in the Bible that discusses Eden explicitly, the other being Gen 2–3. **Every precious stone:** Precious gemstones are associated with the sanctuary of God and the worship of him. Precious stones are mentioned as being in the vicinity of Eden (Gen 2:12). Ezekiel's list of gemstones compares to those on the breastplate of the high priest (Ex 28:15–20; 39:10–12) and the foundation of the heavenly Jerusalem (Rev 21:19–20). The sanctuary symbolism may be connected with the fact that Tyre provided much of the expertise and material for the Solomonic Temple (1 Kings 5:1–12; 7:13–47; 9:11, 14, 26–28; 10:11–12, 22; 2 Chron 2:13–14; 9:10–11).

28:14 With an anointed guardian cherub: Or more likely, "As an anointed guardian cherub". The king of Tyre is being described as if he were one of the angels who guarded the divine presence in the garden paradise at creation. • Since this cannot be literally true of the king of Tyre, Christian tradition has applied the literal sense to Satan, understood to have been the primary angel to whom the governance of the world was entrusted. **holy mountain of God:** The garden of Eden was on a mountain. This is presumed also in Genesis, where the river that flows out of Eden is described as the headwaters of four rivers that in turn irrigate the whole earth (Gen 2:10–14). **stones of fire:** The holy gemstones that sparkled with light like fire. Beautiful and rare stones were employed to add beauty, dignity, and mystery to the sanctuary where God's presence dwelt and was worshiped.

28:16 I cast you as a profane thing: Mystically understood to reflect the ejection of Satan from heaven. See note on 28:11–19.

---

[p] Heb obscure.
[q] Or *lapis lazuli*.
[r] Heb uncertain.
[s] Heb uncertain.

18By the multitude of your iniquities,
in the unrighteousness of your trade
you profaned your sanctuaries;
so I brought forth fire from the midst of you;
it consumed you,
and I turned you to ashes upon the earth
in the sight of all who saw you.
19All who know you among the peoples
are appalled at you;
you have come to a dreadful end
and shall be no more for ever."

Prophecy against Sidon

20 The word of the LORD came to me: 21"Son of
man, set your face toward Si′don, and prophesy
against her 22and say, Thus says the Lord GOD:
"Behold, I am against you, O Si′don,
and I will manifest my glory in the midst of you.
And they shall know that I am the LORD
when I execute judgments in her,
and manifest my holiness in her;
23for I will send pestilence into her,
and blood into her streets;
and the slain shall fall in the midst of her,
by the sword that is against her on every side.
Then they will know that I am the LORD.
24 "And for the house of Israel there shall be no
more a brier to prick or a thorn to hurt them among
all their neighbors who have treated them with contempt. Then they will know that I am the Lord GOD.

Future Blessings for Israel

25 "Thus says the Lord GOD: When I gather the
house of Israel from the peoples among whom they
are scattered, and manifest my holiness in them
in the sight of the nations, then they shall dwell in
their own land which I gave to my servant Jacob.
26And they shall dwell securely in it, and they shall
build houses and plant vineyards. They shall dwell
securely, when I execute judgments upon all their
neighbors who have treated them with contempt.
Then they will know that I am the LORD their God."

Prophecy against Egypt

29 In the tenth year, in the tenth month, on the
twelfth day of the month, the word of the
LORD came to me: 2"Son of man, set your face against
Pharaoh king of Egypt, and prophesy against him
and against all Egypt; 3speak, and say, Thus says
the Lord GOD:
"Behold, I am against you,
Pharaoh king of Egypt,
the great dragon that lies
in the midst of his streams,
that says, 'My Nile is my own;
I made it.'[t]
4I will put hooks in your jaws,
and make the fish of your streams stick to your scales;
and I will draw you up out of the midst of your streams,
with all the fish of your streams
which stick to your scales.
5And I will cast you forth into the wilderness,
you and all the fish of your streams;
you shall fall upon the open field,
and not be gathered and buried.
To the beasts of the earth and to the birds of the air
I have given you as food.
6 "Then all the inhabitants of Egypt shall know
that I am the LORD. Because you[u] have been a staff
of reed to the house of Israel; 7when they grasped
you with the hand, you broke, and tore all their
shoulders; and when they leaned upon you, you
broke, and made all their loins to shake;[v] 8therefore
thus says the Lord GOD: Behold, I will bring a sword
upon you, and will cut off from you man and beast;
9and the land of Egypt shall be a desolation and a
waste. Then they will know that I am the LORD.

28:20–26: Joel 3:4–8; Zech 9:2.

28:21 Sidon: The mother city of Tyre. Older and located farther north on the Lebanese coast, Sidon was eventually overshadowed politically and economically by her daughter city. Ethnic, cultural, political, and economic ties between the two cities were so strong they are mentioned 30 times in the Old and New Testaments as a pair, but always with Tyre first: "Tyre and Sidon".

28:24 no more a brier to prick: Sidon was part of the tribal territory of Asher (Josh 19:28), but the Asherites were unable to conquer the city (Judg 1:31). The Israelites dwelt inland of Sidon throughout their history and even enjoyed good relations with them (1 Kings 5:6) during the united monarchy, but later both Tyre and Sidon grew antagonistic toward Israel, and while not posing a major military threat, these Phoenician cities became an irritant and nuisance to the Israelites.

[t] Syr Compare Gk: Heb *I have made myself.*
[u] Gk Syr Vg: Heb *they.*
[v] Syr: Heb *stand.*

28:26 dwell securely: The prophet seems to borrow this phrase from Leviticus, in the covenant blessing passages Lev 25:18–19 and 26:5.

29:1 tenth year . . . tenth month . . . twelfth day: Most likely January 7, 587 B.C.

29:3 king of Egypt: Pharaoh Hophra (Jer 44:30). Known to the Greeks as Apries, he reigned 589–570 B.C. An unpopular and unsuccessful Pharaoh, he was eventually overthrown by one of his generals, fled Egypt, and was probably killed while attempting to regain his throne. **the great dragon that lies in . . . streams:** The imagery of a crocodile.

29:4 fish . . . stick to your scales: The imagery of parasitic fish, like lampreys or remoras, that attach to their host.

29:6 a staff of reed: Nile reeds could be tall and thick but could bear little weight. Help from Egypt looked promising, but always failed when called upon to support Judah's rebellions against Babylon.

29:7 tore all their shoulders: The image is of a crutch placed under the arm, only to splinter and injure the user.

"Because you[w] said, 'The Nile is mine, and I
made it,' 10therefore, behold, I am against you, and
against your streams, and I will make the land of
Egypt an utter waste and desolation, from Migdol
to Sye'ne, as far as the border of Ethiopia. 11No
foot of man shall pass through it, and no foot of
beast shall pass through it; it shall be uninhabited
forty years. 12And I will make the land of Egypt a
desolation in the midst of desolated countries; and
her cities shall be a desolation forty years among
cities that are laid waste. I will scatter the Egyptians
among the nations, and disperse them among
the countries.

13 "For thus says the Lord GOD: At the end of
forty years I will gather the Egyptians from the
peoples among whom they were scattered; 14and I
will restore the fortunes of Egypt, and bring them
back to the land of Path'ros, the land of their origin;
and there they shall be a lowly kingdom. 15It shall
be the most lowly of the kingdoms, and never again
exalt itself above the nations; and I will make them
so small that they will never again rule over the
nations. 16And it shall never again be the reliance
of the house of Israel, recalling their iniquity, when
they turn to them for aid. Then they will know that
I am the Lord GOD."

17 In the twenty-seventh year, in the first month,
on the first day of the month, the word of the LORD
came to me: 18"Son of man, Nebuchadrez'zar king
of Babylon made his army labor hard against Tyre;
every head was made bald and every shoulder
was rubbed bare; yet neither he nor his army got
anything from Tyre to pay for the labor that he
had performed against it. 19Therefore thus says
the Lord GOD: Behold, I will give the land of Egypt
to Nebuchadrez'zar king of Babylon; and he shall
carry off its wealth[x] and despoil it and plunder it;
and it shall be the wages for his army. 20I have given
him the land of Egypt as his recompense for which
he labored, because they worked for me, says the
Lord GOD.

21 "On that day I will cause a horn to spring forth
to the house of Israel, and I will open your lips among
them. Then they will know that I am the LORD."

Lamentation for Egypt

30 The word of the LORD came to me: 2"Son of
man, prophesy, and say, Thus says the Lord
GOD:

"Wail, 'Alas for the day!'
3 For the day is near,
the day of the LORD is near;
it will be a day of clouds,
a time of doom for the nations.
4A sword shall come upon Egypt,
and anguish shall be in Ethiopia,
when the slain fall in Egypt,
and her wealth is carried away,
and her foundations are torn down.
5Ethiopia, and Put, and Lud, and all Arabia, and
Libya,[y] and the people of the land that is in league,
shall fall with them by the sword.

6"Thus says the LORD:
Those who support Egypt shall fall,
and her proud might shall come down;

29–32: Is 19; Jer 46; Zech 14:18–19.

29:10 Migdol to Syene: From north to south, like the Israelite expression "from Dan to Beersheba". Migdol means "tower, fortress" in Hebrew and probably indicates the extreme northeastern fortress city that guarded the approach to Egypt from the east along the Mediterranean coast. Syene is modern Aswan, the first cataract as one travels south up the Nile, the traditional boundary between Egypt and Nubia (= biblical Cush). **Ethiopia:** In Hebrew, Cush. Known in classical literature as Nubia, this ancient, powerful African nation occupied the territory bordering the Nile from Aswan to Khartoum in what is now southern Egypt and northern Sudan—far north of modern Ethiopia.

29:14 Pathros: A traditional name for Upper Egypt, which began along the Nile just south of the Delta region (near modern Cairo) and extended upriver to Syene (Aswan), the border of Cush/Nubia.

29:17 twenty-seventh year ... first month ... first day: Most likely April 26, 571 B.C. This is the latest date given in the Book of Ezekiel. The oracle appears to be an addendum to Ezekiel's denunciations of Tyre and prediction that Nebuchadnezzar would destroy the city. It is probably included here, rather than immediately after the Tyrian oracles, because it promises Egypt as a consolation prize to Nebuchadnezzar for his failure to loot Tyre. Nebuchadnezzar did besiege the city, and apparently the king of Tyre finally submitted to Babylonian rule, but the city was not destroyed immediately in the way Ezekiel describes. That would have to wait for Alexander the Great, who captured and destroyed the city in 332 B.C., killing or enslaving all the inhabitants.

29:18 neither ... got anything: The Tyrian king submitted and paid tribute, and so the city was not captured and looted, which was the usual way soldiers enriched themselves from warfare.

29:20 they worked for me: Babylon's army was God's instrument of judgment on Tyre.

30:1–19 A lament for Egypt. This is in keeping with Ezekiel's pattern: he typically gives an oracle of destruction, followed by a lament, followed by an oracle against the king, followed by a complementary lament.

30:3 The day of the LORD: A liturgical term for a feast day or other religious celebration. Ezekiel, like several other prophets, turns this term with festive connotations upside down, employing it as a reference to a day of judgment.

30:4 Ethiopia: Ancient Nubia, known in the Bible as Cush.

30:5 Ethiopia, and Put, and Lud: See notes on 27:10 and 30:4. **Libya:** The Hebrew is *kûb*, which is probably a scribal error for *lûb*, an ethnic group allied with the Libyans. The usual Hebrew name for Libya is Put (see Nahum 3:9).

30:6 Migdol to Syene: From north to south. See note on 29:10.

[w] Gk Syr Vg: Heb *he*.
[x] Or *multitude*.
[y] Gk Compare Syr Vg: Heb *Cub*.

from Migdol to Sye′ne
they shall fall within her by the sword,
says the Lord GOD.
7 And she[z] shall be desolated in the midst of desolated countries
and her cities shall be in the midst of cities that are laid waste.
8 Then they will know that I am the LORD,
when I have set fire to Egypt,
and all her helpers are broken.

9 "On that day swift[a] messengers shall go forth
from me to terrify the unsuspecting Ethiopians; and
anguish shall come upon them on the day of Egypt's
doom; for behold, it comes!

10 "Thus says the Lord GOD:
I will put an end to the wealth[b] of Egypt,
by the hand of Nebuchadrez′zar king of Babylon.
11 He and his people with him, the most terrible of the nations,
shall be brought in to destroy the land;
and they shall draw their swords against Egypt,
and fill the land with the slain.
12 And I will dry up the Nile,
and will sell the land into the hand of evil men;
I will bring desolation upon the land and everything in it,
by the hand of foreigners;
I, the LORD, have spoken.

13 "Thus says the Lord GOD:
I will destroy the idols,
and put an end to the images, in Memphis;
there shall no longer be a prince in the land of Egypt;
so I will put fear in the land of Egypt.
14 I will make Path′ros a desolation,
and will set fire to Zoan,
and will execute acts of judgment upon Thebes.
15 And I will pour my wrath upon Pelu′sium,
the stronghold of Egypt,
and cut off the multitude of Thebes.
16 And I will set fire to Egypt;
Pelu′sium shall be in great agony;
Thebes shall be breached,
and its walls broken down.[c]
17 The young men of On and of Pibe′seth shall fall by the sword;
and the women shall go into captivity.
18 At Tehaph′nehes the day shall be dark,
when I break there the dominion of Egypt,
and her proud might shall come to an end;
she shall be covered by a cloud,
and her daughters shall go into captivity.
19 Thus I will execute acts of judgment upon Egypt.
Then they will know that I am the LORD."

Prophecy against Pharaoh

20 In the eleventh year, in the first month, on
the seventh day of the month, the word of the LORD
came to me: 21 "Son of man, I have broken the arm of

30:9 Ethiopians: Nubians. Nubia conquered Egypt, and Nubian Pharaohs ruled during the 25th Pharaonic Dynasty (ca. 744–656 B.C.), uniting Egypt and Cush/Nubia into a large Cushite empire. Ezekiel is writing about 60 years after a native Egyptian dynasty (the Saites, from their capital at Sais in the delta) managed to regain control of Upper and Lower Egypt in the wake of an Assyrian invasion that drove back the Nubians. The close association of Egypt and Nubia, however, is still fresh in cultural memory.

30:13 Memphis: The ancient capital of Egypt and one of its oldest and most important cities. It was located just south of modern Cairo, near the confluence of the Delta branches of the Nile. **No longer be a prince in ... Egypt:** Within 50 years of Ezekiel's writing, Egypt was conquered by the Persians and permanently lost self-rule. Persian, Hellenistic, Roman, Byzantine, and Arab Muslim dynasties or governors would rule Egypt for the rest of its existence. The majority of the population of modern Egypt (about 90 percent) are Muslim Arabs, who conquered the nation in the A.D. 640s. The Christian Copts (about 10 percent of the population) are the actual descendants of the ancient Egyptians.

30:14 Pathros: Upper Egypt. See note on 29:14. **Zoan:** An ancient city in the eastern Nile Delta. **Thebes:** The natural capital of Upper Egypt (Pathros) and the site of modern Luxor. Its name in Hebrew is *no'*.

30:15 Pelusium: The eastern-most city of the Nile Delta, located at the mouth of a branch of the Nile. Famed for its flax and beer, throughout history Pelusium bore the brunt of attacks on Egypt from the east along the Mediterranean coast and therefore was heavily fortified. Its name in Hebrew is *sîn*.

30:17 On: Heliopolis, an ancient Egyptian city important as a religious center, especially for the worship of Amon-Re (or Amun-Ra), the sun god. The northern suburbs of Cairo now surround the ancient site. **Pibeseth:** Bubastis, in the southeastern Nile Delta, a city dedicated to the cat goddess Bastis and remarkable for its many feline mummies.

30:18 Tehaphnehes: A city about halfway between Pibeseth/Bubastis and Sin/Pelusium on the eastern-most (Tanitic) delta branch of the Nile. It was a popular city for Judean refugees from the Babylonian conquest (see Jer 2:16; 43:7, 8, 9; 44:1; 46:14), as it was easy to reach but not as heavily militarized as Pelusium.

30:19 I will execute acts of judgment upon Egypt: This line is reminiscent of Ex 12:12: "On all the gods of Egypt I will execute judgments: I am the LORD." Ezekiel intentionally evokes the memory of the plagues of the Exodus.

30:20 eleventh year ... first month ... seventh day: April 29, 587 B.C. The formal date announcement marks the beginning of a new oracle that will extend to 30:26. Around this time, Pharaoh Hophra (Apries) sent an army to relieve the Babylonian siege of Jerusalem, an event that provoked false and short-lived hope for the rebellious Jerusalemites.

30:21 the arm of Pharaoh: In Egyptian art and rhetoric, the "arm" of Pharaoh was a metaphor for his strength.

[z] Gk: Heb *they*.
[a] Gk Syr: Heb *in ships*.
[b] Or *multitude*.
[c] Cn: Heb *and Memphis, distresses by day*.

Pharaoh king of Egypt; and behold, it has not been
bound up, to heal it by binding it with a bandage,
so that it may become strong to wield the sword.
22Therefore thus says the Lord GOD: Behold, I am
against Pharaoh king of Egypt, and will break his
arms, both the strong arm and the one that was
broken; and I will make the sword fall from his hand.
23I will scatter the Egyptians among the nations,
and disperse them throughout the lands. 24And I
will strengthen the arms of the king of Babylon, and
put my sword in his hand; but I will break the arms
of Pharaoh, and he will groan before him like a man
mortally wounded. 25I will strengthen the arms of
the king of Babylon, but the arms of Pharaoh shall
fall; and they shall know that I am the LORD. When I
put my sword into the hand of the king of Babylon,
he shall stretch it out against the land of Egypt;
26and I will scatter the Egyptians among the nations
and disperse them throughout the countries. Then
they will know that I am the LORD."

The Towering Cedar

31 In the eleventh year, in the third month, on
the first day of the month, the word of the
LORD came to me: 2"Son of man, say to Pharaoh king
of Egypt and to his multitude:

"Whom are you like in your greatness?
3 Behold, I will liken you[d] to a cedar in Lebanon,
with fair branches and forest shade,
and of great height,
its top among the clouds.[e]
4The waters nourished it,
the deep made it grow tall,
making its rivers flow[f]
round the place of its planting,
sending forth its streams
to all the trees of the forest.
5So it towered high
above all the trees of the forest;
its boughs grew large
and its branches long,
from abundant water in its shoots.
6All the birds of the air
made their nests in its boughs;
under its branches all the beasts of the field
brought forth their young;
and under its shadow
dwelt all great nations.
7It was beautiful in its greatness,
in the length of its branches;
for its roots went down
to abundant waters.
8The cedars in the garden of God could not rival it,
nor the fir trees equal its boughs;
the plane trees were as nothing
compared with its branches;
no tree in the garden of God
was like it in beauty.
9I made it beautiful
in the mass of its branches,
and all the trees of Eden envied it,
that were in the garden of God.

10 "Therefore thus says the Lord GOD: Because
it[g] towered high and set its top among the clouds,[h]
and its heart was proud of its height, 11I will give
it into the hand of a mighty one of the nations; he
shall surely deal with it as its wickedness deserves.
I have cast it out. 12Foreigners, the most terrible
of the nations, will cut it down and leave it. On
the mountains and in all the valleys its branches
will fall, and its boughs will lie broken in all the
watercourses of the land; and all the peoples of
the earth will go from its shadow and leave it.
13Upon its ruin will dwell all the birds of the air,
and upon its branches will be all the beasts of
the field. 14All this is in order that no trees by the
waters may grow to lofty height or set their tops
among the clouds,[h] and that no trees that drink
water may reach up to them in height; for they are
all given over to death, to the nether world among
mortal men, with those who go down to the Pit.

15 "Thus says the Lord GOD: When it goes
down to Sheol I will make the deep mourn for[i] it,
and restrain its rivers, and many waters shall be
stopped; I will clothe Lebanon in gloom for it, and all
the trees of the field shall faint because of it. 16I will
make the nations quake at the sound of its fall, when
I cast it down to Sheol with those who go down to
the Pit; and all the trees of Eden, the choice and best
of Lebanon, all that drink water, will be comforted
in the nether world. 17They also shall go down to
Sheol with it, to those who are slain by the sword;

31:6: Ezek 17:23; Dan 4:12–21; Mt 13:32; Mk 4:32; Lk 13:19. **31:8 (Gk):** Rev 2:7.

31:1 eleventh year ... third month ... first day: June 21, 587 B.C.

31:3 a cedar in Lebanon: The moist climate and high elevations of mountainous Lebanon were famed for their magnificent evergreens, especially cedars, whose fragrant wood was highly valued.

31:8 the garden of God: Eden. **plane trees:** Trees from the same family and similar in appearance to American sycamores. **no tree in the garden of God was like it:** Ezekiel attributes Satanic pride to the Pharaoh of Egypt, much as he did to the king of Tyre in chap. 28. Both are described as trying to rival God in their strength and beauty, and both are cast down as a result.

31:14 set their tops among the clouds: A metaphor for kings claiming divinity for themselves.

[d] Cn: Heb *Behold, Assyria.*
[e] Gk: Heb *thick boughs.*
[f] Gk: Heb *going.*
[g] Syr Vg: Heb *you.*
[h] Gk: Heb *thick boughs.*
[i] Gk: Heb *mourn for, I have covered.*

yes, those who dwelt under its shadow among the
nations shall perish.[j] 18Whom are you thus like in
glory and in greatness among the trees of Eden? You
shall be brought down with the trees of Eden to the
nether world; you shall lie among the uncircumcised,
with those who are slain by the sword.

"This is Pharaoh and all his multitude, says the
Lord GOD."

Lamentation over Pharaoh

32 In the twelfth year, in the twelfth month, on
the first day of the month, the word of the
LORD came to me: 2"Son of man, raise a lamentation
over Pharaoh king of Egypt, and say to him:

"You consider yourself a lion among the nations,
but you are like a dragon in the seas;
you burst forth in your rivers,
trouble the waters with your feet,
and foul their rivers.
3Thus says the Lord GOD:
I will throw my net over you
with a host of many peoples;
and I[k] will haul you up in my dragnet.
4And I will cast you on the ground,
on the open field I will fling you,
and will cause all the birds of the air to settle on
you,
and I will gorge the beasts of the whole earth
with you.
5I will strew your flesh upon the mountains,
and fill the valleys with your carcass.[l]
6I will drench the land even to the mountains
with your flowing blood;
and the watercourses will be full of you.
7When I blot you out, I will cover the heavens,
and make their stars dark;
I will cover the sun with a cloud,
and the moon shall not give its light.
8All the bright lights of heaven
will I make dark over you,
and put darkness upon your land,
says the Lord GOD.

9 "I will trouble the hearts of many peoples, when
I carry you captive[m] among the nations, into the
countries which you have not known. 10I will make
many peoples appalled at you, and their kings shall
shudder because of you, when I brandish my sword
before them; they shall tremble every moment, every
one for his own life, on the day of your downfall.
11For thus says the Lord GOD: The sword of the king
of Babylon shall come upon you. 12I will cause your
multitude to fall by the swords of mighty ones, all of
them most terrible among the nations.

"They shall bring to nothing the pride of Egypt,
and all its multitude shall perish.
13I will destroy all its beasts
from beside many waters;
and no foot of man shall trouble them any more,
nor shall the hoofs of beasts trouble them.
14Then I will make their waters clear,
and cause their rivers to run like oil,
says the Lord GOD.
15When I make the land of Egypt desolate
and when the land is stripped of all that fills it,
when I strike all who dwell in it,
then they will know that I am the LORD.
16This is a lamentation which shall be chanted; the
daughters of the nations shall chant it; over Egypt,
and over all her multitude, shall they chant it, says
the Lord GOD."

17 In the twelfth year, in the first month,[n] on the
fifteenth day of the month, the word of the LORD
came to me: 18"Son of man, wail over the multitude of
Egypt, and send them down, her and the daughters
of majestic nations, to the nether world, to those
who have gone down to the Pit:
19'Whom do you surpass in beauty?
Go down, and be laid with the uncircumcised.'

20 They shall fall amid those who are slain by
the sword,[o] and with her shall lie all her multitudes.[p] 21The mighty chiefs shall speak of them,
with their helpers, out of the midst of Sheol: 'They
have come down, they lie still, the uncircumcised,
slain by the sword.'

31:18 among the uncircumcised: The Egyptians, like most ancient Near Eastern peoples, practiced circumcision and regarded uncircumcision as disgusting and characteristic of uncivilized barbarians.

32:1 twelfth year ... twelfth month ... first day: March 3, 585 B.C.

32:2 a lion among the nations: The lion was a common symbol of royalty employed in many Near Eastern cultures. **a dragon in the seas:** Most Near Eastern cultures had creation myths that involved the slaying of a chaos-monster that dwelled in the primordial sea.

32:5 strew your flesh upon the mountains: Some ancient Near Eastern myths described the world being made by the chief god slaying a chaos-monster or dragon and then creating the world from its carcass. This prophecy seems to invert that narrative, as the destruction of Pharaoh, the chaos-monster, leads to a kind of uncreation.

32:11 The sword of ... Babylon shall come: Nebuchadnezzar invaded Egypt in 568 B.C.

32:17 twelfth year ... first month ... fifteenth day: Most likely March 18, 585 B.C. Ezekiel describes Egypt descending to the realm of the dead, there to find other nations whom Babylon had conquered and dispatched.

32:21 Sheol: The place of the dead in the ancient Israelite world view, similar to Hades in Greek thought. It is not necessarily a place of punishment (thus not hell), but a place of languishing and waiting in a liminal state (CCC 633). See word study: *Sheol* at Num 16:30. **Uncircumcised:** See note on 31:18.

---

[j] Compare Gk: Heb obscure.
[k] Gk Vg: Heb *they.*
[l] Symmachus Syr Vg: Heb *your height.*
[m] Gk: Heb *bring your destruction.*
[n] Gk: Heb lacks *in the first month.*
[o] Gk Syr: Heb *sword, the sword is delivered.*
[p] Gk: Heb *they have drawn her away and all her multitudes.*

22 "Assyria is there, and all her company, their graves round about her, all of them slain, fallen by the sword; 23whose graves are set in the uttermost parts of the Pit, and her company is round about her grave; all of them slain, fallen by the sword, who spread terror in the land of the living.

24 "E′lam is there, and all her multitude about her grave; all of them slain, fallen by the sword, who went down uncircumcised into the nether world, who spread terror in the land of the living, and they bear their shame with those who go down to the Pit. 25They have made her a bed among the slain with all her multitude, their graves round about her, all of them uncircumcised, slain by the sword; for terror of them was spread in the land of the living, and they bear their shame with those who go down to the Pit; they are placed among the slain.

26 "Me′shech and Tu′bal are there, and all their multitude, their graves round about them, all of them uncircumcised, slain by the sword; for they spread terror in the land of the living. 27And they do not lie with the fallen mighty men of old[q] who went down to Sheol with their weapons of war, whose swords were laid under their heads, and whose shields[r] are upon their bones; for the terror of the mighty men was in the land of the living. 28So you shall be broken and lie among the uncircumcised, with those who are slain by the sword.

29 "E′dom is there, her kings and all her princes, who for all their might are laid with those who are slain by the sword; they lie with the uncircumcised, with those who go down to the Pit.

30 "The princes of the north are there, all of them, and all the Sidonians, who have gone down in shame with the slain, for all the terror which they caused by their might; they lie uncircumcised with those who are slain by the sword, and bear their shame with those who go down to the Pit.

31 "When Pharaoh sees them, he will comfort himself for all his multitude, Pharaoh and all his army, slain by the sword, says the Lord GOD. 32For he[s] spread terror in the land of the living; therefore he shall be laid among the uncircumcised, with those who are slain by the sword, Pharaoh and all his multitude, says the Lord GOD."

The Watchman's Duty

33 The word of the LORD came to me: 2"Son of man, speak to your people and say to them, If I bring the sword upon a land, and the people of the land take a man from among them, and make him their watchman; 3and if he sees the sword coming upon the land and blows the trumpet and warns the people; 4then if any one who hears the sound of the trumpet does not take warning, and the sword comes and takes him away, his blood shall be upon his own head. 5He heard the sound of the trumpet, and did not take warning; his blood shall be upon himself. But if he had taken warning, he would have saved his life. 6But if the watchman sees the sword coming and does not blow the trumpet, so that the people are not warned, and the sword comes, and takes any one of them; that man is taken away in his iniquity, but his blood I will require at the watchman's hand.

7 "So you, son of man, I have made a watchman for the house of Israel; whenever you hear a word from my mouth, you shall give them warning from me. 8If I say to the wicked, O wicked man, you shall surely die, and you do not speak to warn the wicked to turn from his way, that wicked man shall die in his iniquity, but his blood I will require at your hand. 9But if you warn the wicked to turn from his way, and he does not turn from his way; he shall die in his iniquity, but you will have saved your life.

10 "And you, son of man, say to the house of Israel, Thus have you said: 'Our transgressions and our sins are upon us, and we waste away because of them; how then can we live?' 11Say to them, As I live, says the Lord GOD, I have no pleasure in the death of the wicked, but that the wicked turn from his way and live; turn back, turn back from your evil ways; for why will you die, O house of Israel? 12And you, son of man, say to your people, The righteousness of the righteous shall not deliver him

33:1–9: Ezek 3:16–21. **33:11:** Ezek 18:23, 32.

32:22 Assyria: The Assyrian Empire (911–609 B.C.) was notorious for its brutality toward conquered peoples. It destroyed the Northern Kingdom of Israel and exiled most of the inhabitants in 722 B.C. The Assyrians themselves were vanquished by a Babylonian-led coalition of armies in a series of battles between 612 and 605 B.C.

32:24 Elam: An important nation in southwestern Persia (modern Iran) that was allied with the Assyrian Empire. The Elamites were noted for their fierceness in battle.

32:26 Meshech and Tubal: Two related nations of Asia Minor. See note on 27:13.

32:29 Edom: See note on 25:12.

32:30 Sidonians: See notes on 27:8 and 28:21.

33:1 The word of the LORD came: Marks a major shift in the book. Ezekiel's oracles against the nations are complete (chaps. 27–32). Now the prophet's attention shifts increasingly to the future of Judah and Israel.

33:2 If I bring the sword: Metonymy for invasion by a hostile army.

33:4 his blood shall be upon his own head: A metaphor meaning "He is responsible for his own death."

33:8 his blood I will require at your hand: I.e., you will be morally responsible for his death.

33:10–20 A unit that shares much in common with 18:1–32.

[q] Gk Old Latin: Heb *of the uncircumcised.*
[r] Cn: Heb *iniquities.*
[s] Cn: Heb *I.*

when he transgresses; and as for the wickedness of the wicked, he shall not fall by it when he turns from his wickedness; and the righteous shall not be able to live by his righteousness[t] when he sins. [13]Though I say to the righteous that he shall surely live, yet if he trusts in his righteousness and commits iniquity, none of his righteous deeds shall be remembered; but in the iniquity that he has committed he shall die. [14]Again, though I say to the wicked, 'You shall surely die,' yet if he turns from his sin and does what is lawful and right, [15]if the wicked restores the pledge, gives back what he has taken by robbery, and walks in the statutes of life, committing no iniquity; he shall surely live, he shall not die. [16]None of the sins that he has committed shall be remembered against him; he has done what is lawful and right, he shall surely live.

17 "Yet your people say, 'The way of the Lord is not just'; when it is their own way that is not just. [18]When the righteous turns from his righteousness, and commits iniquity, he shall die for it. [19]And when the wicked turns from his wickedness, and does what is lawful and right, he shall live by it. [20]Yet you say, 'The way of the Lord is not just.' O house of Israel, I will judge each of you according to his ways."

The Fall of Jerusalem

21 In the twelfth year of our exile, in the tenth month, on the fifth day of the month, a man who had escaped from Jerusalem came to me and said, "The city has fallen." [22]Now the hand of the LORD had been upon me the evening before the fugitive came; and he had opened my mouth by the time the man came to me in the morning; so my mouth was opened, and I was no longer mute.

The Survivors in Judah

23 The word of the LORD came to me: [24]"Son of man, the inhabitants of these waste places in the land of Israel keep saying, 'Abraham was only one man, yet he got possession of the land; but we are many; the land is surely given us to possess.' [25]Therefore say to them, Thus says the Lord GOD: You eat flesh with the blood, and lift up your eyes to your idols, and shed blood; shall you then possess the land? [26]You resort to the sword, you commit abominations and each of you defiles his neighbor's wife; shall you then possess the land? [27]Say this to them, Thus says the Lord GOD: As I live, surely those who are in the waste places shall fall by the sword; and him that is in the open field I will give to the beasts to be devoured; and those who are in strongholds and in caves shall die by pestilence. [28]And I will make the land a desolation and a waste; and her proud might shall come to an end; and the mountains of Israel shall be so desolate that none will pass through. [29]Then they will know that I am the LORD, when I have made the land a desolation and a waste because of all their abominations which they have committed.

30 "As for you, son of man, your people who talk together about you by the walls and at the doors of the houses, say to one another, each to his brother, 'Come, and hear what the word is that comes forth from the LORD.' [31]And they come to you as people come, and they sit before you as my people, and they hear what you say but they will not do it; for with their lips they show much love, but their heart is set on their gain. [32]And behold, you are to them like one who sings love songs[u] with a beautiful voice and plays well on an instrument, for they hear what you say, but they will not do it. [33]When this comes—and come it will!—then they will know that a prophet has been among them."

Israel's False Shepherds

34 The word of the LORD came to me: [2]"Son of man, prophesy against the shepherds of Israel,* prophesy, and say to them, even to the shepherds, Thus says the Lord GOD: Ho, shepherds of Israel who have been feeding yourselves! Should

---

33:15 restores the pledge: I.e., returns the property that a poor person left as collateral for a small personal loan.

33:17 The way of the Lord is not just: See notes on 18:19–32.

33:21 twelfth year . . . tenth month . . . fifth day: January 8, 585 B.C., about five months after the fall of Jerusalem, which is thought by some to have occurred in late summer 586 B.C.

33:22 I was no longer mute: God had imposed an intermittent muteness on Ezekiel at the beginning of his career (3:26–27). He could speak only by divine permission.

33:24 Abraham was only one man . . . the land is surely given us: The few survivors in Judah who were not taken as captives to Babylon after the destruction of Jerusalem were convinced that divine Providence had given them possession of all the land of Judah, including the real estate of the exiles.

33:25 eat flesh with the blood: Meat had to be drained (Lev 17:10–16) before it could be cooked and eaten, for the "life of every creature is the blood of it" (Lev 17:14).

33:32 like one who sings love songs: Ezekiel's contemporaries found him entertaining but did not take his warnings to heart.

34:1 The word of the LORD came: Marks another major shift in the book. Chapters 34–37 contain the greatest concentration of covenantal, eschatological, and messianic prophecies of the book, comparable to Jeremiah's so-called Book of Comfort (Jer 30–33). Many of the prophecies in these chapters can be understood as being fulfilled in Jesus and his ministry as recorded in the Gospels. Ezekiel even predicts the coming of a new covenant, although his preferred term for it is "covenant of peace".

34:2 the shepherds of Israel: There was a widespread and ancient tradition throughout the Near East, including Israel, of depicting the king as a shepherd of his people (e.g., 2 Sam 5:2). The wicked shepherds excoriated in this chapter are probably the last several kings of Judah.

---

[t] Heb *by it.*

[u] Cn: Heb *like a love song.*

*34:2, *shepherds of Israel:* cf. Jn 10:1–30.

not shepherds feed the sheep? [3]You eat the fat, you clothe yourselves with the wool, you slaughter the fatlings; but you do not feed the sheep. [4]The weak you have not strengthened, the sick you have not healed, the crippled you have not bound up, the strayed you have not brought back, the lost you have not sought, and with force and harshness you have ruled them. [5]So they were scattered, because there was no shepherd; and they became food for all the wild beasts. [6]My sheep were scattered, they wandered over all the mountains and on every high hill; my sheep were scattered over all the face of the earth, with none to search or seek for them.

7 "Therefore, you shepherds, hear the word of the LORD: [8]As I live, says the Lord GOD, because my sheep have become a prey, and my sheep have become food for all the wild beasts, since there was no shepherd; and because my shepherds have not searched for my sheep, but the shepherds have fed themselves, and have not fed my sheep; [9]therefore, you shepherds, hear the word of the LORD: [10]Thus says the Lord GOD, Behold, I am against the shepherds; and I will require my sheep at their hand, and put a stop to their feeding the sheep; no longer shall the shepherds feed themselves. I will rescue my sheep from their mouths, that they may not be food for them.

God, the True Shepherd

11 "For thus says the Lord GOD: Behold, I, I myself will search for my sheep, and will seek them out. [12]As a shepherd seeks out his flock when some of his sheep[v] have been scattered abroad, so will I seek out my sheep; and I will rescue them from all places where they have been scattered on a day of clouds and thick darkness. [13]And I will bring them out from the peoples, and gather them from the countries, and will bring them into their own land; and I will feed them on the mountains of Israel, by the fountains, and in all the inhabited places of the country. [14]I will feed them with good pasture, and upon the mountain heights of Israel shall be their pasture; there they shall lie down in good grazing land, and on fat pasture they shall feed on the mountains of Israel. [15]I myself will be the shepherd of my sheep, and I will make them lie down, says the Lord GOD. [16]I will seek the lost, and I will bring back the strayed, and I will bind up the crippled, and I will strengthen the weak, and the fat and the strong I will watch over;[w] I will feed them in justice.

17 "As for you, my flock, thus says the Lord GOD: Behold, I judge between sheep and sheep, rams and he-goats. [18]Is it not enough for you to feed on the good pasture, that you must tread down with your feet the rest of your pasture; and to drink of clear water, that you must foul the rest with your feet? [19]And must my sheep eat what you have trodden with your feet, and drink what you have fouled with your feet?

20 "Therefore, thus says the Lord GOD to them: Behold, I, I myself will judge between the fat sheep and the lean sheep. [21]Because you push with side and shoulder, and thrust at all the weak with your horns, till you have scattered them abroad, [22]I will save my flock, they shall no longer be a prey; and I will judge between sheep and sheep. *[23]And I will set up over them one shepherd, my servant David, and he shall feed them: he shall feed them and be their shepherd. [24]And I, the LORD, will be their God, and my servant David shall be prince among them; I, the LORD, have spoken.

25 "I will make with them a covenant of peace and banish wild beasts from the land, so that they may dwell securely in the wilderness and sleep in

34:5: Mt 9:36; Mk 6:34. **34:16:** Lk 19:10. **34:23:** Ezek 37:24.

34:4 with force and harshness: An allusion to the Jubilee laws, which forbade Israelites from enslaving each other and thereby ruling over another "with force and harshness" (Lev 25:46, 53).

34:5 wild beasts: A metaphor for the Gentiles.

34:6 My sheep were scattered: An allusion to the Israelite and Judean Diaspora beginning in 722 B.C. with the destruction of northern Israel. Not only were many Israelites captured and deported by the Assyrians and later by the Babylonians, but untold numbers of others migrated to Egypt and other nations to avoid the warfare and bloodshed taking place in the land of Israel.

34:13 I will bring them out: This New Exodus (or Second Exodus) theme is very strong in Isaiah, Jeremiah, and Ezekiel. The gathering of twelve apostles around Jesus must be seen in light of these prophecies that promise the regathering of the twelve tribes in the latter days.

34:14 I will feed them ... upon the mountain heights: This and the surrounding verses form the literary backdrop for the accounts of the Feeding of the Five Thousand in the Gospels. Mark (Mk 6:39) and John (Jn 6:10) call attention to the plentiful grass at the mountainous site where Jesus performs this miracle and to how everyone was fed until they were satisfied (Mk 6:42; Jn 6:11). Jesus is shown as the divine Shepherd who provides Israel with good pasture (CCC 754). **mountain heights of Israel:** A poetic reference to Jerusalem (17:23; 20:40).

34:17 sheep and sheep, rams and he-goats: Now the oracle moves to criticize the wealthy and the leadership classes, who are not royalty (shepherds) but an elite caste (fat sheep).

34:23 one shepherd, my servant David: The messianic Son of David who will come to rule Israel.

34:25 a covenant of peace: Ezekiel's preferred term for the reality described by Jeremiah as the "new covenant" (Jer 31:31). Ezekiel describes it as a *berît shālôm*, "covenant of peace", because it evokes the tranquility of Eden. The Edenic imagery continues: no wild beasts, safety in the wilderness, sleeping in the forests. These are memories of Eden, prior to the Fall, when man and nature were at perfect peace (CCC 64).

[v] Cn: Heb *when he is among his sheep*.
[w] Gk Syr Vg: Heb *destroy*.
*34:23–31: The Messiah and his kingdom.

the woods. [26]And I will make them and the places round about my hill a blessing; and I will send down the showers in their season; they shall be showers of blessing. [27]And the trees of the field shall yield their fruit, and the earth shall yield its increase, and they shall be secure in their land; and they shall know that I am the LORD, when I break the bars of their yoke, and deliver them from the hand of those who enslaved them. [28]They shall no more be a prey to the nations, nor shall the beasts of the land devour them; they shall dwell securely, and none shall make them afraid. [29]And I will provide for them prosperous[x] plantations so that they shall no more be consumed with hunger in the land, and no longer suffer the reproach of the nations. [30]And they shall know that I, the LORD their God, am with them, and that they, the house of Israel, are my people, says the Lord GOD. [31]And you are my sheep, the sheep of my pasture,[y] and I am your God, says the Lord GOD."

Prophecy against Mount Seir

35 The word of the LORD came to me: [2]"Son of man, set your face against Mount Se'ir, and prophesy against it, [3]and say to it, Thus says the Lord GOD: Behold, I am against you, Mount Se'ir, and I will stretch out my hand against you, and I will make you a desolation and a waste. [4]I will lay your cities waste, and you shall become a desolation; and you shall know that I am the LORD. [5]Because you cherished perpetual enmity, and gave over the people of Israel to the power of the sword at the time of their calamity, at the time of their final punishment; [6]therefore, as I live, says the Lord GOD, I will prepare you for blood, and blood shall pursue you; because you are guilty of blood,[z] therefore blood shall pursue you. [7]I will make Mount Se'ir a waste and a desolation; and I will cut off from it all who come and go. [8]And I will fill your mountains with the slain; on your hills and in your valleys and in all your ravines those slain with the sword shall fall. [9]I will make you a perpetual desolation, and your cities shall not be inhabited. Then you will know that I am the LORD.

10 "Because you said, 'These two nations and these two countries shall be mine, and we will take possession of them,'—although the LORD was there— [11]therefore, as I live, says the Lord GOD, I will deal with you according to the anger and envy which you showed because of your hatred against them; and I will make myself known among you,[a] when I judge you. [12]And you shall know that I, the LORD, have

---

34:26 my hill: Mt. Zion, the site of Jerusalem. **I will send down the showers in their season:** This statement and the surrounding verses rework the covenant blessings of Lev 26:3-4, only now focused on Mt. Zion. Jerusalem had no spiritual significance when Leviticus was written.

34:27 secure in their land: Almost all the imagery here is reworked from the covenantal blessings listed in Lev 26:5-13.

34:31 you are my sheep: An image common in the Psalms (especially Ps 95:7; 100:3; cf. Ps 23:1-2; 74:1; 78:52).

35:2 Mount Seir: Could refer to all Edom, as Mt. Zion sometimes represents all Israel. This oracle against Edom (35:1-15) seems oddly placed here, as we would have expected it to appear with the oracles against the nations in chaps. 25-32. Yet the relationship between Israel and Edom was particularly close and, thus, all the more bitter when the Edomites took advantage of the decimated Judeans in the wake of the Babylonian conquest. The oracle is included among the oracles of hope for Israel (chaps. 34-37) because the vindication of Israel includes judgment on those who treacherously despoiled her. For more on Edom, see note on 25:12.

35:5 gave ... Israel to the ... sword: They denied sanctuary to Israelite refugees, leaving them to be slaughtered by the Babylonian army.

35:7 all who come and go: The traders who passed through Mt. Seir and on whom the Edomites depended for their economic survival.

35:10 these two countries shall be mine: The kingdom of Israel in the north and the kingdom of Judah in the south. The Edomites plotted to take control of, or at least pillage, the entire traditional territory of Israel.

[x]Gk Syr Old Latin: Heb *for renown.*
[y]Gk Old Latin: Heb *pasture you are men.*
[z]Gk: Heb *you have hated blood.*
[a]Gk: Heb *them.*

Word Study

Prince (34:24)

Nāśî' (Heb.): Ezekiel's preferred title for the coming Davidic Messiah. The reason he prefers "prince" over "king" (Heb., *melek*) is probably due to his deep respect for the Law of Moses, which shaped his language and world view. The term *nāśî'* is an ancient and traditional term for a tribal leader that is used frequently with a positive connotation throughout the Pentateuch (e.g., Ex 22:28; Lev 4:22; Num 1:16). The term *melek*, on the other hand, is used only of foreign rulers in the Bible until Deut 17:14–15, where Moses grudgingly allows Israel to have a human king "like all the other nations"—but this "king" whom the Israelites choose will eventually be sent with them into exile (Deut 28:36)! So, the connotation of *nāśî'* in the books of Moses is a traditional leader in keeping with Israel's unique customs and covenant with the Lord, whereas a human *melek* has the connotations of covenant infidelity and the imitation of Gentile, pagan culture. For Moses, Israel's true king can only be the Lord (Deut 33:5); any human ruler should be content to be a "prince" who worships the Lord as the divine "king".

heard all the revilings which you uttered against the mountains of Israel, saying, 'They are laid desolate, they are given us to devour.' 13And you magnified yourselves against me with your mouth, and multiplied your words against me; I heard it. 14Thus says the Lord GOD: For the rejoicing of the whole earth I will make you desolate. 15As you rejoiced over the inheritance of the house of Israel, because it was desolate, so I will deal with you; you shall be desolate, Mount Se′ir, and all E′dom, all of it. Then they will know that I am the LORD.

Blessings on Israel

36 "And you, son of man, prophesy to the mountains of Israel, and say, O mountains of Israel, hear the word of the LORD. 2Thus says the Lord GOD: Because the enemy said of you, 'Aha!' and, 'The ancient heights have become our possession,' 3therefore prophesy, and say, Thus says the Lord GOD: Because, yes, because they made you desolate, and crushed you from all sides, so that you became the possession of the rest of the nations, and you became the talk and evil gossip of the people; 4therefore, O mountains of Israel, hear the word of the Lord GOD: Thus says the Lord GOD to the mountains and the hills, the ravines and the valleys, the desolate wastes and the deserted cities, which have become a prey and derision to the rest of the nations round about; 5therefore thus says the Lord GOD: I speak in my hot jealousy against the rest of the nations, and against all E′dom, who gave my land to themselves as a possession with wholehearted joy and utter contempt, that they might possess[b] it and plunder it. 6Therefore prophesy concerning the land of Israel, and say to the mountains and hills, to the ravines and valleys, Thus says the Lord GOD: Behold, I speak in my jealous wrath, because you have suffered the reproach of the nations; 7therefore thus says the Lord GOD: I swear that the nations that are round about you shall themselves suffer reproach.

8 "But you, O mountains of Israel, shall shoot forth your branches, and yield your fruit to my people Israel; for they will soon come home. 9For, behold, I am for you, and I will turn to you, and you shall be tilled and sown; 10and I will multiply men upon you, the whole house of Israel, all of it; the cities shall be inhabited and the waste places rebuilt; 11and I will multiply upon you man and beast; and they shall increase and be fruitful; and I will cause you to be inhabited as in your former times, and will do more good to you than ever before. Then you will know that I am the LORD. 12Yes, I will let men walk upon you, even my people Israel; and they shall possess you, and you shall be their inheritance, and you shall no longer bereave them of children. 13Thus says the Lord GOD: Because men say to you, 'You devour men, and you bereave your nation of children,' 14therefore you shall no longer devour men and no longer bereave your nation of children, says the Lord GOD; 15and I will not let you hear any more the reproach of the nations, and you shall no longer bear the disgrace of the peoples and no longer cause your nation to stumble, says the Lord GOD."

A New Heart and New Spirit

16 The word of the LORD came to me: 17"Son of man, when the house of Israel dwelt in their own land, they defiled it by their ways and their doings; their conduct before me was like the uncleanness of a woman in her impurity. 18So I poured out my wrath upon them for the blood which they had shed in the land, for the idols with which they had defiled it. 19I scattered them among the nations, and they were dispersed through the countries; in accordance with their conduct and their deeds I judged them. 20But when they came to the nations, wherever they came, they profaned my holy name, in that men said of them, 'These are the people of the LORD, and yet they had to go out of his land.' 21But I had concern for my holy name, which the house of Israel caused to be profaned among the nations to which they came.

22 "Therefore say to the house of Israel, Thus says the Lord GOD: It is not for your sake, O house of Israel, that I am about to act, but for the sake of my holy name, which you have profaned among the nations to which you came. 23And I will vindicate the holiness of my great name, which has been profaned among the nations, and which you have profaned among them; and the nations will know that I am the LORD, says the Lord GOD, when through you I vindicate my holiness before their eyes. 24For I will take you from the nations, and gather you from all the countries, and bring you into your own land. 25I will sprinkle clean water upon you, and

---

36:1 prophesy to ... Israel: The oracle that began with an indictment of Edom in 35:2 continues here, but the tone, subject matter, and audience change: now the prophet speaks about the blessings in store for Israel that are the converse of the judgment on Edom.

36:11 I will multiply ... they shall increase and be fruitful: Ezekiel uses language of the creational blessings in Genesis (1:22, 28; 8:17, 9:1, 7; 28:3; etc.) reiterated in the covenantal blessings of Lev 26:9.

36:17 a woman in her impurity: Ritual impurity that came with a woman's menstrual cycle made marital relations unlawful (Lev 15:19–33). The sense is that the Lord desired to embrace Israel but could not because of its unclean ritual state.

36:24 I will take you from the nations: This is the New or Second Exodus motif common to the prophets, which lies behind the motifs of the restoration of Israel that we find in the Gospels and Acts. See essay: *The New Exodus in Isaiah* at Is 43.

36:25 I will sprinkle clean water upon you: Water was sprinkled to cleanse objects or persons in some rites of the Old Covenant (Num 8:7; 19:17). The Dead Sea Scrolls show that the Essenes of Qumran understood their water washings as a fulfillment of Ezekiel's prophecy. • The Church Fathers understood this passage as a prophecy of Baptism (CCC 694).

---

[b] One Ms: Heb *drive out.*

you shall be clean from all your uncleannesses, and
from all your idols I will cleanse you. 26A new heart
I will give you, and a new spirit I will put within
you; and I will take out of your flesh the heart of
stone and give you a heart of flesh. 27And I will put
my spirit within you, and cause you to walk in my
statutes and be careful to observe my ordinances.
28You shall dwell in the land which I gave to your
fathers; and you shall be my people, and I will be
your God. 29And I will deliver you from all your
uncleannesses; and I will summon the grain and
make it abundant and lay no famine upon you.
30I will make the fruit of the tree and the increase
of the field abundant, that you may never again
suffer the disgrace of famine among the nations.
31Then you will remember your evil ways, and
your deeds that were not good; and you will loathe
yourselves for your iniquities and your abominable
deeds. 32It is not for your sake that I will act, says
the Lord GOD; let that be known to you. Be ashamed
and confounded for your ways, O house of Israel.

33 "Thus says the Lord GOD: On the day that I
cleanse you from all your iniquities, I will cause the
cities to be inhabited, and the waste places shall
be rebuilt. 34And the land that was desolate shall be
tilled, instead of being the desolation that it was
in the sight of all who passed by. 35And they will
say, 'This land that was desolate has become like
the garden of Eden; and the waste and desolate
and ruined cities are now inhabited and fortified.'
36Then the nations that are left round about you
shall know that I, the LORD, have rebuilt the ruined
places, and replanted that which was desolate; I, the
LORD, have spoken, and I will do it.

37 "Thus says the Lord GOD: This also I will let
the house of Israel ask me to do for them: to increase
their men like a flock. 38Like the flock for sacrifices,[c]
like the flock at Jerusalem during her appointed
feasts, so shall the waste cities be filled with flocks
of men. Then they will know that I am the LORD."

The Valley of Dry Bones

37 The hand of the LORD was upon me, and he
brought me out by the Spirit of the LORD,
and set me down in the midst of the valley;[d] it
was full of bones.* 2And he led me round among

36:26: Ezek 11:19; 18:31; 2 Cor 3:3. **36:27:** Ezek 37:14; 1 Thess 4:8. **36:31:** Ezek 6:9; 20:43.

36:26 A new heart . . . a heart of flesh: The stony heart of Israel recalls the hard heart of Pharaoh in the Exodus narrative. The heart was the seat of one's personhood (CCC 368, 1432).

36:27 I will put my spirit within you: The "new spirit" promised in 36:26 turns out to be God's own spirit, the Holy Spirit (CCC 715, 1287). **cause you to walk in my statutes:** The Spirit bestows the ability to follow God's Law (11:19–20). Paul explains this divine gift of obedience in Rom 8:1–17 (cf. Rom 5:5; 13:8–10).

36:28 you shall be my people, and I will be your God: Called the "covenant formula" this phrase stated the nature of the relationship being formed by a covenant (cf. Gen 2:23b). Covenants could form a brotherly bond (1 Kings 20:32–34), a father-son bond (2 Sam 7:14), or a husband-wife bond (Gen 2:23; Hos 2:2, 16–23). The logic and pattern of Hos 2:2, 16–23, leads us to see a marital dimension to this declaration, "You shall be my people, and I will be your God" (cf. 16:59–63; Is 54:5; Jer 3:20; 31:32) (CCC 219, 1611).

36:29 summon the grain: These two verses describe the cessation of the covenant curses of Lev 26:3–39.

36:35 like the garden of Eden: Ezekiel now states explicitly truths presented earlier in imagery. See note on 34:25.

36:37–38 See note on 34:31.

37:1 The hand of the LORD was upon me: This vision lacks a formal date, which is the usual marker of a significant break in thought. Chapter 37:1–14 is a distinct oracle, but it takes up and develops the promise of the New or Second Exodus alluded to in the previous oracle (36:24). **bones:** In Mosaic ritual law, human remains were unclean and contagious, i.e., they communicated uncleanness to anyone who made physical contact with them. The raising of these bones, which brings them from a state of death to new life, will also render them clean; compare the theme of cleansing from uncleanness in the previous chapter (36:25).

[c] Heb *flock of holy things*.
[d] Or *plain*.
*37:1, *full of bones*: This vision foretells the restoration of Israel after the Exile (verse 12). It has sometimes been thought, wrongly, to foretell the resurrection of the body.

Word Study

Spirit (37:1)

Rûaḥ (Heb.): a noun that translates "spirit", "wind", or "breath". It is a very important term in the OT, from the *rûaḥ* that blows over the waters of creation (Gen 1:2) to God stirring up the *rûaḥ* of Cyrus, king of Persia, to restore the Jews to their homeland at the end of last book of the Jewish canon, 2 Chronicles (2 Chron 36:22). That said, owing to the flexibility and different senses of the term, it is not always apparent in English translations when *rûaḥ* appears in the original text. Ezekiel 37:1–14 is a case in point. In just a handful of verses, *rûaḥ* designates the "Spirit" of God (Ezek 37:1, 14), the "breath" of life (Ezek 37:5–6), the "spirit" of man (Ezek 37:8–10), and the four "winds" of the world (Ezek 37:9). The English reader cannot see the continuity and how the prophet is engaged in wordplay that connects the wind that is so crucial to life on earth, the breath that serves as the sign of life in each animal and human, and God's Spirit as the ultimate source of life in the cosmos. Theologically, it appears that Ezekiel understood the wind that blows over the earth and the breath in every living being as gifts and images of the Spirit of God, the Holy Spirit, whom we invoke in the liturgy as *Creator Spiritus*, "Creator Spirit".

them; and behold, there were very many upon the valley;[d] and behold, they were very dry. 3And he said to me, "Son of man, can these bones live?" And I answered, "O Lord GOD, you know." 4Again he said to me, "Prophesy to these bones, and say to them, O dry bones, hear the word of the LORD. 5Thus says the Lord GOD to these bones: Behold, I will cause breath[e] to enter you, and you shall live. 6And I will lay sinews upon you, and will cause flesh to come upon you, and cover you with skin, and put breath[e] in you, and you shall live; and you shall know that I am the LORD."

7 So I prophesied as I was commanded; and as I prophesied, there was a noise, and behold, a rattling; and the bones came together, bone to its bone. 8And as I looked, there were sinews on them, and flesh had come upon them, and skin had covered them; but there was no spirit in them. 9Then he said to me, "Prophesy to the spirit, prophesy, son of man, and say to the spirit,[f] Thus says the Lord GOD: Come from the four winds, O spirit,[f] and breathe upon these slain, that they may live." 10So I prophesied as he commanded me, and the spirit came into them, and they lived, and stood upon their feet, an exceedingly great host.

11 Then he said to me, "Son of man, these bones are the whole house of Israel. Behold, they say, 'Our bones are dried up, and our hope is lost; we are clean cut off.' 12Therefore prophesy, and say to them, Thus says the Lord GOD: Behold, I will open your graves, and raise you from your graves, O my people; and I will bring you home into the land of Israel. 13And you shall know that I am the LORD, when I open your graves, and raise you from your graves, O my people. 14And I will put my Spirit within you, and you shall live, and I will place you in your own land; then you shall know that I, the LORD, have spoken, and I have done it, says the LORD."

The Two Sticks

15 The word of the LORD came to me: 16"Son of man, take a stick and write on it, 'For Judah, and the children of Israel associated with him'; then take another stick and write upon it, 'For Joseph (the stick of E'phraim) and all the house of Israel associated with him'; 17and join them together into one stick, that they may become one in your hand. 18And when your people say to you, 'Will you not show us what you mean by these?' 19say to them, Thus says the Lord GOD: Behold, I am about to take the stick of Joseph (which is in the hand of E'phraim) and the tribes of Israel associated with him; and I will join[g] with it the stick of Judah, and make them one stick, that they may be one in my hand. 20When the sticks on which you write are in your hand before their eyes, 21then say to them, Thus says the Lord GOD: Behold, I will take the sons of Israel from the nations among which they have gone, and will gather them from all sides, and bring them to their own land; 22and I will make them one nation in the land, upon the mountains of Israel; and one king shall be king over them all; and they shall be no longer two

37:5, 10: Rev 11:11. **37:14:** Ezek 36:27; 1 Thess 4:8.

37:5 I will cause breath to enter you: The term for "breath" can also be translated "spirit" (Heb., *rûaḥ*), which may be the meaning here. At any rate, this passage should be read in conjunction with the promise above in 36:27: "I will put my spirit (*rûaḥ*) within you."

37:11 Our bones are dried up: I.e., there is no hope for the future of our nation, faith, and culture.

37:12 I will open your graves: This statement works on two levels. On the one hand, it is a metaphor for restoring the nation of Israel from exile. On another level, it is a promise that, if necessary, God will raise individual Israelites from the dead in order that they may participate in the eschatological blessings. See essay: *Resurrection in the Old Testament* at 2 Mac 7. • Ezekiel, by the gift of prophecy, transcended time and space and stood before the moment of the resurrection. Seeing the future as something present, he set it before our eyes in his account (St. Gregory of Nyssa, *On the Soul and the Resurrection*).

37:13 you shall know that I am the LORD, when I . . . raise you: This text lies in the background of the account of the raising of Lazarus in Jn 11:38–44. In light of this verse, the reader of John discovers that Jesus is the Lord God of Israel when he raises Lazarus from the dead.

37:15 The word of the LORD came: Introduces another distinct oracle, 37:15–28, but continues to develop the theme of national restoration found in the earlier oracles and visions of chaps. 36–37.

37:16 Judah: The Southern Kingdom that remained loyal to the Davidic king in Jerusalem after the death of Solomon (1 Kings 12). The majority of this kingdom consisted of families of the tribe of Judah. However, the smaller tribe of Benjamin was also a part of this kingdom, and the tribe of Simeon, whose territory all lay within the boundaries of Judah, had been completely assimilated by Judah by about the ninth century B.C. In addition, the majority of the Levites probably lived in Jerusalem and other cities of Judah. After the fall of the Northern Kingdom of Israel in 722 B.C., the population of southern Judah swelled with refugees from the northern tribes. **Joseph (the stick of Ephraim):** The Northern Kingdom of Israel, which governed the "northern tribes". This kingdom, with few exceptions, was ruled by a king from the wealthiest and most populous tribe, Ephraim. The large tribe of Joseph had been broken into two half-tribes: Ephraim and Manasseh, Joseph's two sons. Ephraim was younger but was given the birthright of the elder son (Gen 48:8–20). The Book of Genesis leads one to expect that the hopes of Israel rest primarily with Joseph's sons (Gen 48:15–16, 19–20). They received the well-watered central hill country of Canaan as their tribal portions.

37:22 I will make them one nation: The division of the tribal family of Israel into Northern and Southern Kingdoms after the death of Solomon was a spiritual and cultural scar on the soul of the People of God. Ezekiel prophesies a future reunification (CCC 715). • In the NT, the remnant of the northern Israelites are the Samaritans. John 4 and Acts 8:14–17, 25 should be read against the background of these prophecies.

[d] Or *plain*.
[e] Or *spirit*.
[f] Or *wind* or *spirit*.
[g] Heb *join them*.

nations, and no longer divided into two kingdoms. [23]They shall not defile themselves any more with their idols and their detestable things, or with any of their transgressions; but I will save them from all the backslidings in which they have sinned, and will cleanse them; and they shall be my people, and I will be their God.

24 "My servant David shall be king over them; and they shall all have one shepherd. They shall follow my ordinances and be careful to observe my statutes. [25]They shall dwell in the land where your fathers dwelt that I gave to my servant Jacob; they and their children and their children's children shall dwell there for ever; and David my servant shall be their prince for ever. [26]I will make a covenant of peace with them; it shall be an everlasting covenant with them; and I will bless[h] them and multiply them, and will set my sanctuary in the midst of them for evermore. [27]My dwelling place shall be with them; and I will be their God, and they shall be my people. [28]Then the nations will know that I the LORD sanctify Israel, when my sanctuary is in the midst of them for evermore."

Prophecy against Gog

38 *The word of the LORD came to me: [2]"Son of man, set your face toward Gog, of the land of Ma'gog, the chief prince of Me'shech and Tu'bal, and prophesy against him [3]and say, Thus says the Lord GOD: Behold, I am against you, O Gog, chief prince of Me'shech and Tu'bal; [4]and I will turn you about, and put hooks into your jaws, and I will bring you forth, and all your army, horses and horsemen, all of them clothed in full armor, a great company, all of them with buckler and shield, wielding swords; [5]Persia, Cush, and Put are with them, all of them with shield and helmet; [6]Gomer and all his hordes; Beth'-togar'mah from the uttermost parts of the north with all his hordes—many peoples are with you.

7 "Be ready and keep ready, you and all the hosts that are assembled about you, and be a guard for them. [8]After many days you will be mustered; in the latter years you will go against the land that is restored from war, the land where people were gathered from many nations upon the mountains of Israel, which had been a continual waste; its people were brought out from the nations and now dwell securely, all of them. [9]You will advance, coming on like a storm, you will be like a cloud covering the land, you and all your hordes, and many peoples with you.

10 "Thus says the Lord GOD: On that day thoughts will come into your mind, and you will devise an evil scheme [11]and say, 'I will go up against the land of unwalled villages; I will fall upon the quiet people who dwell securely, all of them dwelling without walls, and having no bars or gates'; [12]to seize spoil and carry off plunder; to assail the waste places which are now inhabited, and the people who were gathered from the nations, who have gotten cattle and goods, who dwell at the center of the earth. [13]Sheba and De'dan and the merchants of Tar'shish and all its villages will say to you, 'Have you come to seize spoil? Have you assembled your hosts to carry off plunder, to carry away silver and gold, to take away cattle and goods, to seize great spoil?'

14 "Therefore, son of man, prophesy, and say to Gog, Thus says the Lord GOD: On that day when my people Israel are dwelling securely, you will bestir yourself[i] [15]and come from your place out of the uttermost parts of the north, you and many peoples with you, all of them riding on horses, a great host, a mighty army; [16]you will come up against my

37:26: Heb 13:20. **37:27:** Ex 25:8; 29:45; Lev 26:12; Jer 31:1; 2 Cor 6:16; Rev 21:3. **38:2, 9, 15:** Rev 20:8.

37:24 My servant David shall be king: A descendant of David shall again reign over God's people.

37:26 covenant of peace: See note on 34:25. **everlasting covenant:** The Hebrew is *berît ʿôlām*. This is unlike the Mosaic covenant, which Israel broke, triggering the covenantal curses of Lev 26 and Deut 28 mentioned so frequently in Ezekiel's oracles. **bless them and multiply them:** The blessing of creation, first given in Gen 1:28 and repeated to the patriarchs throughout Genesis and elsewhere in Scripture. **in the midst of them:** Or "within them".

37:27 My dwelling place: The Hebrew is *mishkan*, "tent" or "tabernacle", the term used for the wilderness Tabernacle in the Pentateuch. **shall be with them:** Literally, "shall be upon them" or "shall be over them".

[h] Tg: Heb *give*.
[i] Gk: Heb *will you not know?*
*38–39: Gog and Magog. Gog—an obscure name probably meaning "darkness"—here represents the forces of evil. He is destroyed by Yahweh. Magog probably means no more than "land of Gog." The names appear to be used here as ciphers for Nebuchadnezzar and Babylon.

38:1 The word of the LORD came to me: Begins a long oracle against a certain ruler known as Gog that extends until the end of chap. 39. We would expect a date formula to introduce such a distinct unit, but there is none.

38:2 Gog: Probably the ruler known to the ancient Greeks as Gyges, the king of Lydia, a powerful state in central Asia Minor. Gyges ruled in the mid-600s B.C. In the lifetime of Ezekiel, Gyges' great-grandson Alyattes is ruling the kingdom. Ezekiel may be treating Gog as a dynastic name. Just as he calls the future Davidic monarch simply "David" (34:23–24; 37:24–25), so he calls all the rulers of Gog's/Gyges kingdom simply "Gog". **land of Magog:** Probably a Hebrew adoption of a Babylonian phrase meaning "land of Gog". **Meshech and Tubal:** States near Lydia in western Asia Minor. See note on 27:13.

38:5 Cush: Nubia. See note on 29:10. **Put:** Lybia. See note on 30:5.

38:6 Gomer: A wild tribe that lived north of the Black Sea, possibly in the Crimean Peninsula, known to the Greeks as the Cimmerians. **Beth-togarmah:** See note on 27:14.

38:13 Sheba and Dedan: Arabian kingdoms. See notes on 27:20 and 27:22. **Tarshish:** Probably a Phoenician port in Spain. See note on 27:12.

people Israel, like a cloud covering the land. In the latter days I will bring you against my land, that the nations may know me, when through you, O Gog, I vindicate my holiness before their eyes.

17 "Thus says the Lord GOD: Are you he of whom I spoke in former days by my servants the prophets of Israel, who in those days prophesied for years that I would bring you against them? 18 But on that day, when Gog shall come against the land of Israel, says the Lord GOD, my wrath will be roused. 19 For in my jealousy and in my blazing wrath I declare, On that day there shall be a great shaking in the land of Israel; 20 the fish of the sea, and the birds of the air, and the beasts of the field, and all creeping things that creep on the ground, and all the men that are upon the face of the earth, shall quake at my presence, and the mountains shall be thrown down, and the cliffs shall fall, and every wall shall tumble to the ground. 21 I will summon every kind of terror[j] against Gog,[k] says the Lord GOD; every man's sword will be against his brother. 22 With pestilence and bloodshed I will enter into judgment with him; and I will rain upon him and his hordes and the many peoples that are with him, torrential rains and hailstones, fire and brimstone. 23 So I will show my greatness and my holiness and make myself known in the eyes of many nations. Then they will know that I am the LORD.

The Fall of Gog

39 "And you, son of man, prophesy against Gog, and say, Thus says the Lord GOD: Behold, I am against you, O Gog, chief prince of Me'shech and Tu'bal; 2 and I will turn you about and drive you forward, and bring you up from the uttermost parts of the north, and lead you against the mountains of Israel; 3 then I will strike your bow from your left hand, and will make your arrows drop out of your right hand. 4 You shall fall upon the mountains of Israel, you and all your hordes and the peoples that are with you; I will give you to birds of prey of every sort and to the wild beasts to be devoured. 5 You shall fall in the open field; for I have spoken, says the Lord GOD. 6 I will send fire on Magog and on those who dwell securely in the islands; and they shall know that I am the LORD.

7 "And my holy name I will make known in the midst of my people Israel; and I will not let my holy name be profaned any more; and the nations shall know that I am the LORD, the Holy One in Israel. 8 Behold, it is coming and it will be brought about, says the Lord GOD. That is the day of which I have spoken.

9 "Then those who dwell in the cities of Israel will go forth and make fires of the weapons and burn them, shields and bucklers, bows and arrows, handpikes and spears, and they will make fires of them for seven years; 10 so that they will not need to take wood out of the field or cut down any out of the forests, for they will make their fires of the weapons; they will despoil those who despoiled them, and plunder those who plundered them, says the Lord GOD.

11 "On that day I will give to Gog a place for burial in Israel, the Valley of the Travelers[l] east of the sea; it will block the travelers, for there Gog and all his multitude will be buried; it will be called the Valley of Ha'mon-gog.[m] 12 For seven months the house of Israel will be burying them, in order to cleanse the land. 13 All the people of the land will bury them; and it will redound to their honor on the day that I show my glory, says the Lord GOD. 14 They will set apart men to pass through the land continually and bury[n] those remaining upon the face of the land, so as to cleanse it; at the end of seven months they will make their search. 15 And when these pass through the land and any one sees a man's bone, then he shall set up a sign by it, till the buriers have buried it in the Valley of Ha'mon-gog. 16 (A city Hamo'nah[o] is there also.) Thus shall they cleanse the land.

17 "As for you, son of man, thus says the Lord GOD: Speak to the birds of every sort and to all beasts of the field, 'Assemble and come, gather from all sides to the sacrificial feast which I am preparing for you, a great sacrificial feast upon the mountains of Israel, and you shall eat flesh and drink blood. 18 You shall eat the flesh of the mighty, and drink the blood of the princes of the earth—of rams, of lambs, and of goats, of bulls, all of them fatlings of Bashan. 19 And you shall eat fat till you are filled, and drink blood till you are drunk, at the sacrificial feast which I am preparing for you. 20 And you shall be filled at my table with horses and riders, with mighty men and all kinds of warriors,' says the Lord GOD.

Israel to be Restored

21 "And I will set my glory among the nations; and all the nations shall see my judgment which

---

38:22: Rev 8:7; 14:10. **39:4, 17–20:** Rev 19:17, 18, 21.

39:11 Valley of the Travelers: Translation uncertain, but possibly meaning "the valley of those who have passed on", i.e., to Sheol, the realm of the dead. **Valley of Hamon-gog:** The Hebrew is *gê' hamôn gôg*, "Valley of the hoard of Gog", possibly a pun on *gê-hinnôm*, the ravine southwest of Jerusalem used for Molech worship, child sacrifice, and the burning of refuse—called Gehenna in the New Testament (Mt 5:22, 29, 30; 10:28; 18:9; 23:15, 33; Mk 9:43, 45, 47; Lk 12:5; Jas 3:6).

39:16 A city Hamonah: From *hāmôn*, a multitude. Probably a cryptic reference to Jerusalem.

[j] Gk: Heb *a sword to all my mountains.*
[k] Heb *him.*
[l] Or *Abarim.*
[m] That is *the multitude of Gog.*
[n] Gk Syr: Heb *bury the travelers.*
[o] That is *Multitude.*

I have executed, and my hand which I have laid on them. 22The house of Israel shall know that I am the LORD their God, from that day forward. 23And the nations shall know that the house of Israel went into captivity for their iniquity, because they dealt so treacherously with me that I hid my face from them and gave them into the hand of their adversaries, and they all fell by the sword. 24I dealt with them according to their uncleanness and their transgressions, and hid my face from them.

25 "Therefore thus says the Lord GOD: Now I will restore the fortunes of Jacob, and have mercy upon the whole house of Israel; and I will be jealous for my holy name. 26They shall forget their shame, and all the treachery they have practiced against me, when they dwell securely in their land with none to make them afraid, 27when I have brought them back from the peoples and gathered them from their enemies' lands, and through them have vindicated my holiness in the sight of many nations. 28Then they shall know that I am the LORD their God because I sent them into exile among the nations, and then gathered them into their own land. I will leave none of them remaining among the nations any more; 29and I will not hide my face any more from them, when I pour out my Spirit upon the house of Israel, says the Lord GOD."

The Vision of Measuring the Temple

40 *In the twenty-fifth year of our exile, at the beginning of the year, on the tenth day of the month, in the fourteenth year after the city was conquered, on that very day, the hand of the LORD was upon me, 2and brought me in the visions of God into the land of Israel, and set me down upon a very high mountain, on which was a structure like a city opposite me.[p] 3When he brought me there, behold, there was a man, whose appearance was like bronze, with a line of flax and a measuring reed in his hand; and he was standing in the gateway. 4And the man said to me, "Son of man, look with your eyes, and hear with your ears, and set your mind upon all that I shall show you, for you were brought here in order that I might show it to you; declare all that you see to the house of Israel."

5 And behold, there was a wall all around the outside of the temple area, and the length of the measuring reed in the man's hand was six long cubits, each being a cubit and a handbreadth in length; so he measured the thickness of the wall, one reed; and the height, one reed. 6Then he went into the gateway facing east, going up its steps, and measured the threshold of the gate, one reed deep;[q] 7and the side rooms, one reed long, and one reed broad; and the space between the side rooms, five cubits; and the threshold of the gate by the vestibule of the gate at the inner end, one reed. 8Then he measured the vestibule of the gateway, eight cubits; 9and its jambs, two cubits; and the vestibule of the gate was at the inner end. 10And there were three side rooms on either side of the east gate; the three were of the same size; and the jambs on either side were of the same size. 11Then he measured the breadth of the opening of the gateway, ten cubits; and the breadth of the gateway, thirteen cubits. 12There was a barrier before the side rooms, one cubit on either side; and the side rooms were six cubits on either side. 13Then he measured the gate from

---

40:1—43:17: 1 Kings 6–7; 2 Chron 3–4. **40:2:** Rev 21:10. **40:3, 5:** Rev 21:15.

40:1—48:35 The final section of the book, chaps. 40–48, is the climactic finale of Ezekiel's prophetic career, in which he sees a vision of the restored People of God gathered around a new and perfect Temple.

40:1 twenty-fifth year of our exile: 573 B.C., counting from the exile of King Jehoiachin (597 B.C.) in which Ezekiel was taken, not from the later exile of Zedekiah (586 B.C.) when the Temple was destroyed. **at the beginning of the year:** Literally, "at the head of the year". It is unclear which month is meant. Later Jewish tradition identified four "heads of the year", the two major ones being Nisan 1 (the first month = March–April), the beginning of the liturgical year, and Tishri 1 (the seventh month = September–October), the beginning of civil years and the counting of the sabbatical and Jubilee years. Although some scholars maintain Ezekiel's "head of the year" is Nisan, the traditional Jewish holiday *Rosh Hashshanah* is observed at the beginning of Tishri, and Ezekiel probably also intends to refer to Tishri, in light of his allusions to Lev 25:8–10. **the tenth day of the month:** The tenth day of Tishri was the Day of Atonement and also the day on which the Jubilee Year was proclaimed (Lev 25:8–10). The date of Ezekiel's vision probably relates to the Jubilee Year tradition. Twenty-five years is halfway through a Jubilee Year cycle of fifty years, and Ezekiel's curious language seeming to refer to the tenth day of the month as the "beginning of the year" only has precedent in Lev 25:8–10, in which the Jubilee Year begins on the tenth day of Tishri. Accordingly, Ezekiel is probably seeing this vision in the fall of 573 B.C., a spiritual turning point as Judah has passed over half a Jubilee cycle in exile and may now hope for the restoration that the Jubilee Year always symbolized.

40:2 a very high mountain: The "high mountain" recalls earlier passages of Ezekiel (17:22–23; 20:40) where he describes the location of Jerusalem with similar language. Because of its sanctity, the site of Jerusalem was sometimes poetically described as a very high or even the highest mountain (Ps 48:2; 68:15–18; 76:2–4; 78:68–69; 133:3; Is 2:2–3), even though it was not literally so. **a city opposite me:** A new Jerusalem. Its exact relationship to the old Jerusalem is not completely clear.

40:5 six long cubits ... a cubit and a handbreadth: A cubit and handbreadth were together about 20–22 inches. The measuring reed was therefore about 10–11 feet in length—quite long. **the thickness ... one reed:** A ten-foot-thick wall—a very impressive defensive wall in the ancient world.

40:13 five and twenty cubits: Half of fifty. Many of the measurements Ezekiel takes are multiples of fifty. Some scholars

---

[p] Gk: Heb *on the south.*

[q] Heb *deep, and one threshold, one reed deep.*

*40–48. In these chapters Ezekiel describes the new temple and its worship. The passage is not meant to be taken historically and, in fact, the later builders of the temple made no attempt to take it literally. The prophet is referring to the Messianic times in symbolic language.

the back[r] of the one side room to the back[r] of the
other, a breadth of five and twenty cubits, from
door to door. [14]He measured also the vestibule,
twenty cubits; and round about the vestibule of the
gateway was the court.[s] [15]From the front of the gate
at the entrance to the end of the inner vestibule of
the gate was fifty cubits. [16]And the gateway had
windows round about, narrowing inwards into their
jambs in the side rooms, and likewise the vestibule
had windows round about inside, and on the jambs
were palm trees.

17 Then he brought me into the outer court;
and behold, there were chambers and a pavement,
round about the court; thirty chambers fronted on
the pavement. [18]And the pavement ran along the
side of the gates, corresponding to the length of
the gates; this was the lower pavement. [19]Then he
measured the distance from the inner front of[t] the
lower gate to the outer front of the inner court, a
hundred cubits.

Then he went before me to the north, [20]and
behold, there was a gate[u] which faced toward the
north, belonging to the outer court. He measured
its length and its breadth. [21]Its side rooms, three on
either side, and its jambs and its vestibule were of
the same size as those of the first gate; its length
was fifty cubits, and its breadth twenty-five cubits.
[22]And its windows, its vestibule, and its palm trees
were of the same size as those of the gate which
faced toward the east; and seven steps led up to it;
and its vestibule was on the inside. [23]And opposite
the gate on the north, as on the east, was a gate
to the inner court; and he measured from gate to
gate, a hundred cubits.

24 And he led me toward the south, and behold,
there was a gate on the south; and he measured its
jambs and its vestibule; they had the same size as the
others. [25]And there were windows round about in it
and in its vestibule, like the windows of the others;
its length was fifty cubits, and its breadth twenty-
five cubits. [26]And there were seven steps leading up
to it, and its vestibule was on the inside; and it had
palm trees on its jambs, one on either side. [27]And
there was a gate on the south of the inner court; and
he measured from gate to gate toward the south, a
hundred cubits.

28 Then he brought me to the inner court by the
south gate, and he measured the south gate; it was
of the same size as the others; [29]Its side rooms, its
jambs, and its vestibule were of the same size as the
others; and there were windows round about in it
and in its vestibule; its length was fifty cubits, and
its breadth twenty-five cubits. [30]And there were
vestibules round about, twenty-five cubits long
and five cubits broad. [31]Its vestibule faced the outer
court, and palm trees were on its jambs, and its
stairway had eight steps.

32 Then he brought me to the inner court on the
east side, and he measured the gate; it was of the
same size as the others. [33]Its side rooms, its jambs,
and its vestibule were of the same size as the
others; and there were windows round about in it
and in its vestibule; its length was fifty cubits, and
its breadth twenty-five cubits. [34]Its vestibule faced
the outer court, and it had palm trees on its jambs,
one on either side; and its stairway had eight steps.

35 Then he brought me to the north gate, and he
measured it; it had the same size as the others. [36]Its
side rooms, its jambs, and its vestibule were of the
same size as the others;[v] and it had windows round
about; its length was fifty cubits, and its breadth
twenty-five cubits. [37]Its vestibule[w] faced the outer
court, and it had palm trees on its jambs, one on
either side; and its stairway had eight steps.

38 There was a chamber with its door in the
vestibule of the gate,[x] where the burnt offering was
to be washed. [39]And in the vestibule of the gate
were two tables on either side, on which the burnt
offering and the sin offering and the guilt offering
were to be slaughtered. [40]And on the outside of the
vestibule[y] at the entrance of the north gate were
two tables; and on the other side of the vestibule of
the gate were two tables. [41]Four tables were on the
inside, and four tables on the outside of the side of
the gate, eight tables, on which the sacrifices were
to be slaughtered. [42]And there were also four tables

---

see fifty as symbolic of the Jubilee, the year of restoration of all things, observed on a cycle of fifty years (Lev 25:10).

40:21 Its side rooms, three on either side: Many large city- or Temple-gates have been unearthed, with six or more chambers for guards and storage, arranged in pairs on either side of the central thoroughfare from outside to inside the city walls.

40:22 palm trees: Signs of life, associated with the Temple (1 Kings 6:29, 32, 35; 7:36).

40:35 the north gate ... same size: Symmetry is a sign of harmony and perfection. Ezekiel's Temple is laid out in a great square, with most features symmetrical in all four directions. Sacred numbers like multiples of fifty (the number of Jubilee) and seven (the number of oath-swearing and covenant) recur throughout the description.

40:39 burnt offering: The primary offering of the Mosaic liturgy, the burnt offering required the entire animal to be consumed in flame and smoke (Lev 1:1–17). It expressed the concepts of atonement, reparation, and vicarious self-offering. **sin offering:** A sacrifice offered to gain forgiveness of sins (Lev 4:1–35). **guilt offering:** This offering was made in reparation for sin (Lev 5:1—6:7).

---

[r] Compare Gk: Heb *roof.*
[s] Compare Gk: Heb *and he made the jambs sixty cubits, and to the jamb of the court was the gateway roundabout.*
[t] Compare Gk: Heb *from before.*
[u] Gk: Heb *a hundred cubits on the east and on the north.* [20]*And the gate.*
[v] One Ms Compare verses 29 and 33: Heb lacks *were of the same size as the others.*
[w] Gk Vg Compare verses 26, 31, 34: Heb *jambs.*
[x] Cn: Heb *at the jambs of the gates.*
[y] Cn: Heb *to him who goes up.*

of hewn stone for the burnt offering, a cubit and
a half long, and a cubit and a half broad, and one
cubit high, on which the instruments were to be
laid with which the burnt offerings and the sacrifices were slaughtered. 43And hooks, a handbreadth
long, were fastened round about within. And on the
tables the flesh of the offering was to be laid.

44 Then he brought me from without into the
inner court, and behold, there were two chambers[z] in the inner court, one[a] at the side of the north
gate facing south, the other at the side of the
south[b] gate facing north. 45And he said to me, This
chamber which faces south is for the priests who
have charge of the temple, 46and the chamber which
faces north is for the priests who have charge of
the altar; these are the sons of Za′dok, who alone
among the sons of Levi may come near to the LORD
to minister to him. 47And he measured the court, a
hundred cubits long, and a hundred cubits broad,
foursquare; and the altar was in front of the temple.

48 Then he brought me to the vestibule of the
temple and measured the jambs of the vestibule,
five cubits on either side; and the breadth of the gate
was fourteen cubits; and the sidewalls of the gate
were three cubits[c] on either side. 49The length of the
vestibule was twenty cubits, and the breadth twelve[d]
cubits; and ten steps led up[e] to it; and there were
pillars beside the jambs on either side.

41 Then he brought me to the nave, and measured the jambs; on each side six cubits was
the breadth of the jambs.[f] 2And the breadth of the
entrance was ten cubits; and the sidewalls of the entrance were five cubits on either side; and he measured the length of the nave forty cubits, and its
breadth, twenty cubits. 3Then he went into the inner room and measured the jambs of the entrance,
two cubits; and the breadth of the entrance, six cubits; and the sidewalls[g] of the entrance, seven cubits.
4And he measured the length of the room, twenty
cubits, and its breadth, twenty cubits, beyond the
nave. And he said to me, "This is the most holy place."

5 Then he measured the wall of the temple, six
cubits thick; and the breadth of the side chambers,
four cubits, round about the temple. 6And the side
chambers were in three stories, one over another,
thirty in each story. There were offsets[h] all around
the wall of the temple to serve as supports for the
side chambers, so that they should not be supported
by the wall of the temple. 7And the side chambers
became broader as they rose[i] from story to story,
corresponding to the enlargement of the offset[j]
from story to story round about the temple; on
the side of the temple a stairway led upward, and
thus one went up from the lowest story to the top
story through the middle story. 8I saw also that
the temple had a raised platform round about; the
foundations of the side chambers measured a full
reed of six long cubits. 9The thickness of the outer
wall of the side chambers was five cubits; and the
part of the platform which was left free was five
cubits.[k] Between the platform[l] of the temple and
the 10chambers of the court was a breadth of twenty
cubits round about the temple on every side. 11And
the doors of the side chambers opened on the part
of the platform that was left free, one door toward
the north, and another door toward the south;
and the breadth of the part that was left free was
five cubits round about.

12 The building that was facing the temple yard
on the west side was seventy cubits broad; and the
wall of the building was five cubits thick round
about, and its length ninety cubits.

13 Then he measured the temple, a hundred
cubits long; and the yard and the building with its
walls, a hundred cubits long; 14also the breadth of
the east front of the temple and the yard, a hundred cubits.

15 Then he measured the length of the building
facing the yard which was at the west and its walls[m]
on either side, a hundred cubits.

The nave of the temple and the inner room and
the outer[n] vestibule 16were paneled[o] and round
about all three had windows with recessed[p] frames.
Over against the threshold the temple was paneled
with wood round about, from the floor up to the
windows (now the windows were covered), 17to
the space above the door, even to the inner room, and
on the outside. And on all the walls round about in the

40:46 sons of Zadok: Zadok was a priest who was loyal to Solomon (1 Kings 1:38–39) and established as sole high priest during his reign (1 Kings 2:35). Ezekiel regards the descendants of Zadok as particularly faithful to the Lord and insists that only their line is suited to serve as high priests.

41:4 The most holy place: Or "the Holy of Holies". The Holy of Holies was a perfect cube, 20 cubits on a side. The perfect symmetry expressed the perfection of divinity (cf. the cubical shape of the new Jerusalem in Rev 21:16).

41:6 three stories: Calling to mind the three levels of Solomon's Temple (1 Kings 6:6) and Noah's ark (Gen 6:16).

---

[z] Gk: Heb *and from without to the inner gate were chambers for singers.*
[a] Gk: Heb *which.*
[b] Gk: Heb *east.*
[c] Gk: Heb *and the breadth of the gate was three cubits.*
[d] Gk: Heb *eleven.*
[e] Gk: Heb *and by steps which went up.*
[f] Compare Gk: Heb *tent.*
[g] Gk: Heb *breadth.*
[h] Gk Compare 1 Kings 6:6: Heb *they entered.*
[i] Cn: Heb *it was surrounded.*
[j] Gk: Heb *for the encompassing of the temple.*
[k] Syr: Heb lacks *five cubits.*
[l] Cn: Heb *house of the side chambers.*
[m] Cn: The meaning of the Hebrew term is unknown.
[n] Gk: Heb *of the court.*
[o] Gk: Heb *the thresholds.*
[p] Cn Compare Gk 1 Kings 6:4: The meaning of the Hebrew term is unknown.

inner room and the nave were carved likenesses[q] 18of cherubim and palm trees, a palm tree between cherub and cherub. Every cherub had two faces: 19the face of a man toward the palm tree on the one side, and the face of a young lion toward the palm tree on the other side. They were carved on the whole temple round about; 20from the floor to above the door cherubim and palm trees were carved on the wall.[r]

21 The doorposts of the nave were squared; and in front of the holy place was something resembling 22an altar of wood, three cubits high, two cubits long, and two cubits broad;[s] its corners, its base,[t] and its walls were of wood. He said to me, "This is the table which is before the LORD." 23The nave and the holy place had each a double door. 24The doors had two leaves apiece, two swinging leaves for each door. 25And on the doors of the nave were carved cherubim and palm trees, such as were carved on the walls; and there was a canopy of wood in front of the vestibule outside. 26And there were recessed windows and palm trees on either side, on the sidewalls of the vestibule.[u]

42 Then he led me out into the inner[v] court, toward the north, and he brought me to the chambers which were opposite the temple yard and opposite the building on the north. 2The length of the building which was on the north side[w] was[x] a hundred cubits, and the breadth fifty cubits. 3Adjoining the twenty cubits which belonged to the inner court, and facing the pavement which belonged to the outer court, was gallery[y] against gallery[y] in three stories. 4And before the chambers was a passage inward, ten cubits wide and a hundred cubits long,[z] and their doors were on the north. 5Now the upper chambers were narrower, for the galleries[y] took more away from them than from the lower and middle chambers in the building. 6For they were in three stories, and they had no pillars like the pillars of the outer[a] court; hence the upper chambers were set back from the ground more than the lower and the middle ones. 7And there was a wall outside parallel to the chambers, toward the outer court, opposite the chambers, fifty cubits long. 8For the chambers on the outer court were fifty cubits long, while those opposite the temple were a hundred cubits long. 9Below these chambers was an entrance on the east side, as one enters them from the outer court, 10where the outside wall begins.[b]

On the south[c] also, opposite the yard and opposite the building, there were chambers 11with a passage in front of them; they were similar to the chambers on the north, of the same length and breadth, with the same exits[d] and arrangements and doors. 12And below the south chambers was an entrance on the east side, where one enters the passage, and opposite them was a dividing wall.[e]

13 Then he said to me, "The north chambers and the south chambers opposite the yard are the holy chambers, where the priests who approach the LORD shall eat the most holy offerings; there they shall put the most holy offerings—the cereal offering, the sin offering, and the guilt offering, for the place is holy. 14When the priests enter the holy place, they shall not go out of it into the outer court without laying there the garments in which they minister, for these are holy; they shall put on other garments before they go near to that which is for the people."

15 Now when he had finished measuring the interior of the temple area, he led me out by the gate which faced east, and measured the temple area round about. 16He measured the east side with the measuring reed, five hundred cubits by the measuring reed. 17Then he turned and measured[f] the north side, five hundred cubits by the measuring reed. 18Then he turned and measured[f] the south side, five hundred cubits by the measuring reed. 19Then he turned to the west side and measured, five hundred cubits by the measuring reed. 20He measured it on the four sides. It had a wall around it, five hundred cubits long and five hundred cubits broad, to make a separation between the holy and the common.

The Glory of the Lord Entering the Temple

43 Afterward he brought me to the gate, the gate facing east. 2And behold, the glory of the God of Israel came from the east; and the sound

43:2: Ezek 1:24; Rev 1:15; 14:2; 19:6.

41:18 cherubim: Traditional guardians of the presence of God (Gen 3:24), represented in the Tabernacle (Ex 25:18–20), on the Ark of the Covenant (1 Sam 4:4), and in the Temple of Solomon (1 Kings 6:23–28).

42:20 five hundred cubits: About 800 to 900 feet long. The number 500 is fifty (Jubilee) times ten (fullness, completion).

43:2 glory ... came from the east: The east as the place of God's presence and coming is very old in scriptural tradition: Eden opened to the east, as did the Tabernacle and Temple. Traditions that the Messiah would come from the east led the Essenes at Qumran to establish their community to the east of Jerusalem, on the shores of the Dead Sea.

[q] Cn: Heb *measures and carved.*
[r] Cn Compare verse 25: Heb *and the wall.*
[s] Gk: Heb lacks *two cubits broad.*
[t] Gk: Heb *length.*
[u] Cn: Heb *vestibule. And the side chambers of the temple and the canopies.*
[v] Gk: Heb *outer.*
[w] Gk: Heb *door.*
[x] Gk: Heb *before the length.*
[y] The meaning of the Hebrew word is unknown.
[z] Gk Syr: Heb *a way of one cubit.*
[a] Gk: Heb lacks *outer.*
[b] Cn Compare Gk: Heb *in the breadth of the wall of the court.*
[c] Gk: Heb *east.*
[d] Heb *and all their exits.*
[e] Cn: Heb *And according to the entrances of the chambers that were toward the south was an entrance at the head of the way, the way before the dividing wall toward the east as one enters them.*
[f] Gk: Heb *measuring reed round about. He measured.*

of his coming was like the sound of many waters; and the earth shone with his glory. [3]And[g] the vision I saw was like the vision which I had seen when he came to destroy the city, and[h] like the vision which I had seen by the river Che'bar; and I fell upon my face. [4]As the glory of the LORD entered the temple by the gate facing east, [5]the Spirit lifted me up, and brought me into the inner court; and behold, the glory of the LORD filled the temple.

6 While the man was standing beside me, I heard one speaking to me out of the temple; [7]and he said to me, "Son of man, this is the place of my throne and the place of the soles of my feet, where I will dwell in the midst of the sons of Israel for ever. And the house of Israel shall no more defile my holy name, neither they, nor their kings, by their harlotry, and by the dead bodies[i] of their kings, [8]by setting their threshold by my threshold and their doorposts beside my doorposts, with only a wall between me and them. They have defiled my holy name by their abominations which they have committed, so I have consumed them in my anger. [9]Now let them put away their idolatry and the dead bodies[i] of their kings far from me, and I will dwell in their midst for ever.

10 "And you, son of man, describe to the house of Israel the temple and its appearance and plan,[j] that they may be ashamed of their iniquities. [11]And if they are ashamed of all that they have done, portray[k] the temple, its arrangement, its exits and its entrances, and its whole form; and make known to them all its ordinances and all its laws; and write it down in their sight, so that they may observe and perform all its laws[l] and all its ordinances. [12]This is the law of the temple: the whole territory round about upon the top of the mountain shall be most holy. Behold, this is the law of the temple.

The Altar

13 "These are the dimensions of the altar by cubits (the cubit being a cubit and a handbreadth): its base shall be one cubit high,[m] and one cubit broad, with a rim of one span around its edge. And this shall be the height[x] of the altar: [14]from the base on the ground to the lower ledge, two cubits, with a breadth of one cubit; and from the smaller ledge to the larger ledge, four cubits, with a breadth of one cubit; [15]and the altar hearth, four cubits; and from the altar hearth projecting upward, four horns, one cubit high.[n] [16]The altar hearth shall be square, twelve cubits long by twelve broad. [17]The ledge also shall be square, fourteen cubits long by fourteen broad, with a rim around it half a cubit broad, and its base one cubit round about. The steps of the altar shall face east."

18 And he said to me, "Son of man, thus says the Lord GOD: These are the ordinances for the altar: On the day when it is erected for offering burnt offerings upon it and for throwing blood against it, [19]you shall give to the Levitical priests of the family of Za'dok, who draw near to me to minister to me, says the Lord GOD, a bull for a sin offering. [20]And you shall take some of its blood, and put it on the four horns of the altar, and on the four corners of the ledge, and upon the rim round about; thus you shall cleanse the altar and make atonement for it. [21]You shall also take the bull of the sin offering, and it shall be burnt in the appointed place belonging to the temple, outside the sacred area. [22]And on the second day you shall offer a he-goat without blemish for a sin offering; and the altar shall be cleansed, as it was cleansed with the bull. [23]When you have finished cleansing it, you shall offer a bull without blemish and a ram from the flock without blemish. [24]You shall present them before the LORD, and the priests shall sprinkle salt upon them and offer them up as a burnt offering to the LORD. [25]For seven days you shall provide daily a goat for a sin offering; also a bull and a ram from the flock, without blemish, shall be provided. [26]Seven days shall they make atonement for the altar and purify it, and so consecrate it. [27]And when they have completed these days, then from the eighth day onward the priests shall offer upon the altar your burnt offerings and your peace offerings; and I will accept you, says the Lord GOD."

The Closed Gate

44 Then he brought me back to the outer gate of the sanctuary, which faces east; and it was shut. [2]And he[o] said to me, "This gate shall remain

---

43:4 glory of the LORD: The presence of the Lord, as also filled the Tabernacle in the tent of meeting at Mt. Sinai (Ex 40:34–35) and the dedication of the Solomonic Temple (1 Kings 8:11).

[g] Gk Heb *And like the vision.*
[h] Syr: Heb *and the visions.*
[i] Or *the monuments.*
[j] Gk: Heb *the temple that they may measure the pattern.*
[k] Gk: Heb *the form of.*
[l] Compare Gk: Heb *its whole form.*
[m] Gk: Heb lacks *high.*
[x] Gk: Heb *back.*
[n] Gk: Heb lacks *one cubit high.*
[o] Cn: Heb *the LORD.*

43:8 only a wall between me and them: The royal palace of Judah was built abutting the Temple, which violated the ritual purity of the Temple.

43:12 the whole territory ... shall be most holy: From this verse and others arose the concept that the whole city of Jerusalem participated in the holiness of the Temple. In the time of Jesus, devout Essenes would not relieve themselves or engage in marital relations within Jerusalem, in deference to the holiness of the city.

44:2 This gate shall remain shut: The east gate of the Temple was made especially holy by God's glory entering through it (43:4–5). As a result, it was no longer suitable for common use. • In the Catholic spiritual tradition, it is a commonplace to see the Temple as a type of the Blessed Virgin, and the womb of the Virgin as the "gate" that remains

shut; it shall not be opened, and no one shall enter by
it; for the LORD, the God of Israel, has entered by it;
therefore it shall remain shut. 3Only the prince may
sit in it to eat bread before the LORD; he shall enter
by way of the vestibule of the gate, and shall go
out by the same way."

Those Admitted to the Temple

4 Then he brought me by way of the north
gate to the front of the temple; and I looked, and
behold, the glory of the LORD filled the temple of
the LORD; and I fell upon my face. 5And the LORD
said to me, "Son of man, mark well, see with your
eyes, and hear with your ears all that I shall tell you
concerning all the ordinances of the temple of the
LORD and all its laws; and mark well those who may
be admitted to[p] the temple and all those who are
to be excluded from the sanctuary. 6And say to the
rebellious house,[q] to the house of Israel, Thus says
the Lord GOD: O house of Israel, let there be an end
to all your abominations, 7in admitting foreigners,
uncircumcised in heart and flesh, to be in my
sanctuary, profaning it,[r] when you offer to me
my food, the fat and the blood. You[s] have broken
my covenant, in addition to all your abominations.
8And you have not kept charge of my holy things;
but you have set foreigners to keep my charge in
my sanctuary.

9 "Therefore[t] thus says the Lord GOD: No foreigner, uncircumcised in heart and flesh, of all the
foreigners who are among the people of Israel, shall
enter my sanctuary. 10But the Levites who went far
from me, going astray from me after their idols when
Israel went astray, shall bear their punishment.
11They shall be ministers in my sanctuary, having
oversight at the gates of the temple, and serving
in the temple; they shall slay the burnt offering
and the sacrifice for the people, and they shall
attend on the people, to serve them. 12Because they
ministered to them before their idols and became a
stumbling block of iniquity to the house of Israel,
therefore I have sworn concerning them, says the
Lord GOD, that they shall bear their punishment.
13They shall not come near to me, to serve me as
priest, nor come near any of my sacred things
and the things that are most sacred; but they shall
bear their shame, because of the abominations
which they have committed. 14Yet I will appoint
them to keep charge of the temple, to do all its
service and all that is to be done in it.

The Levitical Priests

15 "But the Levitical priests, the sons of Za'dok,
who kept the charge of my sanctuary when the
people of Israel went astray from me, shall come
near to me to minister to me; and they shall attend
on me to offer me the fat and the blood, says the
Lord GOD; 16they shall enter my sanctuary, and
they shall approach my table, to minister to me,
and they shall keep my charge. 17When they enter

44:4: Rev 15:8.

closed after the entrance of the Lord. The perpetual virginity of the Blessed Mother seems a fitting analogue to the closed gate of the eschatological Temple. • The preservation of the Virgin's condition is evident here. The gate of virginity was closed. Through it the God of Israel entered, and through it he came forth into this world. Her virginal state was preserved inviolate, for the gate remained closed for ever (Rufinus of Aquileia, *Commentary on the Apostles' Creed* 9).

44:7 uncircumcised in heart: Refers to a lack of interior conversion, a rejection of the God of Israel and his law. **and flesh:** Refers to a physical condition, a failure to comply with the rite that marks a man as a member of the covenant made with Abraham (Gen 17:10). Ezekiel is not ruling out the possibility of Gentile conversions, but he does object to the presence in the Temple of foreigners who have not given up paganism or embraced the one true God. **broken my covenant:** Perhaps by failing to enforce the rule of circumcision for those who would worship the Lord or serve in his Temple (cf. Gen 17:14).

44:10 Levites who went far from me: Apparently, many of the Levites were involved in the religious syncretism or outright paganism into which Israel and Judah fell during the period of the monarchy. We do not have many references to this defection in Scripture, but it is historically plausible that many Levites participated in the illicit worship that was promoted by the kings of Israel and even, in some periods, the kings of Judah.

44:13 They shall not ... serve me as priest: Probably means the Levites were excluded from the Holy Place and the Holy of Holies and forbidden to offer the sacrifices, although they could prepare the sacrificial victims. The priesthood proper had always been limited to the descendants of Aaron (Ex 28:1). It is not clear whether this distinction between Aaronite priests and the rest of the Levites was ignored in previous generations, or if the Levites that Ezekiel rebukes are also descendants of Aaron, but nonetheless are now being barred from the fullness of the priestly office.

44:15 the Levitical priests: Ezekiel uses a phrase characteristic of Deuteronomy, "the Levitical priests" (Heb. *hakkōhanîm halleviyim*) but identifies this group as **the sons of Zadok**. Zadok, a descendant of Phinehas, the zealous grandson of Aaron (Num 25:10–12), served as high priest during the reign of David, together with Abiathar, a descendant of Eli (2 Sam 8:17). Under Solomon, Zadok was made sole high priest and Abiathar dispossessed (1 Kings 2:27), to fulfill the curse placed on the house of Eli (1 Sam 3:30–36). In criticizing the non-Zadokite Levites, it is not clear if Ezekiel has in mind the historical infidelity of the Elide Levites as recorded in the books of Samuel and Kings or other more recent infidelities not recorded in the Bible. It is clear, however, that Ezekiel believes only the Zadokites may exercise all the duties attributed to the group called "the Levitical priests" in Deuteronomy. In the New Testament era, the Jewish Essene movement that left us the Dead Sea Scrolls was led by priests who claimed descent from Zadok. **offer me the fat and the blood:** I.e., not simply prepare, but formally offer the sacrifices to God.

44:16 enter my sanctuary ... approach my table: I.e., enter the court of the Temple and minister at the great bronze altar, the "table" of the Lord (cf. Mal 1:7).

[p] Cn: Heb *the entrance of*.
[q] Gk: Heb lacks *house*.
[r] Gk: Heb *it my temple*.
[s] Gk Syr Vg: Heb *they*.
[t] Gk: Heb *for you*.

the gates of the inner court, they shall wear linen
garments; they shall have nothing of wool on them,
while they minister at the gates of the inner court,
and within. 18They shall have linen turbans upon
their heads, and linen breeches upon their loins; they
shall not clothe themselves with anything that causes
sweat. 19And when they go out into the outer court to
the people, they shall put off the garments in which
they have been ministering, and lay them in the holy
chambers; and they shall put on other garments, lest
they communicate holiness to the people with their
garments. 20They shall not shave their heads or let
their locks grow long; they shall only trim the hair
of their heads. 21No priest shall drink wine, when
he enters the inner court. 22They shall not marry
a widow, or a divorced woman, but only a virgin
of the stock of the house of Israel, or a widow who
is the widow of a priest. 23They shall teach my people the difference between the holy and the common,
and show them how to distinguish between the
unclean and the clean. 24In a controversy they shall
act as judges, and they shall judge it according to my
judgments. They shall keep my laws and my statutes
in all my appointed feasts, and they shall keep my
sabbaths holy. 25They shall not defile themselves by
going near to a dead person; however, for father or
mother, for son or daughter, for brother or unmarried
sister they may defile themselves. 26After he is
defiled,[u] he shall count for himself seven days, and
then he shall be clean.[v] 27And on the day that he goes
into the holy place, into the inner court, to minister in
the holy place, he shall offer his sin offering, says the
Lord God.

28 "They shall have no[w] inheritance; I am their
inheritance: and you shall give them no possession
in Israel; I am their possession. 29They shall eat
the cereal offering, the sin offering, and the guilt
offering; and every devoted thing in Israel shall
be theirs. 30And the first of all the first fruits of all
kinds, and every offering of all kinds from all your
offerings, shall belong to the priests; you shall also
give to the priests the first of your coarse meal, that
a blessing may rest on your house. 31The priests
shall not eat of anything, whether bird or beast, that
has died of itself or is torn.

The Holy District

45 "When you allot the land as a possession,
you shall set apart for the Lord a portion of
the land as a holy district, twenty-five thousand
cubits long and twenty[x] thousand cubits broad;
it shall be holy throughout its whole extent. 2Of

44:17 linen garments ... nothing of wool: Linen was a high-cost fabric that drew moisture away from the wearer, removing sweat, keeping the body cool, and resisting odor. As the priests were required to be presentable while serving, it was the only fabric suitable for the priesthood. Later, the Essene community that left us the Dead Sea Scrolls made a practice of wearing only linen, as they regarded themselves as a priestly community. This is the probable background of the young man wearing nothing but a linen cloth in the garden of Gethsemane (Mk 14:51–52), traditionally identified as John Mark, the evangelist. Also, Jesus' garments of linen at his burial (Jn 19:40) suggest, in a spiritual sense, his priesthood.

44:18 linen turbans: Covering the head was a sign of reverence, yet a turban was also a sign of one in authority or leadership. **linen breeches:** To prevent nakedness from being exposed, which was contrary to the reverence due the divine presence (Ex 20:26).

44:19 communicate holiness ... with their garments: This is an unusual concept, as generally when holy and profane objects came in contact, the holy object was rendered common. However, Jesus' garments communicated holiness, as did those of Paul: Mt 9:21; 14:36; Mk 6:56; Lk 8:44; Acts 19:11–12.

44:20 not shave their heads or ... locks grow: A shaven head was a sign of mourning (Deut 21:12) or uncleanness (Lev 13:33; 14:7–9; Num 6:9); and long locks were a sign of luxuriousness (2 Sam 14:25–26), indicating the man did not need to work for a living, as long hair interfered with physical labor. Neither was appropriate for the priesthood.

44:21 No priest shall drink wine: Lest he lose his rationality and misuse his sacred powers in such a way as to profane the sacred things (cf. Lev 10:9; Prov 20:1).

44:22 shall not marry a widow: The wife of the priest could not have had intimate contact with a non-consecrated man. The priest is holy and cannot contact the unclean. Since he is one flesh with his wife, she must also be in a high state of ritual cleanliness.

44:23 the holy and the common ... the unclean and the clean: These four categories were the basis of the Israelite ritual system. A *holy* thing was imbued with the divine presence, whereas a *common* thing was not. A *clean* thing was suitable for sanctification (i.e., it could be made holy), whereas an *unclean* thing could not be sanctified. Lev 11–15 details the regulations for cleanliness, whereas Lev 17–25 details regulations for holiness.

44:24 shall act as judges: Only Deuteronomy introduces a judicial function for the priesthood (Deut 17:8–12; 19:17), as this role is absent in the laws of Exodus through Numbers. Significantly, Moses provides an authoritative means for resolution of disputes over the meaning or application of divine law by establishing the Levitical priests as judges in Deut 17:8–12. Under the Old Covenant, each Israelite did not have the right of private interpretation, to arrive at his personal understanding of divine law. This duty was in the hands of the legitimate priesthood.

44:25 shall not defile themselves: Israelites performed actions rendering themselves ritually unclean as a sign of mourning. Uncleanliness prevented a priest from performing his sacred duties. He was not allowed to do so except for immediate family members.

44:28 shall have no inheritance: The priests were not to own farmlands to support themselves. Rather, they were to live from the offerings the Israelites brought to the Lord. However, this became a type of detachment from temporal things. • In the Gospels, the apostles are called to leave everything, including "houses and lands", in order to cling to Jesus alone (Mt 19:24–28). This hints at their status as a new priesthood of the New Covenant; the judging role of the priests over the tribes of Israel will be given them (Mt 19:28). Their only "part" or "inheritance" (Gk., *meros*) is to be Jesus himself (Jn 13:8), who is the Lord.

45:1 twenty-five thousand cubits ... twenty thousand cubits: Roughly nine miles by seven miles, giving approximately 63 square miles. Washington, D.C., is roughly 68 square miles.

---

[u] Syr Heb *cleansed.*
[v] Syr: Heb lacks *and then he shall be clean.*
[w] Vg: Heb *as an.*
[x] Gk: Heb *ten.*

this a square plot of five hundred by five hundred cubits shall be for the sanctuary, with fifty cubits for an open space around it. 3And in the holy district you shall measure off a section twenty-five thousand cubits long and ten thousand broad, in which shall be the sanctuary, the most holy place. 4It shall be the holy portion of the land; it shall be for the priests, who minister in the sanctuary and approach the LORD to minister to him; and it shall be a place for their houses and a holy place for the sanctuary. 5Another section, twenty-five thousand cubits long and ten thousand cubits broad, shall be for the Levites who minister at the temple, as their possession for cities to live in.[y]

6 "Alongside the portion set apart as the holy district you shall assign for the possession of the city an area five thousand cubits broad, and twenty-five thousand cubits long; it shall belong to the whole house of Israel.

7 "And to the prince shall belong the land on both sides of the holy district and the property of the city, alongside the holy district and the property of the city, on the west and on the east, corresponding in length to one of the tribal portions, and extending from the western to the eastern boundary of the land. 8It is to be his property in Israel. And my princes shall no more oppress my people; but they shall let the house of Israel have the land according to their tribes.

9 "Thus says the Lord GOD: Enough, O princes of Israel! Put away violence and oppression, and execute justice and righteousness; cease your evictions of my people, says the Lord GOD.

Just Weights and Measures

10 "You shall have just balances, a just ephah, and a just bath. 11The ephah and the bath shall be of the same measure, the bath containing one tenth of a homer, and the ephah one tenth of a homer; the homer shall be the standard measure. 12The shekel shall be twenty gerahs; five shekels shall be five shekels, and ten shekels shall be ten shekels, and your mina shall be fifty shekels.[z]

Offerings

13 "This is the offering which you shall make: one sixth of an ephah from each homer of wheat, and one sixth of an ephah from each homer of barley, 14and as the fixed portion of oil,[a] one tenth of a bath from each cor (the cor,[b] like the homer, contains ten baths); 15and one sheep from every flock of two hundred, from the families[c] of Israel. This is the offering for cereal offerings, burnt offerings, and peace offerings, to make atonement for them, says the Lord GOD. 16All the people of the land shall give[d] this offering to the prince in Israel. 17It shall be the prince's duty to furnish the burnt offerings, cereal offerings, and drink offerings, at the feasts, the new moons, and the sabbaths, all the appointed feasts of the house of Israel: he shall provide the sin offerings, cereal offerings, burnt offerings, and peace offerings, to make atonement for the house of Israel.

Feasts

18 "Thus says the Lord GOD: In the first month, on the first day of the month, you shall take a young bull without blemish, and cleanse the sanctuary. 19The priest shall take some of the blood of the sin offering and put it on the doorposts of the temple, the four corners of the ledge of the altar, and the posts of the gate of the inner court. 20You shall do the same on the seventh day of the month for any one who has sinned through error or ignorance; so you shall make atonement for the temple.

21 "In the first month, on the fourteenth day of the month, you shall celebrate the feast of the passover,

---

45:2 five hundred by five hundred cubits ... fifty cubits: Ezekiel's long cubit was somewhere between 20 and 22 inches, so 500 cubits is about 875 feet, 50 cubits about 90 feet. The multiples of fifty in the layout of the sacred precinct and Temple may be references to the Jubilee cycle of fifty years (Lev 25:10), suggesting the Temple is the Jubilee in stone, a kind of architectural expression of the people's liberation.

45:7 the prince: The Davidic king, to whom Ezekiel grants a generous landholding and whom he forbids to encroach on the land of the people. See word study: *Prince* at 34:24.

45:10 You shall have just balances: Ezekiel develops Lev 19:35–37, 27:25, and Deut 25:15. However, he introduces the "bath" (45:11) and the "mina" (45:12), Near Eastern measures unknown in the Pentateuch but apparently introduced into Israelite culture in the Solomonic era (1 Kings 7:26, 38; 10:17).

45:17 the prince's duty: Ezekiel's "prince", the royal Son of David, is primarily a liturgical figure, whose main duty is to support the sanctuary and promote the true liturgy, largely at his own expense. While it was common for the kings of the ancient Near East to patronize the cult of the gods, they typically had many other duties as well. But in Ezekiel's vision, the liturgy is the king's *only* duty.

45:18 first month ... first day ... cleanse the sanctuary: The Law of Moses instituted the Day of Atonement on the tenth day of the seventh month (Tishri 10; Lev 16:1–34). Judaism recognizes this as the holiest day in the liturgical calendar. Here, Ezekiel receives instructions for a day of atonement for the Temple on the first day of the first month (Nisan 1). The ritual is much simpler than that of the Mosaic Day of Atonement. Probably this is intended as an additional annual observance, not a replacement for the Mosaic feast.

45:21 the feast of the passover: Ezekiel modifies the observance of Passover (Num 28:16–25) and the Feast of Unleavened Bread to specify that the "prince" (= the Davidic king) is to provide all the animals and provisions for the Temple sacrifices during these holy days. This once more highlights the main role of the king of Israel in Ezekiel's vision: the one who provides for proper worship and all the atoning sacrifices for the people of Israel at his own expense. Seen in this light,

---

[y] Gk: Heb *twenty chambers.*
[z] Gk: Heb *twenty shekels, twenty-five shekels, fifteen shekels shall be your mina.*
[a] Cn: Heb *oil, the bath the oil.*
[b] Vg: Heb *homer.*
[c] Gk: Heb *watering places.*
[d] Gk Compare Syr: Heb *shall be to.*

and for seven days unleavened bread shall be eaten. 22On that day the prince shall provide for himself and all the people of the land a young bull for a sin offering. 23And on the seven days of the festival he shall provide as a burnt offering to the LORD seven young bulls and seven rams without blemish, on each of the seven days; and a he-goat daily for a sin offering. 24And he shall provide as a cereal offering an ephah for each bull, an ephah for each ram, and a hin of oil to each ephah. 25In the seventh month, on the fifteenth day of the month and for the seven days of the feast, he shall make the same provision for sin offerings, burnt offerings, and cereal offerings, and for the oil.

Other Ordinances of the Temple

46 "Thus says the Lord GOD: The gate of the inner court that faces east shall be shut on the six working days; but on the sabbath day it shall be opened and on the day of the new moon it shall be opened. 2The prince shall enter by the vestibule of the gate from without, and shall take his stand by the post of the gate. The priests shall offer his burnt offering and his peace offerings, and he shall worship at the threshold of the gate. Then he shall go out, but the gate shall not be shut until evening. 3The people of the land shall worship at the entrance of that gate before the LORD on the sabbaths and on the new moons. 4The burnt offering that the prince offers to the LORD on the sabbath day shall be six lambs without blemish and a ram without blemish; 5and the cereal offering with the ram shall be an ephah, and the cereal offering with the lambs shall be as much as he is able, together with a hin of oil to each ephah. 6On the day of the new moon he shall offer a young bull without blemish, and six lambs and a ram, which shall be without blemish; 7as a cereal offering he shall provide an ephah with the bull and an ephah with the ram, and with the lambs as much as he is able, together with a hin of oil to each ephah. 8When the prince enters, he shall go in by the vestibule of the gate, and he shall go out by the same way.

9 "When the people of the land come before the LORD at the appointed feasts, he who enters by the north gate to worship shall go out by the south gate; and he who enters by the south gate shall go out by the north gate: no one shall return by way of the gate by which he entered, but each shall go out straight ahead. 10When they go in, the prince shall go in with them; and when they go out, he shall go out.

11 "At the feasts and the appointed seasons the cereal offering with a young bull shall be an ephah, and with a ram an ephah, and with the lambs as much as one is able to give, together with a hin of oil to an ephah. 12When the prince provides a freewill offering, either a burnt offering or peace offerings as a freewill offering to the LORD, the gate facing east shall be opened for him; and he shall offer his burnt offering or his peace offerings as he does on the sabbath day. Then he shall go out, and after he has gone out the gate shall be shut.

13 "He shall provide a lamb a year old without blemish for a burnt offering to the LORD daily; morning by morning he shall provide it. 14And he shall provide a cereal offering with it morning by morning, one sixth of an ephah, and one third of a hin of oil to moisten the flour, as a cereal offering to the LORD; this is the ordinance for the continual burnt offering.[e] 15Thus the lamb and the meal offering and the oil shall be provided, morning by morning, for a continual burnt offering.

16 "Thus says the Lord GOD: If the prince makes a gift to any of his sons out of[f] his inheritance, it shall belong to his sons, it is their property by

---

Ezekiel's "prince" is a type of Christ. Ezekiel also specifies larger numbers and amounts of sacrificial animals and grain offerings than originally prescribed by Moses (Num 28:16–25).

46:1 The gate ... that faces east ... shall be opened: The east-facing outer gate was to remain perpetually shut, according to 44:1–3, but the east-facing inner gate could be opened on solemn days, allowing the prince and the people to observe the sacrifices taking place within the inner court.

46:6 six lambs ... without blemish: Moses prescribed only two (Num 28:9–10). All the amounts specified for sacrifice on the Sabbath and new moon are different from those specified by Moses (Num 28:9–15). The significance of the changes is not clear, but perhaps the point is simply that all the particulars of the liturgy will be changed in the coming age.

46:9 north gate ... south gate: The reason for this regulation is unclear. Some suggest it is a practical measure to manage the flow of the crowds through the Temple precincts. Spiritually, there could be a reference to personal transformation: to return through the same gate represents lack of change, yet everyone should be transformed by the experience of divine worship and, therefore, should process through the opposite gate, indicating change and progress.

46:10 the prince ... with them: An expression of solidarity between prince and people. He is to identify with the people and set the example for them in worship.

46:13 a lamb ... morning by morning: The *tāmîd*, or continual burnt offering. This sacrifice, offered twice a day, was the most foundational and characteristic sacrifice of the sanctuary, the "beating heart" of the ancient Israelite liturgy. Curiously, Moses specified two lambs, one to be offered in the morning and the other in the evening (Ex 29:38–39; Num 28:3–4). Ezekiel seems to omit the evening sacrifice, prescribing only the offering of a lamb in the morning.

46:16 If the prince makes a gift: Ezekiel makes an amendment to the Jubilee laws of Lev 25. The original Jubilee legislation did not have any provision for dealing with royal property because the laws of Leviticus did not foresee Israel having a king. Ezekiel addresses this gap in the legal system by specifying how the Jubilee Year (the fiftieth year, when all property reverted to its ancestral owner) should apply to crown property. The principle is that all property in Israel should stay within the line of inheritance of its original owners.

---

[e] Cn: Heb *perpetual ordinances continually.*

[f] Gk: Heb *it is his inheritance.*

inheritance. [17]But if he makes a gift out of his inheritance to one of his servants, it shall be his to the year of liberty; then it shall revert to the prince; only his sons may keep a gift from his inheritance. [18]The prince shall not take any of the inheritance of the people, thrusting them out of their property; he shall give his sons their inheritance out of his own property, so that none of my people shall be dispossessed of his property."

19 Then he brought me through the entrance, which was at the side of the gate, to the north row of the holy chambers for the priests; and there I saw a place at the extreme western end of them. [20]And he said to me, "This is the place where the priests shall boil the guilt offering and the sin offering, and where they shall bake the cereal offering, in order not to bring them out into the outer court and so communicate holiness to the people."

21 Then he brought me forth to the outer court, and led me to the four corners of the court; and in each corner of the court there was a court—[22]in the four corners of the court were small[g] courts, forty cubits long and thirty broad; the four were of the same size. [23]On the inside, around each of the four courts was a row of masonry, with hearths made at the bottom of the rows round about. [24]Then he said to me, "These are the kitchens where those who minister at the temple shall boil the sacrifices of the people."

Water Flowing from the Temple

47 Then he brought me back to the door of the temple; and behold, water was issuing from below the threshold of the temple toward the east (for the temple faced east); and the water was flowing down from below the right side of the threshold of the temple, south of the altar. [2]Then he brought me out by way of the north gate, and led me round on the outside to the outer gate, that faces toward the east;[h] and the water was coming out on the right side.

3 Going on eastward with a line in his hand, the man measured a thousand cubits, and then led me through the water; and it was ankle-deep. [4]Again he measured a thousand, and led me through the water; and it was knee-deep. Again he measured a thousand, and led me through the water; and it was up to the loins. [5]Again he measured a thousand, and it was a river that I could not pass through, for the water had risen; it was deep enough to swim in, a river that could not be passed through. [6]And he said to me, "Son of man, have you seen this?"

Then he led me back along the bank of the river. [7]As I went back, I saw upon the bank of the river very many trees on the one side and on the other. [8]And he said to me, "This water flows toward the eastern region and goes down into the Ar′abah; and when it enters the stagnant waters of the sea,[i] the water will become fresh. [9]And wherever the river[j] goes every living creature which swarms will live, and there will be very many fish; for this water goes there, that the waters of the sea[k] may become fresh; so everything will live where the river goes. [10]Fishermen will stand beside the sea; from En-ge′di to En-eg′laim it will be a place for the spreading of nets; its fish will be of very many kinds, like the fish of the Great Sea. [11]But its swamps and marshes will not become fresh; they are to be left for salt. [12]And

47:1–2: Zech 14:8; Rev 22:1–2.

46:24 These are the kitchens: Neither the Solomonic Temple nor the Mosaic Tabernacle made explicit provision for where the cooking and baking associated with the offering of sacrifice were to be performed. Ezekiel's visionary Temple, however, has designated locations for these activities (46:19–24), showing that God's future Temple would fully compensate for various deficiencies of previous sanctuaries.

47:1 water ... from ... the temple: See essay: *The River of Life Flowing from the Temple.*

47:4 knee-deep ... up to the loins: This is a supernatural river that grows wider and deeper, although no tributaries flow into it.

47:5 deep enough to swim ... could not be passed through: In a spiritual sense, the river represents the Holy Spirit flowing from Christ, our true Temple, the depth and impassibility of the river representing the fathomlessness of God's nature (CCC 694). • The waters signify either the grace of Baptism or the teaching of the gospel. If these waters flow from the Lord's Temple and carry the teaching of the apostles, then they can make even sterile piles of gravel bring forth fruit, and they can water every plain and desert (St. Jerome, *Commentary on Ezekiel* 14, 47).

47:7 many trees: A motif recalling Eden, the original garden-sanctuary of God (see Rev 22:1–2).

47:8 the Arabah: The desert east of Jerusalem going down to the Jordan and the Dead Sea. **the stagnant waters:** The lifeless waters of the Dead Sea.

47:9 everything will live where the river goes: The river is a type of the Holy Spirit, and the Dead Sea a type of the human condition apart from God's grace (CCC 1137).

47:10 En-gedi: A famous oasis about halfway down the western shore of the Dead Sea. It was renowned in ancient times for its fruitfulness (Song 1:14). **En-eglaim:** Location uncertain. From the way Ezekiel speaks of it, it must be an oasis along the western shore of the Dead Sea, most likely to the south of En-gedi. **the Great Sea:** The Mediterranean.

47:11 swamps and marshes ... left for salt: Salt being a very valuable commodity and also a necessity of life.

47:12 leaves will not wither nor their fruit fail: Like the righteous man in Ps 1:3. **Fruit ... for food ... leaves for healing:** Also a feature of the New Jerusalem in Rev 22:2. • These may be seen as types of the sacraments, which nourish (Eucharist) and heal (Reconciliation, Anointing of the Sick) the nations.

[g]Gk Syr Vg: The meaning of the Hebrew word is uncertain.
[h]Heb obscure.
[i]Compare Syr: Heb *into the sea to the sea those that were made to issue forth.*
[j]Gk Syr Vg Tg: Heb *two rivers.*
[k]Compare Syr: Heb lacks *the waters of the sea.*

on the banks, on both sides of the river, there will grow all kinds of trees for food. Their leaves will not wither nor their fruit fail, but they will bear fresh fruit every month, because the water for them flows from the sanctuary. Their fruit will be for food, and their leaves for healing."

New Boundaries of the Land

13 Thus says the Lord GOD: "These are the boundaries by which you shall divide the land for inheritance among the twelve tribes of Israel. Joseph
shall have two portions. 14And you shall divide it equally; I swore to give it to your fathers, and this land shall fall to you as your inheritance.

15 "This shall be the boundary of the land: On the north side, from the Great Sea by way of Heth'lon to the entrance of Ha'math, and on to Ze'-
dad,[l] 16Bero'thah, Sib'raim (which lies on the border between Damascus and Ha'math), as far as Hazer-hat'ticon, which is on the border of Hau'ran.
17So the boundary shall run from the sea to Ha'zar-e'non, which is on the northern border of Damascus, with the border of Ha'math to the north.[m] This shall be the north side.

47:13–23 The new boundaries of the land of Israel. This section recalls Num 34:1–15 and is very similar to it. Ezekiel is like a new Moses, parceling out the land once again.

47:13 Joseph ... two portions: The right of the first-born son (Deut 21:17). It is interesting that in Ezekiel, Joseph receives this privilege rather than Judah, even though Judah was the royal tribe, and the tribes of Joseph (Ephraim and Manasseh) had been dispersed for a century and a half at the time Ezekiel writes.

47:14 divide it equally: Ezekiel has faith in God's restoration of all twelve tribes, his covenantal faithfulness to all Israel. This faith is also reflected in key NT texts (cf. Rom 11:26; Rev 7:1–8).

47:15 Hethlon: Location unknown. **the entrance of Hamath:** Literally, "Lebo-hamath". It is probably modern Lebweh, about 50 miles north of Damascus. Ezekiel's holy land includes a large part of Syria, which was incorporated into the kingdom of Israel under David and Solomon. **Zedad:** Probably modern Sedad, 35 miles northeast of Lebweh.

47:16 Berothah: A city of the Beqaʿ valley in Lebanon, mentioned in 2 Sam 8:8. **Sibraim:** Exact location unknown. **Hazer-hatticon:** Location unknown. **Hauran:** The mountainous region east of Galilee.

47:17 Hazar-enon: Location unknown. **Damascus:** Capital and chief city of ancient Aram (modern Syria). **Hamath:** An important city-state on the Orontes River about a hundred miles north of Damascus.

[l] Gk: Heb *the entrance of Zedad, Hamath.*
[m] Heb obscure.

The River of Life Flowing from the Temple

The idea of a primordial garden-sanctuary at the beginning of human history, from which flowed a life-giving river that watered the whole earth, has deep roots in many ancient cultures. Genesis describes a garden-sanctuary on a mountain named Eden, from which flowed a river that divided into four branches (Gen 2:10–14). The four branches are probably reflective of the four cardinal directions or the concept of the "four corners of the earth", expressing the idea that the garden of Eden provided life-giving water to the whole world. Theologically, we can say that communion with God, made possible in his sanctuary, is the source of life for the whole creation.

Later in Israel's history, God's people came to view the Temple in Jerusalem as a kind of successor and sacrament of the garden of Eden. The reverence for the ancient river that flowed from Eden became attached to the spring that supplied water for Jerusalem and its Temple. This spring was named "Gihon" ("the gusher"), recalling one of the branches of the river from Eden (Gen 2:13). It was located on the east slope of ancient Zion, the "City of David" proper, where the king and his court lived. Hezekiah dug a tunnel to bring the waters of the Gihon inside the walls of the city (2 Chron 32:30) to the Pool called Shiloah (Is 8:6; = "Siloam" in Jn 9:7, 11). The Gihon spring attracted religious veneration as the source of life for the holy city, as is reflected in some biblical texts (Ps 46:4; 1 Kings 1:33, 38, 45; Is 8:6). Indeed, the Gihon was seen as a sign of the river or fountain of life that flows from God's presence (Ps 36:9; 68:26; Jer 2:13; 17:13; cf. Rev 22:1–2). Ezekiel and other prophets saw visions of restoration in which a supernatural river would flow from the Temple itself (Ezek 47:1–12; Joel 3:18; Zech 13:1; 14:8).

In the Gospel of John, the Body of Jesus is revealed as the true Temple of God (Jn 2:21). Jesus identifies himself as the fulfillment of Scriptures that say, "Out of his heart shall flow rivers of living water" (Jn 7:38), a paraphrase of the prophetic oracles mentioned above. At the Cross, Jesus' pierced heart flows with a river of blood and water (Jn 19:34). The flow of blood and water calls to mind the drain from the Temple that flowed with the blood of the sacrifices and water of purification during Passover and other festivals. It also points to the Holy Spirit (Jn 7:39), who flows like a river from the sacrifice of Christ. Yet the Spirit comes to us through baptismal water and Eucharistic blood; thus, there is a sacramental symbolism in the blood and water from the side of Christ (Jn 19:34). The Church reads Ezek 47:1–12 every year for the Feast of St. John Lateran, the seat of the Diocese of Rome and mother church of all Christianity. St. John Lateran is seen as an icon of the universal Church, which is the true Temple from which the Holy Spirit flows forth as a life-giving river under the signs of the sacraments.

18 "On the east side, the boundary shall run from
Ha'zar-e'non[n] between Hau'ran and Damascus;
along the Jordan between Gilead and the land of
Israel; to the eastern sea and as far as Ta'mar.[o] This
shall be the east side.
19 "On the south side, it shall run from Ta'mar
as far as the waters of Meribath'-ka'desh, thence
along the Brook of Egypt to the Great Sea. This
shall be the south side.
20 "On the west side, the Great Sea shall be
the boundary to a point opposite the entrance of
Ha'math. This shall be the west side.
21 "So you shall divide this land among you
according to the tribes of Israel. 22You shall allot it
as an inheritance for yourselves and for the aliens
who reside among you and have begotten children
among you. They shall be to you as native-born
sons of Israel; with you they shall be allotted an
inheritance among the tribes of Israel. 23In whatever
tribe the alien resides, there you shall assign him his
inheritance, says the Lord GOD.

The Tribal Portions

48 "These are the names of the tribes: Beginning at the northern border, from the sea by
way[p] of Heth'lon to the entrance of Ha'math, as far
as Ha'zar-e'non (which is on the northern border of
Damascus over against Hamath), and[q] extending
from the east side to the west,[r] Dan, one portion.
2Adjoining the territory of Dan, from the east side
to the west, Asher, one portion. 3Adjoining the
territory of Asher, from the east side to the west,
Naph'tali, one portion. 4Adjoining the territory of
Naph'tali, from the east side to the west, Manas'seh,
one portion. 5Adjoining the territory of Manas'seh,
from the east side to the west, E'phraim, one portion.
6Adjoining the territory of E'phraim, from the east
side to the west, Reuben, one portion. 7Adjoining the
territory of Reuben, from the east side to the west,
Judah, one portion.
8 "Adjoining the territory of Judah, from the
east side to the west, shall be the portion which
you shall set apart, twenty-five thousand cubits
in breadth, and in length equal to one of the tribal
portions, from the east side to the west, with the
sanctuary in the midst of it. 9The portion which
you shall set apart for the LORD shall be twenty-five
thousand cubits in length, and twenty[s] thousand
in breadth. 10These shall be the allotments of the
holy portion: the priests shall have an allotment
measuring twenty-five thousand cubits on the
northern side, ten thousand cubits in breadth on
the western side, ten thousand in breadth on the
eastern side, and twenty-five thousand in length
on the southern side, with the sanctuary of the
LORD in the midst of it. 11This shall be for the con-
secrated priests, the sons[t] of Za'dok, who kept my
charge, who did not go astray when the people of
Israel went astray, as the Levites did. 12And it shall
belong to them as a special portion from the holy
portion of the land, a most holy place, adjoining
the territory of the Levites. 13And alongside the
territory of the priests, the Levites shall have an
allotment twenty-five thousand cubits in length
and ten thousand in breadth. The whole length
shall be twenty-five thousand cubits and the

47:18 Gilead: The ancient name for the territory on the east side of the Jordan River bounded by the Yarmuk River on the north and the Jabbok River on the south. The Ammonites and/or Arameans often encroached upon or controlled this territory, which had been given to the tribe of Gad. **Tamar:** A city south of the Dead Sea (1 Kings 9:18), in the Judean desert, a region sometimes claimed by Edom.

47:19 Meribath-kadesh: Probably an alternate name for Kadesh-barnea (Num 32:8; Deut 1:2, 19; 2:14; Josh 10:41, etc.), an important oasis in southeastern Judah, located on what is now the border between Israel and Egypt. **Brook of Egypt:** Not the Nile, but the modern Wadi el-Arish, which forms the natural border between Egypt and Israel.

47:20 the entrance of Hamath: See note on 47:15.

47:22 for the aliens who reside among you: Unlike Moses, Ezekiel does not command that foreign inhabitants of the land be driven out. Rather, he solves the problem of non-Israelite residents of the holy land by assimilating them with the tribes in whose territory they settled (47:23). This can be seen as a type of the inclusion of the Gentiles within the Church, the "Israel of God" (Gal 6:16).

48:1–35 This section invites comparison with the division of the Promised Land by tribes in Josh 13–21. There are notable differences, however. The allotments of Joshua followed natural divisions and features of the land, whereas in Ezekiel each tribe receives an equal east-west strip of territory from the Jordan Valley to the Mediterranean. Also, instead of cities of refuge (Josh 20:1–9) and cities for the Levites (Josh 21:1–42), there is a large strip of territory in the approximate center of the nation—seven tribes to the north and five to the south—for the Temple-city and its personnel: the priests, the Levites, and the "prince" (= Davidic king), whose main responsibility is the maintenance of the Temple.

48:1–5 Tribes located north of the sacred district of the city and Temple. **Dan**, **Asher**, **Naphtali**, **Manasseh**, and **Ephraim** are listed by location from north to south, as in ancient times. The tribal placements that follow are unexpected: the territory formerly occupied by **Reuben** was on the east side of the Jordan, rather than the west side, and the territory formerly occupied by **Judah** was south of Jerusalem, rather than north of it.

48:1 Hethlon ... Hamath ... Hazar-enon: See notes on 47:15 and 47:17.

48:8–22 In the center of the nation, Ezekiel sees a kind of sacred "federal district" with ample provision for the Temple, its surrounding city, and its functionaries: priests, Levites, and the royal prince. Oddly, although Moses gave no territory to the Levites (only cities, Num 18:20), in Ezekiel's vision, they do receive a tribal territory adjacent the sanctuary.

48:11 the sons of Zadok: See notes on 40:46 and 44:15.

---

[n] Cn: Heb lacks *Hazar-enon*.
[o] Compare Syr: Heb *you shall measure*.
[p] Compare 47:15: Heb *by the side of the way*.
[q] Cn: Heb *and they shall be his*.
[r] Gk Compare verses 2–8: Heb *the east side the west*.
[s] Compare 45:1: Heb *ten*.
[t] One Ms Gk: Heb *of the sons*.

breadth twenty[u] thousand. [14]They shall not sell
or exchange any of it; they shall not alienate this
choice portion of the land, for it is holy to the LORD.
15 "The remainder, five thousand cubits in
breadth and twenty-five thousand in length, shall
be for ordinary use for the city, for dwellings and
for open country. In the midst of it shall be the city;
[16]and these shall be its dimensions: the north side
four thousand five hundred cubits, the south side four
thousand five hundred, the east side four thousand
five hundred, and the west side four thousand five
hundred. [17]And the city shall have open land: on the
north two hundred and fifty cubits, on the south
two hundred and fifty, on the east two hundred
and fifty, and on the west two hundred and fifty.
[18]The remainder of the length alongside the holy
portion shall be ten thousand cubits to the east, and
ten thousand to the west, and it shall be alongside
the holy portion. Its produce shall be food for the
workers of the city. [19]And the workers of the city,
from all the tribes of Israel, shall till it. [20]The whole
portion which you shall set apart shall be twenty-
five thousand cubits square, that is, the holy portion
together with the property of the city.
21 "What remains on both sides of the holy
portion and of the property of the city shall belong to
the prince. Extending from the twenty-five thousand
cubits of the holy portion to the east border, and
westward from the twenty-five thousand cubits to
the west border, parallel to the tribal portions, it
shall belong to the prince. The holy portion with
the sanctuary of the temple in its midst, [22]and the
property of the Levites and the property of the city,[v]
shall be in the midst of that which belongs to the
prince. The portion of the prince shall lie between
the territory of Judah and the territory of Benjamin.
23 "As for the rest of the tribes: from the east
side to the west, Benjamin, one portion. [24]Adjoining
the territory of Benjamin, from the east side to the
west, Simeon, one portion. [25]Adjoining the territory
of Simeon, from the east side to the west, Is'sachar,
one portion. [26]Adjoining the territory of Is'sachar,
from the east side to the west, Zeb'ulun, one portion.
[27]Adjoining the territory of Zeb'ulun, from the east
side to the west, Gad, one portion. [28]And adjoining
the territory of Gad to the south, the boundary
shall run from Ta'mar to the waters of Meribath'-
ka'desh, thence along the Brook of Egypt to the
Great Sea. [29]This is the land which you shall allot as
an inheritance among the tribes of Israel, and these
are their several portions, says the Lord GOD.
30 "These shall be the exits of the city: On
the north side, which is to be four thousand five
hundred cubits by measure, [31]three gates, the gate

48:16: Rev 21:16. **48:31–35:** Rev 21:12–13.

48:14 They shall not sell or exchange: There was a strong opposition in the Mosaic Law to the sale of ancestral property to persons of other families and tribes. The Jubilee was instituted to prevent any permanent alienation of property (Lev 25:8–55).

48:19 workers . . . from all the tribes: The holy city, site of the Temple and the national capital, was not to be the possession of one tribe, but the common possession of all the tribes. The Temple city was a microcosm of the whole nation.

48:20 twenty-five thousand cubits square: There may be numerical symbolism here: twenty-five thousand is fifty times fifty times ten. Fifty is the number of the Jubilee in Israelite tradition (Lev 25:10), associated with restoration, fulfillment of promises, and permanent possession of the holy land. Ten is associated with wholeness and completion (Ten Commandments, Ex 20). Ezekiel's vision is a kind of great Jubilee for Israel, whose central expression is the sacred Temple and its city.

48:22 the portion of the prince: This calls to mind Jerusalem, which lay on the border between the tribal territories of Judah and Benjamin (Josh 15:8, 63; 18:28; Judg 1:8, 21). Historically, Benjamin lay to the north and Judah to the south. In Ezekiel's vision, Judah lies north and Benjamin south!

48:23–28 Tribes located south of the sacred district of the city and Temple. Historically, **Benjamin** and **Simeon** were southern tribes; but **Issachar**, **Zebulun**, and **Gad** formerly had territory near the Sea of Galilee in the north. Ezekiel assigns these tribes new allotments in the territory that once belonged to Judah (and Simeon).

48:30–34 The city has twelve gates, one for each tribe, indicating that each tribe has an equal claim and portion in the city and the Temple. The Temple and city, then, become a kind of sacred microcosm of the nation. • Compare the description of the gates of the heavenly Jerusalem in Rev 21:12–14.

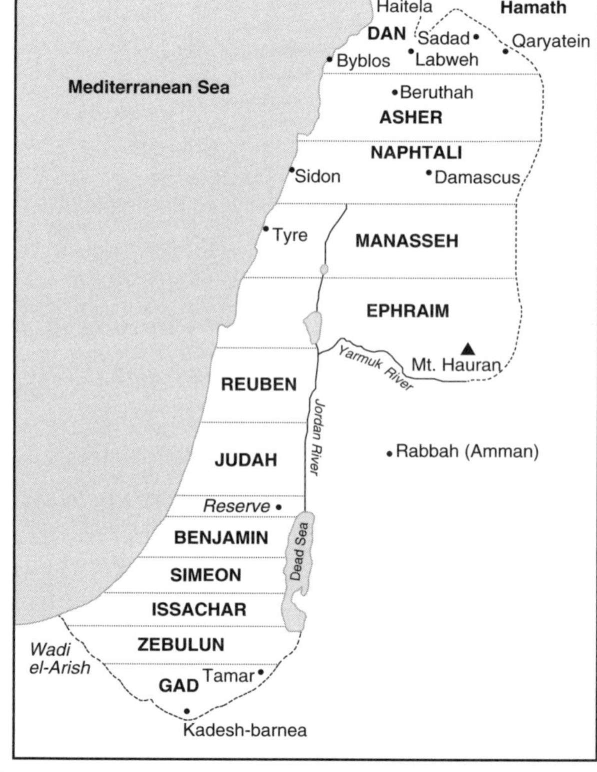

[u]Gk: Heb *ten*.
[v]Cn: Heb *and from the property of the Levites and from the property of the city*.

of Reuben, the gate of Judah, and the gate of Levi,
the gates of the city being named after the tribes
of Israel. 32On the east side, which is to be four
thousand five hundred cubits, three gates, the gate
of Joseph, the gate of Benjamin, and the gate of Dan.
33On the south side, which is to be four thousand
five hundred cubits by measure, three gates, the
gate of Simeon, the gate of Is'sachar, and the gate
of Zeb'ulun. 34On the west side, which is to be
four thousand five hundred cubits, three gates,[w]
the gate of Gad, the gate of Asher, and the gate of
Naph'tali. 35The circumference of the city shall be
eighteen thousand cubits. And the name of the city
henceforth shall be, The LORD is there."

48:35 the name of the city ... The LORD is there": The identity of this visionary city is an enigma. On the one hand, texts such as 20:40 and 34:26 seem to envision the restoration of Jerusalem, referring to it as the "holy mountain" or "hill" of God. On the other hand, the holy city of chaps. 40–48 could not be Jerusalem, because Ezekiel's schematic arrangement of the tribes would place the city and its surrounding precincts farther north than the actual location of Jerusalem in Israel's traditional boundaries. Ezekiel, indeed, sees a city that will fulfill all the functions and significance of Jerusalem of old, but he is not committed to the city being on the same geographical location. This detachment of the holy city from a particular geographical spot enabled the city to be understood in non-geographical terms. • The NT understands the Church, as the Body of Christ (Jn 2:21), to be this new holy city (Heb 12:22–24; Rev 21:2; cf. Eph 5:22–32).

[w] One Ms Gk Syr: Heb *their gates three.*

STUDY QUESTIONS

Ezekiel

Chapter 1

For understanding

1. **1:1.** What is the best explanation for how the prophet specifies the date from which he counts? If that is true, when was the prophet born? What was the typical age for priests to begin their ministry? Where is the river Chebar, and what do we know of it from ancient texts?
2. **1:4–28.** What is Ezekiel's vision about? What is the mobile throne of God borne on four cherubim known as in Judaism? With what are cherubim associated? How many are depicted in the Holy of Holies? What reality represented by the Ark of the Covenant in the Holy of Holies does Ezekiel behold? With what other terms and images is this theophany described? As the God who appeared in those places now shows himself to Ezekiel, how is the cherubim-throne unlike the ark in the Temple, and what locations is it able to visit? What has God's presence come to do?
3. **1:10.** What do the man, the lion, the ox, and the eagle each represent? According to St. Gregory the Great, how do the four creatures denote the four evangelists?
4. **1:15.** What do the wheels on the throne denote? Though they may seem redundant, since cherubim have wings, why does Ezekiel use multiple motifs? What do the wings connote, and what do the wheels connote? Despite what many Israelites thought, where can God's presence move?
5. **1:22.** What does the rare and archaic Hebrew word *raqîaʿ* recall? What message does the creation story marked by Temple-building motifs communicate? What does the firmament "shining like crystal" resemble? As one of the key reference points for interpreting this vision, to whose legacy does mention of Sinai link Ezekiel?

For application

1. **1:1.** What was the date of your most significant religious experience (e.g., your Baptism, Confirmation, conversion)? Why would it be helpful for you occasionally to bring such dates to mind?
2. **1:5–14.** Ezekiel describes the appearance of the four angels who carry the throne of God. How does their appearance differ from the way you envision an angel? According to the notes for these verses, how does the symbolism of their appearance (to Ezekiel) explain what angels as pure spirits are capable of doing?
3. **1:13.** According to the note for this verse, the fire is a sign of God's Spirit. Where else in Scripture is the Spirit's presence indicated by fire?
4. **1:20.** Read the note for this verse. If the spirit of the four living creatures is in the wheels, animating their movement, where might the spirit of a sculptor be? Or the spirit of a writer?

Chapter 2

For understanding

1. **Word Study: Son of Man (2:1).** How can the Hebrew phrase *ben-ʾādām* be translated? Although we are never told the meaning of this title, which appears 93 times in the book, or why the Lord uses it to address Ezekiel, what are two possible explanations for its use? When Jesus calls himself "Son of man", what does he probably intend to evoke? To whom may he also wish to connect himself? How is Jesus Christ like Ezekiel?
2. **2:2.** To what area of theology does Ezekiel make a substantial contribution? What do we note about Ezekiel and the Spirit? What does this represent about mankind?
3. **2:4.** In what way does the call and mission of Moses lie in the background of this passage?
4. **2:10.** Why were scrolls usually inscribed only on the interior? What does this double-sided inscription recall?

For application

1. **2:2.** How does the Holy Spirit enter the soul of the Christian? What does sanctifying grace do to the soul? What is the Christian's role in connection with receiving the Spirit?
2. **2:3.** Note that Ezekiel is sent to preach to his own people, not to pagans. To whom have recent popes sent believers in the New Evangelization? What is "new" in the New Evangelization, and why is it necessary?
3. **2:4–5.** When Jesus says that a prophet is "not without honor except in his own country and in his own house" (Mt 13:57), what does he mean? Why should honor be denied him there?
4. **2:6.** When it comes to sharing the gospel with relatives or friends, what most causes you fear? What do you do when such fears arise? If you give way to fear, such as by keeping silent when you feel you should speak out, how do you face the Lord?

Chapter 3

For understanding

1. **3:3.** To what is Ezekiel's eating of the scrolls analogous? What does it signify? What is the intimate contact with God entailed by being the recipient of divine revelation like, even when the message is severe?
2. **3:12.** How does Ezekiel's call vision conclude? Of what is the sound of the great earthquake that Ezekiel hears reminiscent, and what does it mean?
3. **3:14.** As a key verse for understanding the life and mission of Ezekiel, whose name means "God strengthens", what can the hand of the Lord being strong on the prophet mean?
4. **3:16–21.** For what is Ezekiel responsible? As long as he does so, what benefit will be his?
5. **3:22–27.** How do these verses further specify Ezekiel's initial call?

For application

1. **3:1.** For what does the expression "to devour the Word of God" mean? How hungry are you for that Word? What motivates you to consume it?
2. **3:7.** Read the note for this verse. If every true prophet is rejected by his audience, what is the point of speaking to them? If you know ahead of time that your brother will reject anything religious you say to him, why make the effort?
3. **3:10.** How do you approach the reading of Scripture? As you read and meditate on Scripture, what should you do when you encounter passages that are confusing or hard to understand? For example, how do you deal with the "hard sayings" like God's placement of certain people "under the ban"?
4. **3:17–21.** Who are the watchmen for the Church? What is their responsibility toward the Christian people? As a member of the Body of Christ, how do you participate in that responsibility?

Chapter 4

For understanding

1. **4:1—5:17.** What are sign-acts, which Ezekiel performs in these chapters? What arguably are two sign-acts that Jesus performs?
2. **4:4.** Because, in Israel, directions were taken facing east, which direction was north and which was south? Why, apparently, does the prophet lie on his left side, and again on his right? What may be the significance and origins of the numbers 390 and 40? How does the Greek LXX read? Of what can we at least be certain? How does the principle that one day in the life of a man is equivalent to one year in the life of a nation lie behind the 40 days of the Lord's temptation? If the prophet probably did not lie motionless 24 hours a day, how did he most likely make his point by lying on his side in public?
3. **4:9.** What does the combination of wheat and barley, beans and lentils, millet and spelt make? What were the taste and texture like? In this sign-act, what is Ezekiel prophesying?
4. **4:16.** What language does this prophecy reuse? Due to sin, what is being triggered, and what are being inverted?

For application

1. **4:1–3.** Before the age of computers, how might soldiers strategize an attack against an enemy? In planning a series of plays for a football game, why does the coach have players watch the movement of symbols on a board? Why perform a sign-act if all the prophet has to do is speak the message?
2. **4:4–5.** In modeling the punishment of Israel since its exile began in 722 B.C., Ezekiel, who prophesied around 130 years later, is probably modeling the Northern Kingdom's punishment in exile, lying down in public facing north for an extended period, one day representing one year. What message do you think he is trying to communicate to his fellow exiles about Israel?
3. **4:6–7.** In these verses, Ezekiel turns to face south, representing the siege and destruction of Jerusalem (including Ezekiel's own exile and that of his contemporaries), for a shorter period. Again, what message do you think he is trying to communicate?
4. **4:14.** Compare Ezekiel's complaint with that of Peter in Acts 10:14. What are the similarities, and what are the differences? To whose direction are both responding?

Chapter 5

For understanding

1. **5:1–17.** In this sign-act, which of the various fates that await the inhabitants of Jerusalem does Ezekiel dramatize in outlandish fashion? What will happen to the very small number who survive?
2. **5:1.** What did the sword symbolize? On whom was shaving sometimes imposed? What does the hair represent?
3. **5:2.** What does "a third part" mean?
4. **5:10.** Where is the idea found that parents will be reduced to eating their children to stay alive in siege conditions? Who is the only one who mentions the idea of children eating their own parents?

For application

1. **5:5–8.** Every parent must discipline children who rebel against parental authority. What is the probable difference in quality between the discipline given a child who submits readily and that given to one who stubbornly resists discipline?
2. **5:13.** Read literally, what picture does this verse draw of God's character? By anthropomorphizing God in this way, what point is Ezekiel trying to make about God's judgment on Jerusalem? What is God's actual regard for Jerusalem?
3. **5:14–17.** By using capital punishment as a deterrent, what message do states hope to send potential offenders? What message should the fate of Jerusalem send to the nations around Judah in these verses?

Chapter 6

For understanding

1. **6:3.** In ancient Near Eastern religion, with what were all notable geographic features like mountains and hills associated? What were their deities called upon to do? Here, what creative adaptation of this motif does Ezekiel make?
2. **6:13.** To what is "upon every high hill ... under every green tree" a shorthand reference?
3. **6:14.** What does the expression "from the wilderness to Riblah" mean? To which wilderness area is this a reference? Where is Riblah?

For application

1. **6:3.** In prophesying against the mountain shrines of Israel, why does Ezekiel begin the word of the Lord with "Behold, I, even I, ..."? What is another way of emphasizing the same thing?

2. **6:5.** Read the note for this verse. In the modern era, what act of desecration might make a sacred space unclean and unsuitable for worship? How would a desecrated site be repaired so that the space is once again usable for worship?
3. **6:9.** Ezekiel speaks here of God breaking "wanton hearts" and blinding eyes that stray after idols. What is the Lord's purpose in such breaking and blinding? According to v. 17 of Ps 51, what kind of heart is acceptable to God?

Chapter 7

For understanding

1. **7:1–27.** What is hard to know about the structure of this chapter? Despite that, what is its obvious message?
2. **7:10.** If the literal translation is "the staff has blossomed", to what is it a reference? If the blossoming of Aaron's staff was an omen of blessing, what is the blossoming staff now? What does Ezekiel frequently do with positive images and language from the Pentateuch?
3. **7:13.** What did the Jubilee Year laws of Lev 25:10–55 stipulate? In the coming destruction, what will happen to all the functions of Israelite society?
4. **7:26.** In the face of the failure of leadership in Israel, what were prophets, priests, and elders supposed to do?

For application

1. **7:2.** What does the "four corners of the land" mean? How much of the "four corners" of the United States would a disaster like a pandemic affect?
2. **7:4.** The expression "Then you will know that I am the Lord" appears often in Ezekiel. In what contexts does it usually appear? What seems to be its rhetorical purpose?
3. **7:5–7.** Note how the idea of an end or a doom coming is repeated here and in the following verses. To the hearer of these words, what effect is the repetition supposed to have? Have you ever faced bad situations from which there seemed to be no escape? If so, what were they?
4. **7:10–11.** When a person dabbles in potentially addictive activities, how quickly can they blossom into poisonous fruit? What are some examples? What are some consequences?

Chapter 8

For understanding

1. **8:1.** What is probably the date given in this verse? What does the formal recording of the date signal? In this case, what does it introduce? Despite the predictions that his message would be ignored or rejected, how did Ezekiel's contemporaries regard him?
2. **8:3.** Though physically in Babylon, where is Ezekiel transported in a visionary state? What is the "image of jealousy"? To what image may it be similar?
3. **8:11.** Of how many elders was it traditional for Israel's national ruling council to be composed? What is the meaning regarding the entire leadership of Israel? Who is Ja-azaniah the son of Shaphan? Who was Shaphan?
4. **8:16.** What is the importance of the area between the porch and the altar? Why does Ezekiel have a penchant for the number 25? What was the significance of the 25 men having their backs to the Temple of the Lord? Since they were facing east, what did that mean they were doing? What was the importance of the sun to all ancient Near Eastern societies? Though Manasseh had promoted the sun-cult within Israel, where was it explicitly forbidden?

For application

1. **8:3.** In this verse, who is being provoked to jealousy? Why would God be jealous of an idol? If as a committed believer you were to see a statue of a demon in the sanctuary of a cathedral, what word would best describe your reaction?
2. **8:6.** While governments hostile to religion try to drive God from his sanctuary, who is making that effort in this verse? How might certain Christians, either deliberately or in effect, drive God from his churches?
3. **8:12.** Read the note for this verse. Compare this image with that of a Christian home with images of Jesus and Mary together with a statue of Buddha and a yoga mat near stands of burning incense. What conclusions about the owners' Christian faith might you draw?
4. **8:17.** Read the note for this verse. What are some examples of gestures or physical positions that are intended to convey insult to another person or group? What would cause you to make such a gesture? Why is this so offensive to God?

Chapter 9

For understanding

1. **9:2.** Who are the six men in this verse? What is the significance of the number six in the Bible? Alternatively, if the angelic scribe is included with the six, what does the new total of seven indicate? What was the significance of the linen and the writing case? Where is there an association of priests with angels? As ministers of worship, how were the priests of Israel regarded?
2. **9:4.** What letter of the Hebrew alphabet was the man in linen to put on foreheads? In the old Hebrew script used prior to the Babylonian Exile, how was it written? How is it represented in the Latin capital *T* and lowercase *t*? What significance did early Christian commentators see in the cross on the forehead? According to St. Horsiesi, how should we make the sign of the cross?
3. **9:6.** How does this vision resemble the original Passover? Only now, who is it that falls under judgment?

For application

1. **9:2.** The note for this verse says that six is a number "of ill omen" in the Bible. In our culture, what is a number of ill omen? What does it mean for us?

2. **9:4.** Why do Christians make the sign of the cross? When do you sign your forehead with that sign or draw it on the foreheads of others? How often do you make the larger sign of the cross (forehead, chest, one shoulder, other shoulder)? Aside from being a ritual gesture, what does the sign mean to you?
3. **9:6.** Scripture says that judgment begins with the house of God (1 Pet 4:17). Why there? Should such judgment be welcomed or feared?

Chapter 10

For understanding

1. **10:2.** What is assumed that is burning on an altar? How was this represented in the Jerusalem Temple?
2. **10:14.** Curiously, though the description of faces from 1:10 is repeated, with what is only the face of the ox (or bull) replaced here? Though the reason for this is obscure, from v. 10:22, what do we see that the prophet's intention was?
3. **10:18.** What is Ezekiel witnessing about God's presence? Of what is this an ominous sign?

For application

1. **10:2.** As in Rev 8:5, where an angel takes live coals from a censer and throws them on the earth, here the man clothed in linen takes coals from the altar of incense and scatters them over the city. What seems to be the purpose in both instances?
2. **10:4.** What does the cloud that filled the house represent? In Catholic churches, what does the burning of a sanctuary lamp represent?
3. **10:18–19.** The note for this verse says that the Lord's departure from the Temple is an omen of its impending destruction. What were some of the ominous details Jesus gave about the destruction of the Second Temple (Mk 13:5ff.; Mt 24:4ff.)?

Chapter 11

For understanding

1. **11:3.** What is the probable meaning of "the time is not near to build houses"? What does "this city is the caldron, and we are the flesh" mean?
2. **11:7.** How does God change what the wealthy meant as a positive metaphor? Although the wealthy of the city thought they would be as happy in Jerusalem as chunks of meat cozily simmering in a stew, what will happen to them?
3. **11:16.** What is a major theme of Ezekiel about God's relationship with Israel? Who will repopulate Judah and Jerusalem, and when? From whom does Jesus himself descend?
4. **11:23.** What mountain on the east side of Jerusalem is meant here? What does this vision of Ezekiel help explain about this mountain? From which direction will God reenter the Temple?

For application

1. **11:2–3.** What is an opportunist? According to the note for v. 3, how are the figures of Ja-azaniah and Pelatiah behaving as opportunists? Have you ever felt that someone else's misfortune was an advantage for you? How did you take advantage of the opportunity?
2. **11:12.** Do the "ordinances of the nations that are round about you" have any good moral quality to them? What are some examples? If that is the case, what is the problem with "walking according to" those ordinances? How do they fall short of the Lord's ordinances?
3. **11:17–20.** Americans believe in the benefit of "second chances". Has the Lord ever granted you a "second chance" in life? If so, has it proven to be illusory or beneficial? If the latter, in what way has it improved your life, especially with the Lord?
4. **11:25.** Read this verse carefully. Do you think Ezekiel's message to the exiles was good or bad news for them? Why do you think so?

Chapter 12

For understanding

1. **12:4.** How would men go into exile? In the ancient Near East, why were exiles typically taken away naked? This practice was so common that the Hebrew verb "to exile [someone]" is actually a form of what verb?
2. **12:12.** Who is the prince referred to here? Since many Judeans did not recognize a nephew-to-uncle succession imposed by a foreign conqueror as legitimate, whom did they continue to regard as heads of the royal house?
3. **12:22.** What does the proverb "the days grow long, and every vision comes to nothing" mean? By what was the proverb probably inspired?
4. **12:27.** Since it was not uncommon for prophets to speak of the distant future, how did they speak about the Messiah? But in this instance, when would Ezekiel's prophecies of doom be fulfilled?

For application

1. **12:2.** Jesus expected his disciples to perceive what they saw and understand what they heard, and he complained when they seemed obtuse (e.g., Mk 8:16–18). When you read a Scripture passage and it comes alive, do you notice how often you have read it before without insight? As you examine your spiritual experience, what patterns of grace seem to be developing in it?
2. **12:3, 7.** If you have ever played the game of charades, how good are you at guessing the meaning of the mime? How good are you at solving riddles? In prayer, how often do you ask for the eyes to see and understand the direction in which the Lord is leading your life?
3. **12:16.** Occasionally, someone confined to prison will admit that his punishment is deserved and even that it may have been the best thing that happened to him. Upon reflection, has a personal setback that changed your circumstances ever proven a benefit for you? Did it in any way change your relationship with the Lord?
4. **12:25.** According to 2 Pet 3:7–10, why does the promised day of final judgment seem to be delayed? When does he say it will happen? What is your expectation for how soon that day is likely to come?

Chapter 13

For understanding

1. **13:3.** Because prophets could exercise great public influence, what type of person was it natural that the role should attract? What type of prophecy was roundly criticized by the biblical prophets?
2. **13:10.** To what does "when the people build a wall, these prophets daub it with whitewash" probably refer? What did the false prophets add to this foolish endeavor?
3. **13:18.** What were the women who sewed magic bands actually doing? Apparently, what kind of practice was it?
4. **13:19.** What does it seem that the women who made the "magic" articles did with them? What is not clear about what happened to persons who used these bands?

For application

1. **13:2.** The charism of prophecy is still active in the Church, though prophetic utterances are considered private revelation. According to St. Paul (1 Cor 14:3–5), what is the purpose of this charism? How would the genuineness of this charism be tested?
2. **13:10.** Why did Jesus pronounce woes on the scribes and Pharisees for being "like whitewashed tombs" (Mt 23:27)? Upon whom would he hurl these maledictions today?
3. **13:18f.** Why does the Church forbid occult activity, such as using magic charms, casting spells, and divination? What are the dangers of even playing with it? How does occult activity draw its practitioner away from the Lord?

Chapter 14

For understanding

1. **14:9.** What does Ezekiel use startlingly direct language to emphasize? What shape does Rom 1:18–32 reveal that God's "wrath" will take? So what happens to the false prophets, who pursue prophecy as a means to make a living rather than a true calling from God?
2. **14:10.** Who were inquirers? What were both prophet and inquirer seeking? How did they thus end up?
3. **14:12–23.** In this oracle, what does God insist about three great heroes of faith? What is the background here? Although Ezekiel mentions fewer righteous than ten—just three—how do they make up for numbers?
4. **14:14.** For what are Noah, Daniel, and Job renowned? Why cannot even great saints save Israel? While Noah and Job were famous heroes of faith from Israel's hoary past, who was Daniel? What do some commentators argue about a contemporary such as Daniel, and with whom do they seek to identify him? What does it seem unlikely that Ezekiel's readership could have been expected to recognize?

For application

1. **14:3.** As a consultant, would you agree to meet with clients who you knew would reject your advice? If you did agree to meet with them, what would you tell them? How likely is it that the prayer of one with a divided heart will be answered?
2. **14:6.** Why does repentance always call for a turning away from something? If the house of Israel is to turn away from its idols, to what will the turning lead? How does Ezekiel's message to the house of Israel apply to the Church today?
3. **14:12–20.** The Catholic Church has had a succession of saintly popes, including St. John XXIII, St. Paul VI, and St. John Paul II. Why, despite their holiness and their teaching, is the Church still embroiled in crisis after crisis? What will it take for things to change?
4. **14:22–23.** How does the conversion of sinners or the incorporation into the Church of separated Christians comfort those already in the Church? How does the enthusiasm for their new faith encourage the faithful who have never left the Church?

Chapter 15

For understanding

1. **15:2.** Where can the metaphor of Israel as a cultivated vine be found in Scripture? How does Ezekiel invert this traditional image?

For application

1. **15:2–3.** Compare these verses with Jesus' parable about salt that has lost its taste (Lk 14:34–35). What point do Ezekiel and Jesus both want their hearers to get?
2. **15:6–8.** By telling the exiles already in Babylon about the final destruction of Jerusalem, what does Ezekiel hope the exiles will come to understand? If you were granted a vision of hell such as visionaries sometimes are, what would you do with it?

Chapter 16

For understanding

1. **16:1–63.** What does Ezekiel provide in these verses? Because both allegories are so unrelenting and graphic, what did they provoke ancient rabbis to do? Alongside what other texts of Scripture do these passages of Ezekiel take their place, and what theological paradigm do they establish? How do the repercussions continue to be felt in the New Testament?
2. **16:3.** While Jerusalem originally was a city of no consequence to the Israelites, what happened after David conquered it and made it his capital? How quickly was Jerusalem as a Canaanite enclave conquered? Who were the previous inhabitants? What wordplay on a traditional Israelite recitation of faith occurs here? Who were the Arameans? Who were the Amorites? What is Ezekiel again emphasizing? What do some theorize about the Jebusites who inhabited pre-Davidic Jerusalem? To what woman might there be a reference here?

3. **16:46.** Of what did the city of Samaria become the capital? What were smaller villages in the region around a large city considered to be? What was Sodom, and where was it? When was this notoriously wicked city destroyed by divine judgment? With what is its location probably to be identified? While Ezekiel is being very provocative by identifying Jerusalem with Sodom, who else had already done so?
4. **16:60.** If Ezekiel is maintaining a consistent frame of reference, then about which covenant is he talking here? However, if he is shifting the frame and understanding Jerusalem as the whole nation by metonymy, which covenant is perhaps in view? What expression translates the Hebrew *berît ʿôlam*? While Jeremiah describes it as a "new covenant", what terms does Ezekiel prefer?

For application

1. **16:6–14.** According to this parable, what seems to be God's motivation for choosing to rescue Israel? What benefits did he lavish on it? Of all the people on the earth, what is his motive for choosing you, and how has his choice benefited you?
2. **16:15.** Why is beauty sometimes regarded as a curse? How may beautiful persons be tempted to take advantage of their beauty, as do others who want to exploit it? How can a beautiful man or woman protect personal integrity and retain virtue?
3. **16:20–22.** The note for v. 21 alludes to the modern abortion movement. Ancient child sacrifices were offered to gain favor from the gods. To what gods are our unborn children being sacrificed?
4. **16:60.** All baptized Christians are part of the "everlasting covenant" of which Ezekiel speaks. Over the last 2,000 years, how faithful have Christians been to that covenant? Although God is always faithful to his covenant (2 Tim 2:13) and the gates of hell will not prevail over the Church (Mt 16:18), what is her prognosis in this age of defections from doctrine and discipline?

Chapter 17

For understanding

1. **17:3.** Who is the "great eagle" in this verse? What did he do?
2. **17:4.** Who are the topmost of the cedar's young twigs? What is the "land of trade" and the "city of merchants"?
3. **17:11–21.** What events do these verses describe?
4. **17:21.** In the following allegorical messianic prophecy, what will God choose to do and establish? When does Jesus likely allude to this prophecy?

For application

1. **17:1–2.** Why does the Lord speak through his prophets to his people in riddles, allegories, and parables? Why not come out and say directly what he means? From a rhetorical standpoint, what is the advantage for the audience in such an approach?
2. **17:13–14.** In Nebuchadnezzar's policy of removing the rightful king and all the chief men of Israel to Babylon, what hope did Ezekiel have about what God might have in store for the kingdom of Judah? In humbling our pride through adversity, what good does God have in mind for us?
3. **17:24.** Compare this verse with Mary's Magnificat (Lk 1:46–55). How does the Lord bring low the high tree and make high the low tree and dry the green tree to make the dry tree flourish? Has he ever done so with you? And if so, in what way?

Chapter 18

For understanding

1. **18:2.** What is the meaning of the proverb quoted in this verse? What kind of theological fatalism do Ezekiel's contemporaries (wrongly) embrace?
2. **18:6.** According to Mosaic Law, when was a woman ritually unclean? Because intercourse during this time was uncomfortable for the wife and unable to result in conception, what was the main reason for engaging in it? Thus, what made intercourse at that time more than a ritual violation?
3. **18:23.** What misconception entertained by many in ancient and modern times does the prophet correct? What does he say, rather, about the punishment of the wicked? As the Guardian of perfect justice, what can God not simply overlook?
4. **18:25.** What principle does Ezekiel uphold and develop? How should the idea that God "[visits] the iniquity of the fathers upon the children to the third and fourth generation of those who hate me" be understood?

For application

1. **18:10–13.** What qualms of conscience can afflict the parent of a criminal or a psychopath, even though the parent has tried to raise the child well? How is the parent likely to be viewed in the community? How might comfort be given to such a parent?
2. **18:14–17.** Adult children of alcoholics often make use of twelve-step groups intended just for them. If they are not alcoholics themselves, what is their need for such groups? What support do they hope to gain?
3. **18:25–29.** Have moderns actually improved over the ancients in their attitudes toward the salvation of the unjust? What would they think of a Hitler or a Stalin who actually made a valid confession of sins before he died? How does Jesus' parable of the Landowner and the Workers in the Vineyard (Mt 20:1ff.) apply here?
4. **18:31.** How does one get himself "a new heart and a new spirit"? While basic repentance in the form of turning from evil is necessary, what else is needed?

Chapter 19

For understanding

1. **19:1.** What is a "lamentation" (Heb., *qînah*)? In this allegorical lamentation, what do the "lioness" and the "young lions" represent?

2. **19:5.** What kind of symbol does this second young lion also seem to be?
3. **19:10.** To what different allegory does the prophet abruptly shift? Where else in Scripture does the image of either Israel or the royal house as a vine or vineyard occur?
4. **19:13.** Of what royal house does Ezekiel speak? What do archaeological records indicate regarding the treatment of Jehoiachin and his sons?

For application

1. **19:2.** Dynasties and nations are often represented by symbolic animals. What is the symbolic animal for the United States? What do the olive branch and the arrows that it holds represent? If Jesus is the Son of David, how is he represented as an animal in the Book of Revelation?
2. **19:3–4, 6.** The expression "young lion" can refer not only to a person but to an attitude he has. What attitude do these verses suggest that the "young lions" had?
3. **19:12.** Scripture contains around 17 references to an east wind, one that blows from east to west, often associated with destruction. What are some destructive winds that plague the United States? What responses do they occasion in people who experience them?

Chapter 20

For understanding

1. **20:7.** According to Ezekiel, what did God exhort Israelites to abandon while they were still in Egypt, and how did they respond? While this is not explicitly recorded in the Book of Exodus, what does the Book of Joshua imply that the Israelites did, despite the miracles of the Exodus?
2. **20:25.** What statutes are referred to here? In what sense were the statutes of Deuteronomy "not good"? In what sense were they "ordinances by which they could not have life"?
3. **20:26.** Since the phrase "by fire" is not in the Hebrew, what misunderstanding does its inclusion in the RSV2CE reflect? What first-born are referred to? Prior to the laws of Deuteronomy, what were the Israelites required to offer? How did Deuteronomy relax this requirement? What does Ezekiel, a devout priest sensitive to the meaning of the liturgy, recognize?
4. **Topical Essay: What Laws Were Not Good?** As a difficult passage of Scripture that has long puzzled scholars, what is a literal translation of Ezek 20:25–26? What does contemporary scholarship often infer from these verses, a disturbing interpretation that is not supported by the text? To be sure, while wicked Israelites did sacrifice their children to the Ammonite god Molech, to the Canaanite god Baal, and others as well, what evidence is lacking about first-born children? If, then, Ezek 20:25–26 is not about child sacrifice, what are these verses talking about? How would a careful reading of the Pentateuch explain why Ezekiel describes Deuteronomy in this way?
5. **20:34.** In the original Exodus, when God brought his people out of Egypt into the desert of Sinai, what did his covenant with them involve? In the future, when God will again bring Israel out of the lands where they sojourn, what will he do with them?

For application

1. **20:7.** What are some of the "detestable things your eyes feast on"? What effects do they have on you? What has the Holy Spirit led you to cast away so as to be free to seek him?
2. **20:8–9, 13b–14, 21b–22.** What ideas are repeated here in almost the same words? What is God's motive for sparing his people? How do such stories of repeated rebellion and redemption reflect the experiences of everyday life with the Lord?
3. **20:26.** The note for this verse explains how Deuteronomy relaxed certain requirements of Exodus, Leviticus, and Numbers. How has the Catholic Church relaxed certain disciplinary requirements that were in force a hundred years ago (e.g., fasting and penitential obligations)? Why would rules like these be relaxed in the first place? Why is it not always good to relax disciplinary regulations?
4. **20:43.** What is the "Jesus Prayer"? Why should a person eager to know the Lord recite it?

Chapter 21

For understanding

1. **21:10.** What is the rod? How were criminals punished for non-capital crimes? Because Israel has not repented in response to the moderate punishments God has sent, but rather has increased its crimes, what becomes its punishment?
2. **21:19.** To what does the expression "two ways for the sword" refer? Of what was Ammon the center? Which modern capital is built over ancient Ammon?
3. **21:21.** As a form of ancient divination, how were arrows shaken? What were the teraphim? What was inspecting the livers of sacrificed animals called in the classical world? For what were the marked clay models of livers unearthed by archaeologists used?
4. **21:27.** In the proclamation "a ruin, ruin, ruin I will make it", to what does the pronoun "it" refer? What will happen to any visible signs of the royal house of David? Speaking later of "my servant David" who is to come, what does Ezekiel mean, and what does this explain about the Gospels of Matthew and Luke?

For application

1. **21:6–7.** Have you ever joined in public grief over a national disaster? If so, how did you express this grief, and how was it shared publicly? What was the effect on public morale after the disaster? What religious effect, if any, resulted from it?
2. **21:10.** If you are a parent, what is your approach to disciplining your children? How does it change as they grow older? What do you do if an older child refuses to cooperate and more severe punishments do not work?

3. **21:21.** What forms of divination are used in our culture today? How reliable are they? Why do Scripture and the Church forbid using occult means to determine the future?

Chapter 22

For understanding

1. **22:7–12.** What violations of the Mosaic Law does this representative list include?
2. **22:12.** As what part of speech does the Hebrew word translated here "extortion" occur in the prohibitions of Leviticus and Deuteronomy? Why is forgetting God the greatest and most fundamental sin?
3. **22:26.** About what two axes of distinction on which the Israelite ritual system was based were priests obliged to teach the people? Where does the Book of Leviticus teach these distinctions?
4. **22:30.** When attacking armies would breach (break down) the defensive walls, how would heroic defenders prevent the enemy from entering the city? Although God is coming against Jerusalem in judgment, whom does he seek, and whom does he find? When did Moses perform this intercessory role?

For application

1. **22:7.** Read the note for vv. 7–12. How many of these offenses are committed in our secular culture today? Which moral offenses now rampant in our culture are not listed there?
2. **22:12.** When do you think that collecting interest on a loan can become sinful (cf. CCC 2443–49)? The note for this verse mentions a violation of the first Great Commandment, love of God (Deut 6:5). What about the second "commandment like it", love of neighbor (Lev 19:18)?
3. **22:13.** When we express disapproval at the behavior of another, what prevents our disapproval from becoming judgmentalism? In other words, what may we judge about another person, and what are we forbidden from judging?
4. **22:26.** In catechesis, when should children begin learning the difference between holy and common things and how to handle holy things with respect? For example, how should one handle a Bible (as opposed to an ordinary book), and what should be done with it when it is no longer usable?

Chapter 23

For understanding

1. **23:1–49.** Of what is this chapter a graphic allegory? How is Ezekiel's mission like that of the Catholic author Flannery O'Connor? How is this chapter closely connected to chap. 16? How might Ezekiel's picture of Samaria and Jerusalem as sisters who commit outrageous sexual sins be influenced by the narrative of the two daughters of Lot?
2. **23:4.** How can the name Oholah be understood, and how does that relate to Samaria? How can the name Oholibah be understood, and to what does it refer?
3. **23:23.** Who were Pekod and Shoa and Koa? To whom do the Assyrians mentioned here probably refer?
4. **23:42.** What is the problem with the Hebrew of this verse? Nonetheless, what is the clear general sense?

For application

1. **23:1–4.** The prophets often speak of rebellion against God in terms of sexual sins like fornication and adultery, but nowhere as explicitly as in this chapter. What does that comparison say about the seriousness of these sexual sins? What does the casual attitude to these sins in our culture say about our attitude toward God?
2. **23:8.** What does this verse suggest about the religious condition of Israel before Moses led the nation out of Egypt? Whose sons were Ephraim and Manasseh, and who was their mother (Gen 41:50–52)?
3. **23:31.** How would you render this verse in plain language? In Ezekiel's mind, what has the Southern Kingdom of Judah learned from the fate of the Northern Kingdom of Israel? What then becomes Judah's fate? How often do nations actually apply the lessons of history to their own destinies?

Chapter 24

For understanding

1. **24:7.** According to Mosaic Law, what was supposed to happen to the blood of animals? How did this apply to the inhabitants of Jerusalem?
2. **24:15.** Who was the delight of Ezekiel's eyes?
3. **24:17.** What did ancient mourning rituals include? What would friends and relatives bring? What is God commanding Ezekiel not to do?
4. **24:27.** What was imposed on Ezekiel at the beginning of his ministry? When will his inability to speak be removed?

For application

1. **24:2.** Of which dates marking disasters do you most readily think? Why do these dates stick in your memory? Why do you think the Lord would want Ezekiel to write down this particular date? What lesson is to be learned from it?
2. **24:7.** According to Lev 17:14, anyone who consumes the blood of slaughtered animals is to be cut off from the people. How does that prohibition explain the reaction of Jesus' disciples at being told to drink his blood (Jn 6:53)?
3. **24:15–18.** In our culture, what is considered appropriate behavior and dress for mourning or grieving? What might be considered inappropriate? What message might a person be sending who dresses and acts inappropriately upon the death of a spouse?
4. **24:27.** Compare Ezekiel's release from dumbness with that of Zechariah's, father of John the Baptist (Lk 1:64). Why was dumbness imposed on each in the first place (Ezek 3:25–27; Lk 1:20), and what lessons were Zechariah and Ezekiel's Israelites to learn from it?

Chapter 25

For understanding

1. **25:1–32.** Between the announcement of the siege of Jerusalem in chap. 24 and the announcement of the fall of Jerusalem in chap. 33, against whom are Ezekiel's oracles directed? When may these oracles have been revealed to Ezekiel, or else why have they been gathered together? How does their development move?
2. **25:2.** What was Ammon, and what were its traditional boundaries? From whom did the Ammonites descend? What was their relationship with Israel like? Who was the Ammonite god, and for what was he infamous?
3. **25:8.** What territory did Ammon's sister nation Moab occupy? From whom were the Moabites descended? What was Moab's relationship with Israel like? Who was their god, and who also worshiped him?
4. **25:9.** What are Beth-jeshimoth, Baal-meon, and Kiriathaim? According to the famous *Mesha Stele* (also called the Moabite Stone), when did Mesha take them over? For what was the region of these towns desirable?

For application

1. **25:3.** In Scripture, the exclamation "Aha!" is usually intended for ridicule. What exclamations do we use for the same purpose? Toward whom in the Gospels is this exclamation used, and by whom (Mk 15:29)?
2. **25:6.** At a sporting event, what do applause and stamping of feet signify? How do modern nations express rejoicing at the defeat of an enemy? Over whose defeat should Christians rejoice?
3. **25:8.** Why is Moab's judgment about Judah so offensive to God? Against whom is it ultimately an attack? Why is it wrong to allege that Christianity is no different from other world religions?
4. **25:15.** What is the "law of retaliation"? What is its purpose? How does the Philistines' motive for retaliation, as described in this verse, violate the intent of the "law of retaliation"? What attitude toward getting revenge should replace the "law of retaliation" in Christian life?

Chapter 26

For understanding

1. **26:2.** What function did the port city of Tyre on the southern Lebanese coast serve? Though Tyre enjoyed friendly relations with Israel under David and Solomon, how did that relationship change by the time Jerusalem fell to Nebuchadnezzar in 586 B.C.? What does Tyre's name mean, and to what does it refer? Who besieged the city for 13 years, and who captured and destroyed it? What did Tyre probably hope to do?
2. **26:7.** Though Tyre had become a vassal state of Babylon in 604 B.C., what was it constantly attempting to do? What happened when Nebuchadnezzar arrived? Although ancient sources are unclear, how does the siege seem to have ended?

For application

1. **26:2.** What are some ways modern businesses maneuver to eliminate the competition? Why do some governments try to break up monopolies? Why is it difficult for governments to exercise control over international corporations?
2. **26:7.** Why was Nebuchadrezzar called "king of kings"? What does it mean to call Jesus "king of kings"?

Chapter 27

For understanding

1. **27:2.** What pattern does Ezekiel follow in dealing with Tyre? In both cases, what does he do?
2. **27:8.** What was Sidon? Though Sidon was actually the mother city of Tyre, what happened to its wealth and trade? What was Arvad? What was Zemer?
3. **27:9.** For what city was Gebal another name? For what was it famous, and why was the city named with the Greek word for "book"?
4. **27:22.** What was Sheba? Though the location of Raamah is unknown, with what is it always associated?

For application

1. **27:3–24.** Compare the description of Tyre in these verses with that of "Babylon" in Rev 18. How are the descriptions similar? Which modern cities do you think could make the same claims about their beauty and vitality as these two?
2. **27:12–24.** What is Tyre's main role in all this commerce? If there is nothing necessarily wrong with getting rich as a distribution center for merchandise of all kinds, what sins of Tyre does Ezekiel see behind its downfall (see 26:2; 27:3)? Why does the middleman always seem to grow richer than the original producer?
3. **27:25–36.** Now compare the lament over the destruction of Tyre and "Babylon" in terms of their similarities and what their destruction encompasses. If modern cities or corporate enterprises were to be destroyed in a similar fashion, what kind of lament would our culture raise over them?

Chapter 28

For understanding

1. **28:1–10.** For whom is the oracle against Tyre (chap. 26) and the lament for its people (chap. 27) and the following oracle and lament offered? How has the Christian tradition understood and reflected on the blasphemous things the king of Tyre is described as saying and doing?
2. **28:11–19.** How is the king of Tyre described in this lamentation? What has this passage been understood to reflect? Of what is the devil the author and father? According to St. Cyril of Alexandria, how did he go from being a high angel and God's good servant to becoming Satan, meaning "adversary"?

3. **28:13.** If this is one of only two passages in the Bible that discuss Eden explicitly, what is the other? With what are precious gemstones associated? To what are Ezekiel's list of precious gemstones comparable? With what fact may the sanctuary symbolism be connected?
4. **28:24.** Of whose tribal territory was Sidon a part? Where, relative to Sidon, did Israelites dwell, and what was their relationship with Sidon like during the united monarchy? How did it change afterward?

For application

1. **28:4.** What kind of wisdom does the king of Tyre claim to have, and to what is it limited? What is the kind of wisdom that Scripture urges all mankind to acquire? What are some differences between the two kinds?
2. **28:13.** Read the note for this verse. Which precious stones can you think of that our culture prizes but are not mentioned here? For what do we use them? Although stones such as diamonds do not have the religious symbolism of those Ezekiel lists, what value might they add to our worship?
3. **28:14–16.** The note for v. 14 compares the king of Tyre with the fallen angels. How do these verses describe the goodness of the angels and their fall? How does Jesus refer to the nature of the devil (Jn 8:44)? According to Wis 2:24, what sin of the devil brought death into the world?
4. **28:24.** According to Num 33:55, why would Sidon become a thorn in Israel's side? What happens to those who aspire to holiness if they retain any affection for even the slightest sin?

Chapter 29

For understanding

1. **29:3.** Who was the king of Egypt, and when did he reign? An unpopular and unsuccessful Pharaoh, what happened to his kingship? What is the great dragon that lies in streams?
2. **29:6.** What were Nile reeds like? How does that apply to help from Egypt?
3. **29:10.** What does the expression "Migdol to Syene" mean? What does Migdol mean, and what does it probably indicate? Where is Syene? What is Ethiopia called in Hebrew? Known in classical literature as Nubia, what territory did this ancient, powerful African nation occupy?
4. **29:17.** What does the oracle delivered on April 26, 571 B.C., appear to be, and what did it predict? Why is it probably included here rather than immediately after the Tyrian oracles? Although Nebuchadnezzar did besiege the city and apparently the king of Tyre finally submitted to Babylonian rule, how did the outcome match Ezekiel's description? For what would it have to wait?

For application

1. **29:3.** Assuming Pharaoh is not claiming to have created the Nile, what is he claiming by saying "I made it"? In certain modern corporations, who are some executives who turned their corporations from failure to success? What can they claim to have made?
2. **29:6–7.** Has there been a time when you placed your trust in someone whom you regarded as strong, smart, or competent, and that person failed you? If so, what did the failure of support cost you? What was your relation with that person afterward? What, if any, consequence befell that person?
3. **29:10–12.** What are the causes of some of the major nuclear disasters, such as the Fukushima Daiichi meltdown, that have occurred over the last 50 years? What happened to the habitable areas around them? How should Christians regard the role of the divine will in such cases?
4. **29:21.** In Scripture, what does the horn symbolize? What strength for Israel does Ezekiel see springing up for it? What gives strength to Christians?

Chapter 30

For understanding

1. **30:9.** What did the Nubian Pharaohs who ruled during the 25th Pharaonic Dynasty (ca. 744–656 B.C.) accomplish in Egypt? After what event is Ezekiel writing? What association is still fresh in cultural memory?
2. **30:13.** Within 50 years of Ezekiel's writing, what happened to Egypt? Which dynasties or governors would rule Egypt for the rest of its existence? Who are the majority of the population of modern Egypt? Who are the actual descendants of the ancient Egyptians?
3. **30:15.** Where is Pelusium? Famed for its flax and beer, of what did Pelusium bear the brunt throughout its history? What is its name in Hebrew?
4. **30:20.** Of what does the formal date announcement of April 29, 587 B.C., mark the beginning? Around this time, what did Pharaoh Hophra (Apries) do, and what did the event provoke?

For application

1. **30:3.** What is the "day of the LORD" for us? How near does the New Testament say that is? How soon is "soon"?
2. **30:9.** Look up the word *catastrophe* in a dictionary. What does the word have to do with drama? Is the meaning always negative? What catastrophe awaits your life, assuming you follow the will of God for it?
3. **30:21.** Read the note for this verse. What are some other biblical metaphors for strength? What metaphors do we use to refer to it?
4. **30:24.** According to Ezekiel, how was the balance of power shifting in the ancient Near East, and in whose favor? In modern times, which countries are striving most for the balance of power in the world? How is this balance shifting? Where does the hand of the Lord seem to be in all this?

Chapter 31

For understanding

1. **31:3.** For what were the moist climate and high elevations of mountainous Lebanon famed?
2. **31:8.** What is the garden of God? What are plane trees? To whom does Ezekiel attribute Satanic pride as he did to the king of Tyre? Whom are both described as trying to rival, and what happens to them as a result?
3. **31:18.** How did the Egyptians, like most ancient Near Eastern peoples, regard circumcision, and what did they think of uncircumcision?

For application

1. **31:3–9.** Ezekiel compares the Egyptian Pharaoh to the qualities of a cedar of Lebanon. What tree in our land most represents what the cedar represents? How might the metaphor apply to modern rulers?
2. **31:6.** Compare the description in this verse to Jesus' parable of the Mustard Seed (Lk 13:19). What point is Ezekiel making? In contrast, what point is Jesus making?
3. **31:12–18.** When a mighty nation such as the Union of Soviet Socialist Republics falls, what happens to all the satellite countries that depended on it? How do other world powers take advantage of the situation? What lessons about human nature can be learned from developments such as these?

Chapter 32

For understanding

1. **32:5.** How did some ancient Near Eastern myths describe the world being made? How does this prophecy seem to invert that narrative?
2. **32:17.** What is the most likely date for this prophecy? What does Ezekiel describe Egypt as doing?
3. **32:22.** For what was the Assyrian Empire (911–609 B.C.) notorious? What did it do to the Northern Kingdom of Israel? What eventually happened to the Assyrians themselves?
4. **32:24.** Where was Elam? For what were the Elamites noted?

For application

1. **32:2.** What images of themselves do the major powers of our world have, and how do their enemies view them? What image of yourself do you entertain? Would others agree with it?
2. **32:15.** Consider the desolation that surrounds the Chernobyl nuclear power plant, destroyed in 1986 by a nuclear meltdown. What lessons have we learned from it? How often do these lessons include things of God?
3. **32:18–30.** Although Sheol is not hell as we understand it, what does it mean to Ezekiel? What is Ezekiel's point in cataloging the nations that Egypt will meet there? What lesson can we take from it?
4. **32:31–32.** Since he is in the same state as the nations in Sheol, what comfort can he take from seeing them? Why does misery love company?

Chapter 33

For understanding

1. **33:1.** What does this verse mark? Since Ezekiel's oracles against the nations are complete, to what does his attention shift?
2. **33:22.** What had God imposed on Ezekiel at the beginning of his career? When only could he speak?
3. **33:24.** Of what were the few survivors in Judah who were not taken as captives to Babylon after the destruction of Jerusalem convinced?
4. **33:32.** Why did Ezekiel's contemporaries think of him as being like one who sings love songs?

For application

1. **33:7–9.** How would you apply these verses to the current Church situation? Who is in the prophet's position as watchman for the People of God?
2. **33:12–16.** To what extent is an individual responsible for his own actions? How do maturity, ignorance, duress, or psychological and social factors color one's responsibility (CCC 1734–36)?
3. **33:23–27.** What are "squatter's rights", known legally as "adverse possession"? Under the law of our land, how long may someone occupy a property he does not own before it legally becomes his? On what grounds is Ezekiel denying those remaining in Judah after the fall of Jerusalem any right to adverse possession?
4. **33:31.** In your opinion, how well do people take to heart the homilies they hear at Mass? If the homilist warns of the dangers of a political ideology, how many heed the warning or quarrel with his viewpoint? How do you respond to such homilies?

Chapter 34

For understanding

1. **34:1.** What does this verse mark? What do chaps. 34–37 contain, and to what are they comparable? How can many of the prophecies in these chapters be understood? Of what does Ezekiel even predict the coming, although what is his preferred term for it?
2. **34:13.** What biblical theme is very strong in Isaiah, Jeremiah, and Ezekiel? How must the gathering of twelve apostles around Jesus be seen in light of these prophecies?
3. **34:14.** For what event in the Gospels do this and the surrounding verses form the literary backdrop? To what do Mark (Mk 6:39) and John (Jn 6:10) call attention? Who is Jesus shown to be? To what are the "mountain heights of Israel" a poetic reference?

4. **Word Study: Prince (34:24).** Why does Ezekiel prefer the title "prince" over "king" for the coming Davidic Messiah? For what is the term *nāśîʾ* an ancient and traditional term? For whom is the term *melek*, on the other hand, only used, and what will eventually happen to this "king" whom the Israelites choose? So, what are the connotations of *nāśîʾ* and of a human *melek* in the books of Moses? For Moses, who is Israel's true king, and what should any human ruler be content to be?
5. **34:25.** What is Ezekiel's preferred term for the reality described by Jeremiah as the "new covenant"? Why does Ezekiel describe it as a *berît shālôm*? How does the Edenic imagery as memories of Eden prior to the Fall continue?

For application

1. **34:1–6.** What are some of the causes behind people leaving the Church and the numerical increase of the "nones" (persons who profess no religion)? Who is responsible for finding ways to bring them back to the faith?
2. **34:11–16.** Compare these verses with Jn 10:11–15. How does Jesus fulfill the role of the "good shepherd"?
3. **34:17–24.** Since the Second Vatican Council (1962–1965), how has the flock of the Church shown itself restive, contentious, and inclined to stray? How have the shepherds of the Church, especially the popes, tried to promote unity?
4. **34:25.** Under the covenant of peace, what might the "wild beasts" signify? What kind of security does this covenant provide?

Chapter 35

For understanding

1. **35:2.** To what could Mt. Seir refer? Why does this oracle against Edom (35:1–15) seem oddly placed here? Because the relationship between Israel and Edom was particularly close, what Edomite conduct made it all the more bitter? Why, then, is this oracle included among the oracles of hope for Israel (chaps. 34–37)?
2. **35:5.** What happened to Israelite refugees when the Edomites denied them sanctuary?
3. **35:7.** On whom did the Edomites depend for their economic survival?
4. **35:10.** Which two countries did Edom believe would be theirs? What were they plotting?

For application

1. **35:5.** What is the origin of the word "resent"? Why is it so difficult to let go a grudge? What does the Book of Hebrews say about the effects of a "root of bitterness" on people like Esau (Heb 12:12–17)?
2. **35:11.** Why are anger and envy considered capital sins? To what other sins do they lead?
3. **35:13.** What does God's condemnation of Edom in this verse say about his relationship with Israel? When Saul of Tarsus persecuted early Christians, what did Jesus tell him he was actually doing (Acts 9:4)?

Chapter 36

For understanding

1. **36:16.** What did the ritual impurity that came with a woman's menstrual cycle mean for marital relations? What is the sense of this passage?
2. **36:25.** In some rites of the Old Covenant, why was water sprinkled on objects and persons? What do the Dead Sea Scrolls show about how the Essenes of Qumran understood their water washings? How did the Church Fathers understand this passage?
3. **36:27.** What does the "new spirit" promised in 36:26 turn out to be? What does the Spirit bestow the ability to do?
4. **36:28.** What is the "covenant formula", and what does it state? What bonds could covenants form? What dimension to this declaration, "You shall be my people, and I will be your God", do the logic and pattern of Hos 2:2, 16–23, lead us to see?

For application

1. **36:20–21.** How does the Exile of Israel and Judah to foreign lands constitute a profanation of God's holy name? Even though these people are exiled for their own sin, how does their exile reflect on God himself? Although our sin primarily harms us, how does it profane God's name among those around us?
2. **36:25.** What are the spiritual effects of Baptism (CCC 1263–67)? What are some of the obligations resulting from being baptized (CCC 1269–70)?
3. **36:27.** The note for this verse refers to Rom 8:1–17. What two forces within the person are opposed to each other? What are these two forces concerned with in life (vv. 6–8)? What effort is the Spirit-filled person required to make (v. 13)?
4. **36:31.** About what kind of self-loathing is Ezekiel speaking here? Why is it good to recall your own sinfulness in the face of God's goodness to you? Why is it not good to engage in self-condemnation (cf. Rom 8:1)?

Chapter 37

For understanding

1. **37:1.** Though chap. 37:1–14 is a distinct oracle, what promise does it take up and develop? In Mosaic ritual law, how did human remains impart uncleanness and contagion? What will the raising of these bones, which brings them from a state of death to new life, do for them?
2. **Word Study: Spirit (37:1).** What does the noun *rûaḥ* (Heb.) translate to mean? In what ways is it a very important term in the OT? That said, why is it not always apparent in English translations when *rûaḥ* appears in the original text, and how is Ezek 37:1–14 a case in point? How is the prophet engaged in wordplay? What does it appear that Ezekiel understood, theologically?
3. **37:12.** How does the statement "I will open your graves" operate on two levels? According to St. Gregory of Nyssa, how did Ezekiel, by the gift of prophecy, transcend space and time?

4. **37:16.** What was Judah? Of what did the majority of this kingdom consist? Where were the tribes of Benjamin and Simeon? In addition, where did the majority of the Levites probably live? After the fall of the Northern Kingdom of Israel in 722 B.C., what happened to the population of southern Judah? What was "Joseph (the stick of Ephraim)"? Who ruled this kingdom, with few exceptions? Into which two half-tribes had the large tribe of Joseph been broken? What does the Book of Genesis lead one to expect about the hopes of Israel? What territory did they receive as their tribal portions?

For application

1. **37:1–10.** In addition to their meaning for national renewal, how do these verses describe what happens during personal conversion? What do theologians mean by "enthusiasm", and why are they sometimes suspicious of it?
2. **37:11.** Do you recall any time when you felt cut off from the life of faith, when you lost hope or faith? If so, what was the experience like? How did the Holy Spirit alleviate or resolve it?
3. **37:14.** How does an experience of the Holy Spirit transform the way one lives out the Christian life? What happens to one's experience of ordinary rituals and personal prayer?
4. **37:20–22.** According to St. Paul (Eph 1), what unification did God accomplish through the preaching of the gospel? Rather than an image of two sticks artificially held together, Paul uses the image of grafting (Rom 11:17–24). What does Paul's image imply that Ezekiel's does not?

Chapter 38

For understanding

1. **38:2.** Who, probably, is the ruler here called Gog? When did he rule? In the lifetime of Ezekiel, who ruled his kingdom? How may Ezekiel be treating Gog as a dynastic name? Of what is "land of Magog" probably a Hebrew adoption? Where are Meshech and Tubal?
2. **38:6.** Where was the wild tribe called Gomer located, and how was it known to the Greeks?

For application

1. **38:1–6.** Ezekiel describes the mobilization of a huge army that plans to invade Israel, resettled after the Israelites' return from exile. On a spiritual level, what large armies are arrayed against the Church (e.g., Rev 12:13–17)? What defenses does she have?
2. **38:10.** In ancient times, unwalled villages were virtually defenseless against raiders. Spiritually, how can a vulnerable soul fortify itself against attacks by the evil one and his minions?
3. **38:14–16.** Why does God allow the devil and the world to attack his people? How does he vindicate his holiness in their resistance to these enemies?

Chapter 39

For understanding

1. **39:11.** What might "the Valley of the Travelers" mean? What is the "Valley of Hamon-Gog", and on what name is it possibly a pun?
2. **39:16.** From what is "a city Hamonah" derived, and to what is it probably a cryptic reference?

For application

1. **39:1–6.** The failure of Gog's invasion of Israel as described in these verses sounds almost miraculous. According to historians, what spiritual weapons were brought to bear against superior Muslim forces in the Battle of Lepanto? How are they effective in our own day?
2. **39:7.** What response do Church authorities make when a church building is desecrated? Why should acts of restoration be publicized?
3. **39:11–16.** How is the land cleansed by burying corpses of the enemy after battle? According to Num 19:11, what happens to an Israelite who touches a corpse? How is he purified? How is the human heart purified from the aftereffects of sin?
4. **39:25.** What does it mean for God to be "jealous" for his holy name? How is jealousy in this context like the virtue of zeal?

Chapter 40

For understanding

1. **40:1.** What year is the "twenty-fifth year of our exile" counting from whose exile? When is "the beginning of the year"? How does later Jewish tradition identify four "heads of the year"? Although some scholars maintain Ezekiel's "head of the year" is Nisan, how do we know that Ezekiel probably intends to refer to Tishri? What feast day is on the tenth day of Tishri, and to what tradition does the date of Ezekiel's vision probably relate? Accordingly, when is Ezekiel probably seeing this vision, and what makes it a spiritual turning point?
2. **40:5.** How long were a cubit and handbreadth together, and therefore how long was the measuring reed? How thick was the wall being measured?
3. **40:35.** Of what is symmetry a sign? How is Ezekiel's Temple laid out? What sacred numbers recur throughout the description?
4. **40:39.** As the primary offering of the Mosaic liturgy, what did the burnt offering require? What did it express? What are sin offerings and guilt offerings?

For application

1. **40:5.** What is the purpose of a Temple? Assuming the Temple has already been built, why measure it for Ezekiel's benefit? In Rev 11:1–2, what portion of the Temple was John told to measure, and what did it represent?

2. **40:6–16.** Even if you are not an architect, what do you think the perfect church building should look like? As in styles of architecture such as Gothic and Romanesque, what should the design of church buildings convey to worshipers?
3. **40:35.** The note for this verse stresses the importance of symmetry for Ezekiel's Temple. What design elements are important for the church building you attend, for example, the arrangement of the narthex, the nave, and any transepts?
4. **40:38–43.** In your church building, what furniture is in the sanctuary area? Why are the altar, the ambo, and other pieces placed where they are? What does their placement signify?

Chapter 41

For understanding

1. **41:4.** What is another name for the "most holy place"? How was it shaped? What did its perfect symmetry express?
2. **41:6.** What did the three stories of the side chambers call to mind?
3. **41:18.** What were the cherubim for, and on what locations were they represented?

For application

1. **41:4.** Although in Roman rite churches the Tabernacle is where the Blessed Sacrament is reserved, what is actually the holiest item in the sanctuary? In Eastern churches, why is it located behind an iconostasis?
2. **41:14.** Why does the Temple face east? Toward what direction should church buildings be oriented, if possible? Why?
3. **41:17–20.** What is the function of art in church buildings? What works of art are placed in the church you attend, and what do they represent? Where is the main crucifix located, and why is it there?
4. **41:22.** This verse refers to the altar of incense. In what is incense burned? What is it used for in the liturgy? When is it most likely to be used?

Chapter 42

For understanding

1. **42:20.** How long is 500 cubits? What does the number 500 represent?

For application

1. **42:14.** Why do priests and deacons wear special vestments? What are some of them? Where are these vestments worn?
2. **42.20.** Using the number in the note for this verse, calculate the area of Ezekiel's Temple. Why so large? Why do Christians build churches as large as St. Peter's in Rome or Hagia Sophia in Istanbul?

Chapter 43

For understanding

1. **43:2.** Why does the glory of the Lord come from the east? What sites opened to the east? Where did traditions that the Messiah would come from the east lead the Essenes at Qumran to establish their community?
2. **43:8.** Why does the Lord object to having only a wall between the king's threshold and his own?
3. **43:12.** From this verse and others, what concept arose about the whole city of Jerusalem? In the time of Jesus, what would devout Essenes avoid doing, and why?

For application

1. **43:1–5.** Have you ever had a strong experience of the Lord's presence when entering a church where the Blessed Sacrament is reserved? What was it like? If you have never had such an experience, how do you recognize the Lord's presence in the Blessed Sacrament?
2. **43:8.** Attached to the north wall of the Temple in Jesus' time was the Fortress Antonia, occupied by the Romans. Why was the fortress placed there? Suppose the only thing separating your church from the city administration offices was a wall or partition. What could such a layout imply, and what problems might arise for the church from it?
3. **43:12.** In the Book of Revelation, where is the Temple in the New Jerusalem that comes down from heaven (Rev 21:22)? What takes its place?
4. **43:13–17.** What did ancient altars look like, and of what were they made? Of what are modern altars typically made? How are they shaped? Why do they have that shape rather than that of ancient altars?

Chapter 44

For understanding

1. **44:2.** Why was the east gate of the Temple to remain shut? In the Catholic spiritual tradition, of whom is it a commonplace to see the Temple as a type? What is an appropriate analogue to the closed gate of the eschatological Temple? According to Rufinus of Aquileia, why is the preservation of the Virgin's condition evident here?
2. **44:15.** Although Ezekiel uses a phrase characteristic of Deuteronomy, "the Levitical priests", as whom does he identify this group? When did Zadok, a descendant of Phinehas, the zealous grandson of Aaron (Num 25:10–12), serve as high priest? Under Solomon, why was Abiathar dispossessed of the high priesthood? In criticizing the non-Zadokite Levites, what is it unclear that Ezekiel has in mind? What is clear that he believes about the Zadokites? In the New Testament era, which priests led the Jewish Essene movement?
3. **44:17.** Why were priests to wear linen garments and nothing made of wool? Why did the later Essene community make a practice of wearing only linen garments? What does Jesus' garments of linen at his burial suggest about him?

4. **44:23.** What four categories were the basis of the Israelite ritual system? With what was a holy thing imbued, whereas a common thing was not? For what was a clean thing suitable, whereas an unclean thing was not? How does Leviticus detail these regulations?
5. **44:28.** Since priests were not to own farmlands to support themselves, how were they to live? Of what did this become a type? In the Gospels, why are the apostles called to leave everything, including "houses and lands"? What does this hint at regarding their status? What is to be their only "part" or "inheritance"?

For application

1. **44:7.** Why are catechumens allowed to hear the Liturgy of the Word but not permitted to attend the Liturgy of the Eucharist? What sacrament enables them to participate in the Eucharist?
2. **44:10–14.** The *Catechism* describes three degrees of the Sacrament of Holy Orders (CCC 1554). What are they? What is the role of the deacon, as distinct from that of the priest (CCC 1569–71)?
3. **44:15–16.** In the Christian dispensation, what is the role of the ministerial priest, especially as regards the liturgy (CCC 1562–68)?
4. **44:22.** Read the note for this verse. Why, in the Christian dispensation, is celibacy held in such high regard? In the Latin Church, why is celibacy required (CCC 1579)? In the Eastern churches, what is the practice of priestly celibacy (CCC 1580)?

Chapter 45

For understanding

1. **45:2.** If Ezekiel's long cubit was somewhere between 20 and 22 inches, what are the dimensions of the sanctuary? To what may the multiples of fifty in the layout of the sacred precinct and Temple refer, and what does that suggest?
2. **45:17.** What kind of figure is Ezekiel's "prince", the royal Son of David, and what is his main duty? While it was common for the kings of the ancient Near East to patronize the cult of the gods, and to have many other duties as well, in Ezekiel's vision, what is the king's only duty?
3. **45:18.** When did the Law of Moses institute the Day of Atonement? How important is this holy day in the Jewish liturgical calendar? Here, on what day does Ezekiel receive instructions for a day of atonement for the Temple? How does the ritual compare to the Mosaic Day of Atonement? As what is this day probably intended?
4. **45:21.** Why does Ezekiel modify the observance of Passover (Num 28:16–25) and the Feast of Unleavened Bread? How does this once more highlight the main role of the king of Israel in Ezekiel's vision? Seen in this light, of whom is Ezekiel's "prince" a type? How else does Ezekiel change what Moses originally prescribed?

For application

1. **45:4.** Most parishes in the Latin Church are territorial. What does this usually mean for Catholics within the parish boundaries? What is the benefit of having the priest live near the church at which he ministers?
2. **45:10–11.** In our country, who sets the standards for our system of weights and measures? How confident are you that the scales you use to weigh produce at the supermarket (for example) are honest? What would you do if you were sure the scales were "fixed" (i.e., dishonest)?
3. **45:19.** Compare what the priest does in this verse with what the heads of families were to do on the night of the first Passover (Ex 12:22). In Israelite understanding, what does it mean to "remember" the Passover event? At the Last Supper, what does Jesus mean by telling the disciples to "do this in remembrance" of him?

Chapter 46

For understanding

1. **46:1.** While the east-facing outer gate was to remain perpetually shut according to 44:1–3, when could the east-facing inner gate be opened? What did opening this gate allow the prince and the people to do?
2. **46:9.** What do some suggest is the reason for the regulation in this verse? Spiritually, how could there be a reference to personal transformation?
3. **46:13.** What is the importance of the *tāmîd*, or continual burnt offering? Curiously, how many lambs did Moses specify, and when were they offered? Which sacrifice does Ezekiel seem to omit?
4. **46:24.** For what did neither the Solomonic Temple nor the Mosaic Tabernacle make explicit provision? Since Ezekiel's visionary Temple has designated locations for these activities, what do they show about God's future Temple?

For application

1. **46:2–3.** During the performance of Catholic liturgies such as the Mass, who may enter the sanctuary area of the church? From where do the other participants follow the liturgy? Why is this distance imposed between the congregation and the sanctuary?
2. **46:9.** When someone enters a Catholic church, why does he customarily bless himself with holy water? As he approaches the altar, why does he genuflect toward the Tabernacle before taking his place? If the Tabernacle is located away from the altar, what does he do rather than genuflect?
3. **46:19–20.** In most churches, what is the room called where the bread and wine offered in the Mass are prepared for the offering? What happens with the sacred vessels (the chalice, ciborium, and other vessels) after the liturgy ends? Why should only an instituted acolyte, deacon, or priest cleanse these vessels?

Chapter 47

For understanding

1. **47:5.** In a spiritual sense, what does the river represent? According to St. Jerome, if the waters of Baptism and the apostles' teaching flow from the Lord's Temple, what can they cause to happen?

2. **Topical Essay: The River of Life Flowing from the Temple.** What deep roots does the idea of a primordial garden-sanctuary at the beginning of human history, from which flowed a life-giving river that watered the whole earth, have in many ancient cultures? Later in Israel's history, how did reverence for the ancient river that flowed from Eden become attached to the spring that supplied water for Jerusalem and its Temple? In the Gospel of John, how is the Body of Jesus revealed as the true Temple of God? Why does the Church read Ezek 47:1–12 every year for the Feast of St. John Lateran?
3. **47:13.** Why does the tribe of Joseph have two portions of land? What is interesting about Ezekiel's designation of Joseph rather than Judah for this privilege? What faith is Ezekiel showing in his division of the land?
4. **47:22.** Unlike Moses, what position does Ezekiel take regarding foreign inhabitants of the land? Rather, how does he solve the problem of non-Israelite residents of the holy land? Of what can this be seen as a type?

For application

1. **47:1.** Compare this stream with that in Rev 22:1. From where does each stream flow? According to Jn 7:38, what flows from Jesus' heart? What name is given to the stream of water in Revelation?
2. **47:3–5.** As a symbol of the Holy Spirit (cf. note for v. 9), what is the significance of the stream getting deeper as it flows, despite having no tributaries feeding into it? How does the "depth" of the Holy Spirit increase in the life of the Christian?
3. **47:7–12.** Compare the trees in these verses to the tree of life in Rev 22:2. What are the similarities and differences? What purpose do the leaves of both trees serve?
4. **47:11.** Read the note for this verse. What makes salt a necessity for life? What does Jesus mean by calling his disciples the "salt of the earth" (Mt 5:13)?

Chapter 48

For understanding

1. **48:1–35.** While this section invites comparison with the division of the Promised Land by tribes in Josh 13–21, what are some of the notable differences?
2. **48:8–22.** In the center of the nation, what does the kind of sacred "federal district" that Ezekiel sees look like? Oddly, although Moses gave no territory to the Levites, in Ezekiel's vision what do they receive, and where is it?
3. **48:30–34.** What do the twelve gates of the city, one for each tribe, indicate? What do the Temple and city, then, become?
4. **48:35.** In what way is the identity of this visionary city an enigma? Though Ezekiel, indeed, sees a city that will fulfill all the functions and significance of the Jerusalem of old, to what is he not committed? What enables the city to be understood in non-geographical terms? What does the NT understand this new holy city to be?

For application

1. **48:8–14.** Ideally, where should the parish church be situated within the boundaries of the parish? Aside from its practical benefits, what does that location indicate for the spiritual life of the parish?
2. **48:14.** What happens to a church building that can no longer be used for divine worship (CIC 1222)? Since the altar remains dedicated for worship even if the church building is no longer used for worship, what should happen to it in that case (CIC 1238)?
3. **48:19.** Using this verse as an axiom, who should ultimately be responsible for the care of the church and its property?
4. **48:35.** Compare this verse with Rev 21:3–4. In St. John's vision, where is the Lord? What does his presence mean for his people?

BOOKS OF THE BIBLE

THE OLD TESTAMENT (OT)

Gen	Genesis
Ex	Exodus
Lev	Leviticus
Num	Numbers
Deut	Deuteronomy
Josh	Joshua
Judg	Judges
Ruth	Ruth
1 Sam	1 Samuel
2 Sam	2 Samuel
1 Kings	1 Kings
2 Kings	2 Kings
1 Chron	1 Chronicles
2 Chron	2 Chronicles
Ezra	Ezra
Neh	Nehemiah
Tob	Tobit
Jud	Judith
Esther	Esther
Job	Job
Ps	Psalms
Prov	Proverbs
Eccles	Ecclesiastes
Song	Song of Solomon
Wis	Wisdom
Sir	Sirach (Ecclesiasticus)
Is	Isaiah
Jer	Jeremiah
Lam	Lamentations
Bar	Baruch
Ezek	Ezekiel
Dan	Daniel
Hos	Hosea
Joel	Joel
Amos	Amos
Obad	Obadiah
Jon	Jonah
Mic	Micah
Nahum	Nahum
Hab	Habakkuk
Zeph	Zephaniah
Hag	Haggai
Zech	Zechariah
Mal	Malachi
1 Mac	1 Maccabees
2 Mac	2 Maccabees

THE NEW TESTAMENT (NT)

Mt	Matthew
Mk	Mark
Lk	Luke
Jn	John
Acts	Acts of the Apostles
Rom	Romans
1 Cor	1 Corinthians
2 Cor	2 Corinthians
Gal	Galatians
Eph	Ephesians
Phil	Philippians
Col	Colossians
1 Thess	1 Thessalonians
2 Thess	2 Thessalonians
1 Tim	1 Timothy
2 Tim	2 Timothy
Tit	Titus
Philem	Philemon
Heb	Hebrews
Jas	James
1 Pet	1 Peter
2 Pet	2 Peter
1 Jn	1 John
2 Jn	2 John
3 Jn	3 John
Jude	Jude
Rev	Revelation (Apocalypse)